Contextualism in Psychological Research?

*This book is dedicated to a friendly critic of our position,
James E. Deese,
who died on February 15, 1999.
Deese, who made many contributions to psychology,
came to embrace contextualism late in his life.
We had many interactions with Professor Deese,
who was frequently called upon to evaluate our work,
which generally took a critical stance toward contextualism.
Although Deese disagreed with us on many points,
he was as fair and unbiased a critic as anyone could hope for.
We will remember him as totally dedicated to the
proposition that truth can be arrived at through
open discussion among individuals with competing views.*

Contextualism in Psychological Research?

A Critical Review

E. J. Capaldi
Robert W. Proctor

SAGE Publications
International Educational and Professional Publisher
Thousand Oaks   London   New Delhi

For information:

SAGE Publications, Inc.
2455 Teller Road
Thousand Oaks, California 91320
E-mail: order@sagepub.com

SAGE Publications Ltd.
6 Bonhill Street
London EC2A 4PU
United Kingdom

SAGE Publications India Pvt. Ltd.
M-32 Market
Greater Kailash I
New Delhi 110 048 India

Printed in the United States of America

Library of Congress Cataloging-in-Publication Data

Capaldi, E. John.
    Contextualism in psychological research?: A critical review /
by E. J. Capaldi and Robert W. Proctor.
      p. cm.
    Includes bibliographical references and index.
    ISBN 0-7619-0997-4 (cloth: acid-free paper)
    ISBN 0-7619-0998-2 (pbk.: acid-free paper)
    1. Context effects (Psychology) 2. Relativity. I. Proctor,
Robert W. II. Title.
    BF315.2 .C37   1999
    150.19′8—dc21   99-6362

This book is printed on acid-free paper.

99 00 01 02 03 04 05 7 6 5 4 3 2 1

Acquiring Editor:	C. Deborah Laughton
Editorial Assistant:	Eileen Carr
Production Editor:	Diana E. Axelsen
Editorial Assistant:	Patricia Zeman
Typesetter/Designer:	Lynn Miyata
Cover Designer:	Michelle Lee

Contents

Preface   xi

1. Contextualism: Its Definition, Origins,
   Current Manifestations, and Allies   1

   The Necessity for a Critical Evaluation of Contextualism   2

   Contextualism Defined   6

   Contextualism, Pragmatism, and Postmodernism   9

   Why Psychologists Are Attracted to Contextualism   12

   Objections Encountered in Our Analysis of Contextualism   14
   The Opinion That We Are Rejecting Contextualism Per Se   14
   *The Opinion That Contextualism Does Not Warrant
   Critical Scrutiny*   15
   The Opinion That We Are Denying the Relevance of Context   16
   *The Opinion That Contextualism Cannot Be Evaluated
   by Noncontextualists*   16

   Summary and Conclusions   17

2. Philosophy of Science and Psychology   19

   The Opinion That Philosophy of Science Is Irrelevant   19
   Opinions of Others   20
   *Two Examples of Suggesting How Psychology
   Should Be Practiced*   22

   Early Conceptions of Science   23

Five Major Positions in the Philosophy of Science   25
   Radical Empiricism   25
   Logical Empiricism   27
   Falsificationism   28
   Thomas Kuhn's System and Its Relation to Relativism   29
   Laudan's Version of Normative Naturalism   31
Summary and Conclusions   37

3. The Metaphilosophy of Stephen Pepper   39
The Four Worldviews   40
   Formism   40
   Organicism   40
   Mechanism   41
   Contextualism   42
A Specific Example of Contextualism in Practice   45
Can Contextualism Be Scientific?   46
Pepper With a Pinch of Psalt   48
Summary and Conclusions   52

**4. Philosophic Contextualism and
Modified Contextualism Described   53**
Philosophic Contextualism in Psychology   54
   Rejecting Restriction of Variables   54
   Rejecting Lawfulness   55
   Accepting Novelty   56
   Rejecting Science   58
Modified Contextualism in Psychology   59
   Accepting Restriction of Variables   60
   Accepting Lawfulness   62
   Ignoring or Minimizing Novelty   63
   Accepting Science   64
Comparison of Philosophic Contextualism,
   Modified Contextualism, and Mainstream Science   65
Summary and Conclusions   68

**5. Philosophic Contextualism and Academic Psychology:
A Comparison and Evaluation   69**
Philosophic Contextualism's Ontology   70

Philosophic Contextualism and Methodology   71
   Experimentation in Academic Psychology   71
   Contextualism and Rejection of Experimentation   72
   Contextualism and Alternative Methodologies   75
Can Experimentation Be Replaced?   78
   Our Evaluation of Alternative Methods   79
   Experimentation Is Indispensable   80
The Character of Psychology Under Philosophic Contextualism   82
   General Changes   82
   Specific Changes   84
Some Proposed Practical Applications of Contextualism   87
Summary and Conclusions   88

6. **Developmental Contextualism and Academic Psychology:
   A Comparison and Evaluation**   91
   Origins of Developmental Contextualism   92
   Two Central Characteristics of Developmental Contextualism   93
   Less Central Characteristics of Developmental Contextualism   94
      Active Versus Passive Organism   94
      Linear Causality Versus Mutual Causality   96
      Nonreductionism Versus Reductionism   97
   Developmental Contextualism Compared
      With Academic Psychology   98
   Summary and Conclusions   104

7. **Functional Contextualism and Academic Psychology:
   A Comparison and Evaluation**   105
   Characteristics of Functional Contextualism   108
      The Concept of the Operant   109
      Contextualism and the Act   111
      The Role of the Scientist in Scientific Analysis   113
      The Possibility of Novelty   114
      Truth Criterion   114
   Comparison of Functional Contextualism
      to Academic Psychology   115
      Extrapolation From Principles   115
      Interpretive Schemes   116
      Radical Empiricism   117

Do Contextualism and Mechanism Marry Well?   118
Summary and Conclusions   119

8. Are Mainstream Psychology and the Various Contextualisms in Competition, and Should They Be?   121
Developmental Contextualism   122
Functional Contextualism   123
Philosophic Contextualism   127
Separatism and Its Consequences   129
   Pepper's Position on Separatism   130
   The History of Science and Separatism   131
   Separatism, Counterproductivity, and Anti-Intellectualism   133
   Prediction and Control in Contextualism   135
Summary and Conclusions   136

9. Underdetermination, Incommensurability, and Relativism   137
Limitations of Underdetermination   140
   Humean, or Logical, Underdetermination   140
   Quinean, or Empirical, Underdetermination   142
Implications of Underdeterminations   144
   Relativism   144
   Lack of Progress   146
Incommensurability   148
Backing Off From Underdetermination and Relativism   149
Status of Relativism   151
Summary and Conclusions   154

10. Downplaying Ontology   155
The Basic Rules of the Game   157
   Abstaining From Caricatures   157
   Engage in Relevant Arguments   159
   Proper Evaluation of Methods   162
Generalizability   165
Range of Cognitive Attitudes   170
Contextualism's Greatest Fallacy   172
Summary and Conclusions   173

References   175

Author Index   185

Subject Index   189

About the Authors   193

Preface

traditionally, major movements in psychology have turned rightly to the philosophy of science in an attempt to justify their theoretical and methodological commitments and to direct their future growth. As one example, behaviorism adopted logical positivism and operationism as its philosophy of science. With the decline of logical positivism, the philosophy of science itself turned to various forms of relativism, and of course this had a profound influence in psychology. However, although relativism is declining in importance in the philosophy of science itself, it seems to be inappropriately embraced by psychologists more strongly than ever. Those psychologists who embrace relativism seem to be anachronistic in two major ways. On one hand, they inaccurately characterize mainstream psychologists as logical positivists; on the other hand, they have ignored developments in one of the major recent movements in the philosophy of science—post-Kuhnian naturalism. Perhaps this volume can point the direction to a corrective in both of these respects.

The most well-known relativism adopted by psychologists, of course, is that of Kuhn. Another form of relativism that has had a strong influence in psychology, contextualism, is of primary concern in this book. Our concern with contextualism is not narrowly with that point of view alone. Our intention is to show by a detailed analysis of contextualism that all currently popular forms of relativism are useful to science only in the context of discovery and, at least as matters stand now, not in the context of justification.

Contextualism, a postmodern variety of pragmatism that endorses radical empiricism, is closely related to several other relativistic movements, such as social constructionism. The influence of contextualism and relativism in general seems inexplicably to be on the ascent in psychology and perhaps some of the social sciences but not in the philosophy of science itself. We will identify two quite distinct contextualist camps and ask whether either form of contextualism provides a satisfactory basis for the conduct of empirical and theoretical psychology. We will contrast the two varieties of contextualism with our own conception of the philosophy of science, which we freely adopt from Larry Laudan. This conception, we think, provides a much more up-to-date and better basis than contextualism for the conduct of research and theory in psychology. In addition, unlike contextualism and various forms of relativism, which attempt to repudiate the rest of psychology and to seal themselves off from it, the position that we favor encourages interaction among the various approaches to psychology. Our intention is not merely to show the limitations of contextualism and various other outdated forms of relativism but to provide in the process a more realistic and rational philosophy of science for psychology.

Contextualists, together with other relativists, seek two general outcomes. One is to establish a body of knowledge compatible with their views. We have no quarrel with that objective and indeed would encourage contextualists to be as productive as possible. The second outcome sought by contextualists is to repudiate root and branch scientific psychology as it is practiced in mainstream, or academic, psychology. Their intention in this regard is a major concern of ours. In fact, it is our desire to blunt the intention of the contextualists to marginalize the remainder of psychology that is the major impetus to this book. Despite the fact that we think that many claims of the contextualists are overstated and incorrect, we do not seek in turn to marginalize contextualism; we think that much that is valuable could issue from that perspective. Perhaps this book will encourage meaningful dialogue between contextualists and noncontextualists and, as a result, benefit both positions. However, if contextualists are to make significant contributions to the rest of psychology, they will have to accept methodological canons that they currently find distasteful. Such acceptance could conceivably have the effect of rendering their knowledge products not only interesting but as reliable as the knowledge products of the remainder of psychology.

The intended audience for this book ranges from advanced under-graduate and graduate students to professional psychologists, whether favorably inclined toward contextualism or not. Students will learn from this book that psychology is a multifaceted discipline with many divergent views concerning its proper subject matter, its proper methodology, and its proper form of theorizing. To cite merely one example, what, according to psychologists of various persuasions, are the strengths and weaknesses of experimentation, a popular methodology widely employed in mainstream psychology? The book also provides a useful primer for beginning graduate students, enabling them to understand the various philosophies of science, such as logical positivism, that have been influential within psychology. The book contains a novel, modern, up-to-date analysis of two concepts that have been widely misunderstood in the social sciences: underdetermination and incommensurability. These concepts have provided much of the ammunition for a misplaced emphasis on relativism within psychology and social sciences generally.

Mainstream psychologists can learn from this book that they have many opponents in the psychological community who are highly critical of them. Contextualists and their close allies can learn from this book that mainstream psychologists have many cogent arguments to advance against their position. What is unique about this effort is that it is the first full-length book to critically examine all sides of the many and various issues that are raised by contextualists. It is perhaps this unique aspect of this book that may contribute in the future to more productive dialogue between contextualists and their adversaries. In the final chapter, several suggestions are offered that we hope will facilitate such a dialogue.

We would like to thank the Acquiring Editor, C. Deborah Laughton, for her support and encouragement. We also wish to thank the reviewers of the manuscript, who provided many helpful comments: the late James Deese, David C. Edwards, Tom Leahey, Brent Slife, and Michael Wertheimer. We thank as well Julie Smith, our very efficient secretary, who helped in preparation of the manuscript. Finally, we wish to acknowledge that some material in Chapters 3, 6, and 7 has been freely adapted from a previously published article, Capaldi and Proctor (1994).

Contextualism:

Its Definition, Origins,
Current Manifestations, and Allies

*C*ontextualism is a metatheory in psychology that seeks to replace what it sees as the currently rival dominant metatheory, which contextualists call mechanism. As a metatheory, contextualism is growing rapidly and is being advocated by a diverse variety of psychologists, many of whom otherwise have little in common. To give an idea of such diversity, consider the two ends of the contextualism continuum. On one end are individuals such as Theodore Sarbin, a personality psychologist, and Jerome Bruner, a cultural folk psychologist, both of whom are skeptical about the role of experimentation in psychology. On the other end are individuals such as Hayne Reese, a developmental psychologist, and Steven Hayes, an operant psychologist and follower of B. F. Skinner, both of whom speak approvingly of experimentation.

What are individuals from the Sarbin-Bruner wing of contextualism for and against? In the pursuit of psychological knowledge, they are for using methods such as narrative, hermeneutics, and dramaturgy, methods that are drawn from literature and from European philosophy. The goal of this wing of contextualists is to produce plausible interpretations of human experience. The resultant product will be something that resembles history and literature more than it does physics and experimental psychology. This wing of contextualists doubts that psychologists can isolate general laws of human behavior, views the laboratory as a limited context of dubious usefulness, and suggests that all knowledge is contingent and ephemeral.

Contrast the views of the Sarbin-Bruner wing of contextualism with those that are embraced by the academy. As stated by Chaiklin (1991), these views are that

> psychology is grounded in the assumptions that there is a formally structured universe that can be discovered through methods, particularly experimental ones, that will reveal true, universal laws, preferably of "formal-computational" or "hypothetical-deductive" variety, that are true for all times, places, and persons. (p. 197)

Clearly, psychological science as it is understood by the academy is not something that contextualists of the Sarbin-Bruner wing think is either desirable or attainable.

What are individuals from the Reese-Hayes wing of contextualism for and against? This is more difficult to say because their views resemble in many respects those of mainstream psychologists. For example, these individuals accept prediction and control of behavior as desirable goals, and they seek to accomplish those ends through a variety of methods, including experimentation. Why, then, do they call themselves contextualists? Some do because they are radical empiricists who eschew theorizing of any kind. Others do because they seek to investigate behavior at many interacting levels: physical, chemical, biological, individual, and social. This approach is characterized as multilevel determination. Both the radical empiricists and the multilevel determinists profess to establish psychology as a science. They think that they can do a better job in this regard from a contextualistic perspective than from the so-called mechanistic perspective that they identify as currently dominant in psychology.

THE NECESSITY FOR A CRITICAL EVALUATION OF CONTEXTUALISM

Why does contextualism warrant the attention we are giving it in this book? We can think of at least five reasons.

(1) As we shall show, contextualists hold the rest of psychology in low esteem, with many of them completely rejecting the rest of the field. Contextualism is seen by these individuals as the savior of an otherwise misguided psychology. To allow their assessment of the discipline to go unanswered could be construed as a form of implicit agreement.

The widest and most inclusive of the rejections of academic psychology is undoubtedly that which suggests that all psychology based on the conventional approach to science, which the contextualists call mechanism, is totally misguided (see, e.g., Morris, 1991; Sarbin, 1993). Sometimes academic psychology is identified as embracing logical positivism (e.g., Schneider, 1998; Slife & Williams, 1997). Because practically all of academic psychology supposedly is based on so-called mechanism (or logical positivism), the contextualists' rejection of that approach to psychology is total.

Another sort of rejection of academic psychology is by implication. That is, science based on mechanism is disparaged, and thus psychology is rejected along with the so-called mechanism in general (e.g., Gillespie, 1992; Reese, 1991). This particular form of rejecting science often entails the implication that so-called mechanists are narrow-minded ideologues who impose their will on a variety of unwilling participants through sheer political force (e.g., Sarbin, 1990).

An additional form of rejection of mainstream psychology involves a disparagement of this or that particular area. For example, Gergen (1973) has provided an analysis of social psychology, widely rejected by other social psychologists (Wallach & Wallach, 1994), that essentially disparages mainstream social psychology. As another example, Bruner (1990) has rejected out of hand information processing, one of the major approaches in cognitive psychology. Similarly, Shanon (1993) has rejected that portion of psychology—most of psychology, in his opinion—that employs a representational analysis. As a final example, Hayes and Hayes (1992) indicate that "the contextualistic behaviorist can find little of value in most of cognitive psychology" (p. 237).

A final form of rejection of academic psychology involves a repudiation of all areas in the field that employ experimentation. This particular criticism of academic psychology is not shared by all contextualists. Although contextualists in the Sarbin-Bruner wing reject experimentation, those in the Reese-Hayes wing accept experimentation.

(2) Another reason why a critical evaluation of contextualism is warranted is that contextualism in its current manifestation, being a relatively new phenomenon in psychology, has challenged the remainder of psychology along a variety of specific dimensions. These challenges need to be examined

in detail for their validity, as they will be in this book. To be sure, there have been some scattered and limited evaluations of contextualism (e.g., Staddon, 1993), but even taken together, such evaluations do not constitute the sort of thorough critical analysis that contextualism requires.

(3) Contextualism deserves our attention because it is a rapidly developing metatheory that increasingly has come to be accepted by a greater and greater number of psychologists (see, e.g., Cicirelli, 1994). Some of these individuals (e.g., Jerome Bruner and James Deese) have made significant contributions to mainstream academic psychology in the past. Such contextualists are numerous, and some are too esteemed in terms of past accomplishments to ignore. The growth of contextualism is such that Cicirelli (1994) has stated, "Contextualism is the present fad in metamodels" (p. 42).

(4) Contextualism, along with other closely related varieties of relativism, is the approach to the philosophy of science that most often is advocated in such influential organs as the *American Psychologist,* the one journal that all members of the American Psychological Association receive. If the writings of the contextualists and other relativists were limited to the *American Psychologist,* that would be influence enough. The fact is that just about every recent book on the philosophy of science directed at psychologists embraces some form of relativism while denigrating much of what goes on in the academy. There have been exceptions, such as Bechtel (1988), but these are few and far between.

As for the popularity of contextualism, its many adherents can be found in virtually all areas of psychology—for example, developmental psychology (e.g., Ford & Lerner, 1992), environmental psychology (e.g., Altman & Rogoff, 1987), social-personality psychology (e.g., Mancuso, 1993), clinical psychology (e.g., Hayes, 1987), cognitive psychology (e.g., Gillespie, 1992), and operant psychology (e.g., Hayes, Hayes, & Reese, 1988)—and their numbers appear to be growing. A prime example of contextualism's popularity and influence is indicated by the observation of Szapocznik and Kurtines (1993) that contextualism represents a paradigm shift within psychology. They state,

There is a growing recognition that contemporary psychology is undergoing a paradigm shift. Many challenges are being raised to a psychology concerned primarily with the individual as a focus of study. One important challenge comes from the contextualist view, which has had a broad impact on the field (cf. Liddle, 1987). (p. 400)

(5) A major and final reason for subjecting contextualism to critical scrutiny is that, in our view, it is not the most useful philosophy of science for the task of taking psychology into the next millennium. Contextualism, along with its variants of constructivism and social constructionism, is a variety of relativism, and relativism is becoming a declining force in the philosophy of science. This decline is a result of recognizing relativism's numerous imperfections (see, e.g., Laudan, 1996; Scheffler, 1967; Shapere, 1984). In psychology itself, various forms of relativism—most notably, but not exclusively, that associated with Thomas Kuhn—are becoming increasingly suspect (Gholson & Barker, 1985; Leahey, 1992).

Two of the most malodorous aspects of the various varieties of relativism, seen very clearly in Kuhn's approach, are the tendencies to suggest that it is proper to ignore rival points of view and to recommend various nonscientific procedures for evaluating theories and paradigms. That it is proper for contextualists to ignore other points of view was stated very clearly by Hayes and Hayes (1992). In contrasting contextualism and mechanism, they assert, "The philosophy and goals differ so dramatically that the analytic constructions in one have little utility for the other" (p. 237). Moreover, even within radical behaviorism itself, contextualism and mechanism are seen by Hayes and Hayes as totally incompatible: "The two positions are incompatible, and the differences cannot be resolved by way of a compromise" (p. 231).

As for using nonscientific means for justifying one's approach to psychology, consider the following two recommendations. Feyerabend (1970) has noted disapprovingly that the emphasis on paradigms has resulted in attempts to stifle dissent and marginalize one's rivals:

> More than one social scientist has pointed out to me that now at last he had learned how to turn his field into a "science"—by which of course he meant that he had learned how to *improve* it. The recipe, according to these people, is to restrict criticism, to reduce the number of comprehensive theories to one, and to create a normal science that has this one theory as its paradigm. (p. 198)

An even more insidious recommendation has come from Pfeffer (1993), a follower of Kuhn:

> It would be interesting and useful to study the history of related fields such as political science and economics to understand exactly how paradigm consensus was achieved. My sense is that such consensus

was developed by a group of individuals forming a dense network of connections and unified view, who then intentionally and systematically took over positions of power and imposed their views, at times gradually and at times surreptitiously, on the field. There seems to be nothing in the natural order of things that suggests that mathematical rigor should be valued over empirical richness or realism. Rather, the criteria, the status hierarchy, and the enforcement of rules were and are very much political processes. (p. 618)

These reasons provide abundant justification for an analysis of the sort that we undertake in this book.

CONTEXTUALISM DEFINED

Gillespie (1992) provides a useful definition of contextualism, as follows:

For the contextualist, experience consists of total events that are rich in features. Each event has a texture and quality—or "its intuited wholeness or total character" (Pepper, 1942, p. 238). The resulting felt quality of the event becomes primary to the contextualist; any analysis of experience always starts from the given quality and works down to the particulars. Because the event takes up the knower and the known, contextualism is an interactive, dynamic worldview. Moreover, nothing in the event is permanent or immutable because each particular changes with the flux of time. The contextualist focuses on the richness of experience and on shared meanings that arise out of interactions with others. Truth lies in the process of taking up the whole context of the event, in its "thick description," including its complexities, ambiguities, and contradictions (Geertz, 1973). And so meaning is embodied in our experience of the world. "On the one hand, cognitive activity is intimately tied to the organism's being and acting in the real world. On the other hand, cognitive activity cannot come into being and proceed without the cognitive agent being part of a social world" (Shanon, 1990, p. 163). (p. 18)

What we would alert the reader to in this quotation is that Gillespie (1992) emphasizes immediate, unfiltered experience. For the contextualist, this immediate experience is ever changing and in flux. In addition, immediately given experience is taken as a whole, with analysis of experience being at best a secondary concern.

On the jacket of the recent book, *Varieties of Scientific Contextualism*, edited by Hayes, Hayes, Reese, and Sarbin (1993), it is observed that "contextualism has been receiving increased attention from psychologists and other social scientists frustrated with the dominant mechanistic view within psychology. It is a fresh approach that cuts across old quarrels and polarities." The advantages of contextualism seen by its adherents are exemplified in the following statements. Ford and Lerner (1992) propose that their contextualistic approach will "put the understanding of human development on firmer scientific grounds" (p. x). Similarly, Morris (1991) suggests that contextualism "offers new perspectives that raise new questions, put aside old questions, and provide new answers" (p. 125). According to Gillespie (1992), contextualism is important because "contextualistic thinkers have been especially active in showing the inadequacy of objectivist and reductionist methodologies for understanding human behavior . . . but they have also been actively producing different conceptions of science and theories of cognition" (p. 39). Likewise, Blackman (1993) suggests, "The root metaphor of contextualism provides a different approach to the understanding of natural phenomena from that of the more traditional scientific emphasis (usually reductionist) on mechanisms" (p. 238). Hayes (1993) optimistically sums up these views, stating that "contextualism is being looked to as a framework within which psychology may advance, stripped of needless mechanism and needless philosophical inconsistencies. . . . Contextualism, it seems, is suddenly a progressive alternative" (p. 11).

Contextualists, as we have indicated, have charged that academic or mainstream psychology, by which we mean all areas of psychology that employ widely accepted methods such as experimentation, is empirically and conceptually bankrupt. Contemporary cognitive psychology is a good example of mainstream psychology that, according to Bruner (1990), is not merely practically worthless but entirely worthless. A similar charge has been made by a number of individuals who sail under various banners such as constructivism, social constructionism, and cultural psychology, among others, which are species of contextualism, all of them being forms of relativism.

On what is this wholesale rejection of academic psychology based? Is it based on theories that are demonstrably superior at explaining data? No, there is not a hint of such a demonstration in the writings of the relativists. Actually, the situation is worse. Seldom do the relativists even bother to compare their theories to those of mainstream psychology. Nor is the rejection of mainstream psychology based on theories that are more parsimonious than those espoused by most academicians. Neither parsimony nor any other logical consideration figures prominently in the wholesale rejection of mainstream contemporary theories by contextualists.

If it is not data or logical considerations that are cited by the contextualists in their rejection of mainstream psychology, what is it? Two major reasons seem to be cited most often by contextualists. One is that they judge the worth of a particular approach in terms of whether it is consistent with their metatheory, contextualism. Thus, if a particular approach has arisen on the basis of a so-called mechanistic metatheory, it is rejected out of hand as worthless by the contextualists and their close allies. It does not matter if the theory being rejected is of major explanatory usefulness in some area of psychology. If it is not consistent with the contextualistic metatheory, it is simply rejected as of no possible usefulness. Because most of mainstream psychology is based on a metatheory that is not congenial to the contextualists, little of it finds favor with them. It is ironic that contextualists and their close allies, who reject mainstream psychology in uncompromising terms, consistently portray themselves as unfairly rejected by mainstream psychology.

A second reason why contextualists reject mainstream psychology is as follows. They embrace an epistemology that sees questions that are not normally given much prominence in mainstream psychology as important. For example, Bruner (1990) is interested in questions of the following type: "How does the concept of Self differ in Homeric Greece and in the postindustrial world" (p. 5)? There is nothing wrong with the concerns of the contextualists as such, but that is not to say there is nothing wrong with their approach. On one hand, many of them ask us to solve empirical problems using a variety of methods, derived mainly from nonscientific sources, that to date have not been shown to be effective and have yet to prove their worth. Of course, the future may show such methods to be effective, but that is not the case at present. On the other hand, the contextualists ask us to dismiss that portion of psychology that is based on methods such as experimentation, methods that have proved their worth. The logic of the relativists seems to be as follows: Because you are not answering the questions we deem to be important, then everything you deem to be important is, without exception, worthless.

CONTEXTUALISM, PRAGMATISM,
AND POSTMODERNISM

Contextualism as a philosophy of science stems from a view that is known as pragmatism (see Goodman, 1995, for an excellent reader on the origins and current status of pragmatism). The version of pragmatism adopted by contextualism, which stems from James rather than Peirce, takes the form of radical empiricism and may be regarded as a type of postmodernism. Thus, contextualism has much in common with these other forms of postmodernism, as will be considered in greater detail later. Although the form of pragmatism that adopts radical empiricism is a major force in American philosophy itself, it has not had much influence in the philosophy of science per se. Of course, radical empiricism itself was a major force in the philosophy of science and in science itself from approximately 1880 to 1900, but it has since diminished in influence. Viewed in this way, contextualism and various forms of relativism are a return to old, discarded ways of thinking about science. Despite its checkered past, as we have noted, contextualism has been seen by many of its adherents as a more promising approach to the development of scientific psychology than more traditional and modern approaches.

Certain fundamental features of postmodernism, of which contextualism is a species, are that our inferences about the world are not constrained by the world, knowledge is socially constructed, experimental methodology is not a useful way of gaining information and is therefore passé, and knowledge can be usefully constructed employing a variety of nonexperimental methods such as hermeneutics. Although a variety of contextualists clearly accept all or most tenets of postmodernism, others accept similar principles but may not call themselves contextualists. We have two major reasons for treating and referring to all of these individuals as contextualists. First, as indicated, they share a significant number of similar beliefs. Second, when the writings of these individuals are examined, it is often found that their ideas originate in similar sources. As a major example, many individuals who call themselves constructivists, constructionists, or postmodernists, rather than contextualists, cite Richard Rorty as a major source of ideas compatible with their own. Rorty himself is recognized as possibly the most outstanding theorist of contemporary pragmatism. One of Rorty's major positions is that truth is created rather than discovered. For example, he said approvingly, "About 200 years ago, the idea that truth was made rather than found began to take hold of the imagination of Europe" (Rorty, 1989, p. 107). Fox (1993), a sociologist, in agreement with Rorty, said, "Science as knowledge is fabricated rather than discovered" (p. 16). In agreement with Fox, Nicolson (1995) says that this is "a perspective which is increasingly present at the periphery of social psychology and gaining a robust presence within feminist psychology" (p. 125).

William James is widely regarded as a major father of pragmatism. In certain respects, Rorty's ideas are hardly different from those of James, who said that truth means "that ideas . . . become true just in so far as they help us to get into satisfactory relation with other parts of our experience" (James, 1907/1975, p. 58). James went on to say,

> A new opinion counts as "true" just in proportion as it gratifies the individual's desire to assimilate the novel in his experience to his beliefs in stock. . . . When old truth grows, then, by new truth's addition, it is for subjective reasons. (p. 59)

As Leahey (1992), a prominent historian of psychology, has indicated, toward the end of his life James elaborated a system that he called *radical empiricism,* denoting his increasing acceptance of the implications of pragmatism. From a radical empiricist perspective, the world is pure experience and nothing else. According to James's form of radical empiricism, which was strongly influenced by Ernst Mach, we may not look for any form of reality that may be constraining our experience. This feature of Jamesian pragmatism and contextualism is shared by many of the current postmodern movements, which go by various names and are sympathetic to contextualism in numerous other respects.

As indicated, constructivism, which has proved extremely popular in educational circles, clearly has much in common with contextualism, and each appears to be a species of the other. For example, Fosnot (1996) has said of constructivism, "Based on work in psychology, philosophy, and anthropology, the theory describes knowledge as temporary, developmental, nonobjective, internally constructed, and socially and culturally mediated" (p. ix). The close relationship of constructivism to pragmatism and thus to contextualism is apparent in the following quote from von Glasersfeld (1996), a noted constructivist: "Knowledge does not and cannot have the purpose of producing representations of an independent reality, but instead has an adaptive function" (p. 3).

A view closely related to constructivism is a position called cultural psychology (Shweder & Sullivan, 1993). Cultural psychology is not merely about studying culture but holds the view that truth is determined by the culture in which it is found. Bruner (1990) says of this position, "Is what we know 'absolute,' or is it always relative to some perspective, some point of view? Is there an 'aboriginal reality,' or as Nelson Goodman would put it, is reality a construction?" (p. 24). Bruner suggests that his view is a variety of Rorty's pragmatism. He notes that

> the view that I have been expressing here falls into that category [Rorty's pragmatism]—as "simply anti-essentialism applied to notions like 'truth,' 'knowledge,' 'language,' 'morality' and other similar objects of philosophical theorizing," and he [Rorty] illustrates it by reference to William James's definition of the "true" as "what is good in the way of belief." In support of James, Rorty remarks, "his point is that it is of no use being told that truth is 'correspondence with reality.' " (p. 25)

A milder form of contextualism, which calls itself the transactional worldview, has been applied to environmental psychology (Altman & Rogoff, 1987). Unlike James and Rorty, who see truth as entirely constructed, the transactional view has been seen as having the following characteristics: "openness to seeking general principles, but primary interest in accounting for event[s]; pragmatic application of principles and laws as appropriate to situation[s]; openness to emergent explanatory principles; prediction acceptable but not necessary" (Altman & Rogoff, 1987, p. 13). The transactional view is an instance of what we shall later call modified contextualism, as opposed to the views of Rorty and James, which are characteristic of what we shall call philosophic contextualism.

As the previous treatment may indicate, our concern with contextualism extends to related movements that, like contextualism, adopt radical empiricism as its ontology. We are not concerned, however, with what Guba (1990) describes as critical theory. Critical theory adopts a form of realism as its ontology, coupled with a subjectivist epistemology. Under critical theory, Guba includes "neo-Marxism, materialism, feminism, Freierism, participatory inquiry, and other similar movements" (p. 23).

WHY PSYCHOLOGISTS ARE ATTRACTED
TO CONTEXTUALISM

We see three major reasons why some psychologists are attracted to contextualism, two of which were alluded to earlier. The first, which applies to many but not all contextualists, is the emphasis of contextualism on experience. By this we mean its radical empiricism, which is evident in the previous remarks of Gillespie, Rorty, and Bruner, among others. Most of the modern-day contextualists express a keen dislike for the idea that there is some reality behind experience. They reject theories and laws and express a preference for functional relations. This explains, for example, why such unlikely bedfellows as Sarbin (1993), a personality theorist who advocates the narrative technique as the main means of understanding psychology, and Hayes (1993), a behavior analyst who certainly approves of operant conditioning techniques as a means for advancing psychology, both describe themselves as contextualists. It is of course well-known that Skinnerians are radical empiricists who eschew theorizing (see, e.g., Skinner, 1950), and thus it is not surprising that some of them are attracted to contextualism.

The second reason, in our view, why some psychologists are attracted to contextualism, albeit in a modified form, is that they attempt to understand real-world events in all of their complexity. This is also illustrated in Gillespie's (1992) definition of contextualism, cited earlier, and it certainly characterizes the position of life span developmental psychologists, many of whom favor multilevel determination. For example, Lerner (1993), a life span developmental psychologist, has said,

> Developmental contextualism is a synthetic (multilevel-integrative) and change-oriented view of human development. It rests on two key ideas. First, there are variables from multiple, *qualitatively* distinct levels of analysis, or levels of organization, involved in human life (e.g., biology, psychology, sociology, and history). . . . This perspective is linked to a second key idea: Variables from the several levels of organization comprising human life exist in reciprocal relation. The structure and function of variables from any one level influence, and are influenced by, the structure and function of variables from the other levels. (pp. 301-302)

Later, we shall see that some developmental contextualists, recognizing that not all variables that influence a system can be studied simultaneously, propose to constrain it in various ways. This produces a variety of contextualism that is closer to psychology as it is conventionally practiced than are other varieties of contextualism.

The third reason why some psychologists are attracted to contextualism—and indeed to its various postmodern allies, such as constructivism—is the acceptance of the thesis of underdetermination. Underdetermination in its most radical form holds that any finite set of data may be reconciled with an infinite number of theories. According to this view, to accommodate discrepant findings, a theory might be revised in a variety of ways. These revisions could involve, for example, modifying auxiliary assumptions, redefining certain concepts, and so on, without changing the theory in any significant respect. All of these modified theories would be seen as equivalent with reference to the facts to be explained. Acceptance of the underdetermination thesis implies that no one theory is better than any other theory, and thus one is free to hold whichever theory suits one's convenience.

Although the underdetermination thesis is widely accepted among contextualists, it finds little favor among scientists and some recent philosophers of science. The objection to underdetermination is simply this: Although it is conceivable as a logical proposition, it is totally unrealistic as a practical one. That is, some logical alternative to a currently accepted, satisfactory theory may fail to satisfy many of the various demands imposed by the data at hand. Thus, underdetermination exists only as a logical alternative and not as a realistic alternative.

Are the contextualists and their closely related allies justified in rejecting mainstream academic psychology based on their radical empiricism or phenomenological approach to experience, their emphasis on multilevel determination, and their acceptance of underdetermination? Our answer to this question, which will be developed throughout the book, is that although the contextualists may have something valuable to contribute to psychology, contextualism in no way replaces the contribution of academic psychology. In the final analysis, the contributions of contextualism can be evaluated and judged only by employing some of the various criteria employed within academic psychology to evaluate its methods and procedures, as detailed in Chapter 10. The primary error of the contextualists is in strongly claiming that their approach is the only legitimate approach to psychology. In our view, contextualism is of potential usefulness only for selected aspects of psychology, and even there it has yet to prove its mettle.

OBJECTIONS ENCOUNTERED IN
OUR ANALYSIS OF CONTEXTUALISM

It has been suggested to us by various individuals that we should not be engaging in a critical analysis of contextualism. Interestingly, this suggestion has been offered by both contextualists and noncontextualists, although for different reasons.

The Opinion That We Are Rejecting
Contextualism Per Se

Several individuals have suggested that in subjecting contextualism to critical analysis, we are criticizing contextualism in and of itself. This is far from the truth. On one hand, we encourage all varieties of contextualists to develop their position as they see fit. On the other hand, we insist that there are rational criteria for evaluating knowledge claims, and whatever one's approach to science, knowledge claims are subject to the same set of rational criteria. As a matter of fact, rather than us or people like us rejecting contextualism, many contextualists reject the remainder of psychology, as indicated earlier in this chapter. This is a major aspect of contextualism that disturbs us greatly. For contextualists to accuse noncontextualists of narrow-mindedness in the evaluation of their position, given the contextualists' stated views on this matter, is extremely difficult to understand and is like the proverbial pot calling the kettle black.

As for our second point, it is abundantly clear that, to a considerable extent, contextualists of the Sarbin-Bruner wing do not want their knowledge claims judged by the same sort of rational criteria as those applied to other human affairs. Thus, to take some examples, Bruner (1990) approves of knowledge claims that are merely plausible. Sarbin (1993) approves of knowledge claims that are based on narratives. Gergen and Gergen (1991) ask us to put experimentation aside in favor of hypothetical data rotation. The list goes on and on.

In sum, we encourage contextualists to use any methods that they think worthwhile, such as hermeneutics, in the pursuit of knowledge. We are open to the possibility that such methods may thereby produce useful knowledge not attainable by other methods. But such knowledge will have to be evaluated using at least some of the criteria employed to evaluate knowledge produced by other methods such as experimentation. Contrary to the assertions of some contextualists, the methods they recommend do not rule out the rival possibility that other methods such as experimentation may also produce useful knowledge.

The Opinion That Contextualism Does Not Warrant Critical Scrutiny

To the average academic psychologist, the claims of the contextualists regarding the role of methods and theory in psychology are strange indeed, so much so that they have difficulty taking contextualism seriously. Having described the position of contextualists to some of our colleagues, we have been met with two responses. On one hand, it is suggested that we must be mistaken, that contextualists cannot possibly believe in what we have ascribed to them. On the other hand, it is suggested that if contextualists do indeed believe what we have ascribed to them, then they are not worth listening to and should be ignored.

Regarding the attitude of academic psychologists that contextualists have improbable beliefs, the fault lies as much with contextualists as with our colleagues. The fault of our colleagues seems to be that they are totally unprepared and perhaps unwilling to entertain a position that is essentially a mirror reversal of many of their own attitudes toward science, methods, and knowledge. The fault of the contextualists seems to be that they often express their views in the most uncompromising and inaccurate of manners. As Chaiklin (1991) has noted, "The inaccurate characterization of the 'modern' philosophical and 'academic' psychological traditions makes it impossible to engage in a serious ideological debate about existing forms and methods in relation to a postmodern-inspired psychology" (p. 203). As examples of such overblown rhetoric, we learn from Kvale (1992b), for example, that "modern psychology, whether in the naturalist or the humanist version, has become an intellectual secondhand store, displaying a variety of collections from last year's fashions of the neighboring disciplines—'you name it, we have it' " (p. 45). We also learn from Gergen and Gergen (1991) that all experimentation does is confirm our already established beliefs. To the average academic psychologist whose hypotheses have been shot down by experimental results as often as not, the claim of Gergen and Gergen has all the earmarks of unreality. We could cite many other similar examples of contextualists making claims that seem to the average academic psychologist to lack a reasonable mooring in reality.

We disagree with the suggestion of some of our colleagues that if contextualism is as we describe it, it is best ignored. As we said earlier, we are entirely open to the possibility that the contextualistic approach may have something of value to offer psychology that is not available from other approaches. In addition, the influence of contextualism in psychology is of such extent that it would be foolhardy to ignore it. After all, when people from such diverse traditions as clinical-personality psychology (e.g., Sarbin), human experimental psychology (e.g., Deese), developmental psychology (e.g., Ford and Lerner), and behavior analysis (e.g., Hayes) embrace contextualism, a view that proposes a radically different approach to psychology than that currently practiced, their arguments deserve to be both listened to and critically evaluated. That is, we should neither accept nor reject lightly the direction in which the contextualists proposed to lead the field.

The Opinion That We Are Denying the Relevance of Context

In our critical evaluation of contextualism, some have suggested that we are denying the importance of context. This is certainly not the case, and two separate points deserve to be made here.

First, although contextualism emphasizes the importance of context, it is a view that also emphasizes a variety of other positions. These positions include radical empiricism, that history is its proper metaphor, that novelty is always to be expected, and so on. Our interest is, of course, in critically evaluating contextualism along all of these dimensions, including the claims it makes about other approaches to science. Context is but a small part of this total mix.

Second, we are as enthusiastic as any contextualist in proclaiming our belief that context may be of critical importance in a variety of instances. We go more deeply into this point in Chapter 6. In short, *context* is not synonymous with *contextualism,* and we recognize the importance of context as readily as any contextualist.

The Opinion That Contextualism Cannot Be Evaluated by Noncontextualists

An argument made by some contextualists is that contextualism cannot be evaluated by those who, like us, are not themselves contextualists. An important variant of this argument is that contextualism should and must develop in isolation without reference to other rival systems that may exist, such as mechanism (see Hayes et al., 1988). We consider these points so important, wrongheaded, and inimical to scientific and intellectual practice that we forego treatment of them here and discuss them in detail in a later chapter devoted solely to this topic.

SUMMARY AND CONCLUSIONS

In this chapter, it was indicated that contextualism, including its major variants such as social constructionism and interactionism, sees itself as a powerful metatheory that should replace the current dominant metatheory in academic psychology, mechanism. We identified two major wings of contextualism, one closer than the other to the philosophic roots of contextualism. We considered a number of reasons why a critical evaluation of contextualism and the claims made by contextualists is appropriate at this time. It was indicated that contextualists criticize mainstream psychology on an epistemological and ontological basis, rather than on an empirical one. Contextualism was shown to have its roots in the radical empiricism of Ernst Mach, who heavily influenced William James. We considered various reasons why contextualism is popular among contemporary psychologists. We described various objections that have been raised to the fact that we would undertake an analysis of contextualism. It may be concluded on the basis of the considerations advanced in this chapter that contextualism has its basis in 19th-century thought, rather than only being a product of more recent pragmatism.

Philosophy of Science and Psychology

A variety of positions in the philosophy of science has had a major impact on the way that psychology is practiced. Understanding these positions is indispensable to evaluating the place of contextualism in contemporary psychology. In this chapter, we describe early conceptions of science and five positions in the philosophy of science that have exercised a major influence in psychology. Before doing that, we shall deal with the opinion of some psychologists that delving into the philosophy of science is irrelevant to the practice of scientific psychology.

THE OPINION THAT PHILOSOPHY OF SCIENCE IS IRRELEVANT

It is not uncommon to believe that it is possible to do quite acceptable science in the absence of familiarity with the philosophy of science. We certainly agree with this assessment. There is no doubt that many psychologists who have contributed substantially to the field neither have nor wish to have formal knowledge of the philosophy of science. For example, Tolman (1959),

19

certainly one of the more productive theorists in all of psychology this century, said,

> I am personally antipathetic to the notion that science progresses through intense, self-conscious analysis of where one has got and where one is going. Such analyses are obviously a proper function for the philosopher of science and they may be valuable for many individual scientists. But I myself become frightened and restricted when I begin to worry too much as to what particular logical and methodological canons I should or should not obey. (p. 93)

Although we accept the validity of Tolman's (1959) point, it seems clear to us that one does not need to have explicit knowledge of the philosophy of science to be influenced by it. We would argue that it is the rule, rather than the exception, for individuals to conduct science according to some conception that they have of science, which may be implicit rather than explicit. This conception will determine the topics of interest to the individual and the theories and methods employed. Although we believe that many may not always be aware of their scientific presuppositions, and this is not a bar to doing good research, we hardly think that it is best to be unaware of them. For example, if there is some alternative to an accepted presupposition, we fail to see how being aware of it would be a disadvantage; to the contrary, it might well be an advantage.

To demonstrate the point that one's philosophy of science, whether explicit or implicit, affects one's practice of science, we appeal to two different types of evidence. On one hand, many individuals of otherwise quite different persuasion have made similar claims in strong and certain terms; these diverse individuals clearly think that psychology is practiced by others according to one or another philosophy of science. On the other hand, numerous and convincing examples suggest that individuals themselves conduct science according to some explicit philosophy of science.

Opinions of Others

Consider some opinions of others concerning the influence of the philosophy of science on psychology. Scriven (1964) suggested, "I believe that philosophy has an enormous influence on psychology though it has often been very bad" (p. 182). Spence (1960) said,

A number of psychologists, Tolman, Skinner, and Stevens, stimulated by the writings of Bridgeman, have centered their efforts largely on the empirical component of scientific method. Under the watchword of operationism, they have carefully considered and laid down the requirements that scientific concepts must fulfill in order to insure testability and thus empirical meaning. (p. 3)

Leahey (1992), writing many years after Spence, confirmed his analysis of the importance of operationism and logical positivism to behaviorism in particular and psychology in general. According to Leahey,

In the 1930s logical positivism had provided a philosophical justification for behaviorism, helping to redefine psychology as the study of behavior rather than mind. Positivism modified at least the formulation of the leading learning theories of the era and completely captured the allegiance of young experimental psychologists who hitched their stars to operationism, using it as an analytic tool to define which problems were worth studying and which were blind alleys. (p. 421)

As an example of the influence of positivism on a specific individual, consider the following from John-Steiner (1997):

As a graduate student in the 1950s, I was taught the positivist model of psychological research: A focus on precise, limited problems of behavior. Broader human questions that motivated me were put aside as unscientific. As time went on, however, I found that narrow focus constricting. (p. xiii)

Harré (1990) stated his own experiences with social psychology:

That a field of academic specialism should exist so shot through with conceptual confusions, unexamined assumptions from antique philosophical positions long since demolished, and propounding theories of such gross implausibility seemed to me quite shocking. (p. 342)

Van Langenhove (1995) has said of Harré's position, "Many philosophers of science and more and more psychologists share the above views" (p. 10).

Slife and Williams (1995) suggest that a variety of philosophic theories, which can be collectively grouped under postmodernism, contain "no metaphysical absolutes; no fundamental and abstract truths, laws, or principles that determine what the world is like and what happens in it" (p. 54). They go on to say,

> This position rejects at once psychodynamic instincts and unconscious minds, behavioristic laws of learning and conditioning, humanistic needs and growth potentials, and cognitive structures and processes. Indeed postmodernists tend to be suspicious of structures and abstractions of any sort that can be invoked as explanation. (p. 54)

As the previous quotes amply demonstrate, one's philosophy of science determines to a significant extent one's more specific scientific practices. These range from the sort of empirical endeavors in which one engages to the more formal modes of theorizing that one might or might not embrace. On the other hand, one's philosophy of science may have little relationship to the quality and importance of one's contribution.

Two Examples of Suggesting How Psychology Should Be Practiced

Some examples of individuals explicitly suggesting how science should be practiced are as follows. Lachman, Lachman, and Butterfield (1979), in an influential textbook on cognitive psychology, enthusiastically adopted a Kuhnian perspective on the philosophy of science. They suggested that cognitive psychology should consciously attempt to develop strictly along the lines suggested by Kuhn's philosophy of science. That many cognitive psychologists agreed with Lachman et al. is suggested by Leahey (1992), who said that

> Kuhn's views themselves became popular with many psychologists. As cognitive psychology seemed to replace behaviorism in the later 1960s, references to scientific revolutions and paradigm clashes abounded. Kuhn's doctrine seemed to justify a revolutionary attitude: Behaviorism must be overthrown, it cannot be reformed. (p. 421)

As a second example, Slife and Williams (1997) advocate the development of a specialization that they call theoretical psychology (basically, a philosophical analysis of concepts and methods) and suggest that it is incompatible with the philosophy of science known as logical positivism, citing various reasons why this is so. They go on to say that the practice of theoretical psychology is compatible with various postmodern developments in the philosophy of science, such as feminism, social constructionism, structuralism, phenomenology, existentialism, and hermeneutics, among others.

EARLY CONCEPTIONS OF SCIENCE

A good starting point for understanding the development of science is Plato's view of knowledge. For Plato, knowledge did not grow out of experience. True knowledge was innate and consisted of forms. There was a form for every class of objects that has a general name, such as cat, dog, and so on. Particular cats and dogs were merely imperfect replicas of the ideationally held true forms. Thus, the forms or ideas alone are the only realities and, accordingly, sense experience is not a guide to true knowledge. Plato was therefore a rationalist. As Dampier (1949) notes, "Whatever be the truth of Plato's doctrine of ideas from a metaphysical point of view, the mental attitude which gave it birth is not adapted to further the cause of experimental science" (p. 34).

Plato's student Aristotle gave much more credence to knowledge based on experience. Aristotle distinguished between scientific knowledge and practical knowledge. Scientific knowledge had two characteristics: It was certain, and it was causal. The notion that scientific knowledge was certain lasted much longer than the notion that it was causal. Science as causal knowledge suffered its first major blow, ironically enough, at the hands of Newton. As Dampier (1949) indicated,

Newton's work was assailed by Huygens and Leibniz as unphilosophical, because he offered no explanation of the ultimate cause of gravitational attraction. Newton was the first to see clearly that an attempt at an explanation, if necessary or possible at all, comes at a later stage. He took the known facts, formed a theory which fitted them and could be expressed in mathematical terms, deduced mathematical and logical consequences from the theory, again compared them with the facts by observation and experiment, and saw that the concordance was complete. It was not necessary to know the cause of the attraction; Newton regarded that as a secondary and independent problem, as yet only in the stage suitable for speculation. We might now go further, and say that it is not even necessary to know that such an attraction really exists. All the complex planetary motions *happen as though* each particle in the solar system attracts every other in agreement with the law of mass and inverse square, and that is enough for the mathematical astronomer. (p. 170)

It hardly needs to be added, perhaps, that Newton's approach to science is widely accepted today.

Although Aristotle's notion that science is necessarily causal was rebuffed by Newton, the idea that science provided apodictic, or certain, knowledge continued to be accepted in the 17th and 18th centuries. As Laudan (1996) has observed,

> Bacon, Locke, Leibniz, Descartes, Newton, and Kant are in accord about this way of characterizing science. They may disagree about how precisely to certify the certainty of knowledge, but none quarrels with the claim that science and infallible knowledge are coterminous. (p. 213)

One of the major blows to certain knowledge was delivered by Hume's analysis of induction in the 18th century. As is well known, Hume (1993) indicated that no number of positive instances could serve logically to make a generalization certain. That is, no matter how many white swans are observed, it is logically possible that the next one observed will be black. As a result of Hume's observations and other considerations, the idea that science involves certain knowledge began to be abandoned in the 19th century. However, the idea that science was a unique activity, different from other forms of activity, was still retained. In this period, the distinctive feature of knowledge was said to be its methodology. Commenting on this, Laudan (1996) said,

With certainty no longer available as the demarcation tool, nineteenth century philosophers and scientists quickly forged other tools to do the job. Thinkers as diverse as Comte, Bain, Jevons, Helmholtz, and Mach (to name only a few) began to insist that what really marks science off from everything else is its *methodology*. (p. 213)

As we shall see later, the search for what demarcates scientific knowledge from other sorts of knowledge continued into the 20th century, without resolution.

FIVE MAJOR POSITIONS IN THE PHILOSOPHY OF SCIENCE

Having examined some older conceptions of science, we now describe five major positions that have had a substantial impact on psychology. The first two positions described are varieties of empiricism. One is radical empiricism, or phenomenology, which is the precursor of contextualism. The second is the logical empiricism of the Vienna circle, which was the received view in mainstream psychology until roughly 1960 and which many feel is still influential. The third and fourth views are negative reactions to logical empiricism. These are the views of Popper and Kuhn, respectively. The fifth view, that of Laudan, is a reaction to both logical empiricism and the relativism of Kuhn and others. Our view of the appropriate philosophy of science of usefulness to psychology is that of Laudan or, more generally, the position known as naturalism. Later in the book, we will develop various implications of Laudan's view for the proper conduct of contemporary psychology.

Radical Empiricism

The essence of radical empiricism is the desire to restrict knowledge to that which is immediately observable and nothing else. The earliest of the most prominent radical empiricists were certainly Berkeley and Comte. But Mach was probably the most influential radical empiricist in science, particularly physics, in the period from roughly 1880 to the early 1900s. Mach conceived the task of science to be the bringing of order into elementary observations, which he described as sensations. Mach refused to believe in the existence of unseen entities (e.g., atoms). Mach believed that many scientific concepts went beyond direct experience and were therefore meta-physical. Mach said, "No point of view has absolute permanent validity. Each has importance only for some given end" (Mach, 1906/1959, p. 37). Schlick, quoted by Holton (1988), describes Mach's approach to science as follows:

> There exists in this world nothing whatever other than sensations and their connections. In place of the word "sensations," Mach liked to use rather the more neutral word "elements" . . . scientific knowledge of the world consists, according to Mach, in nothing else than the simplest possible description of the connection between the elements, and it has as its only aim the intellectual mastery of those facts by means of the least possible effort of thought. (p. 240)

The influence of Mach's radical empiricism in physics declined with the publication of Albert Einstein's theory of relativity. Actually, Einstein himself, in his younger days, was a devotee of Mach. With the development of relativity theory, however, Einstein became increasingly skeptical of Mach's views. Einstein (1951) said,

> It was Ernst Mach, who in his *History of Mechanics,* shook this dogmatic faith [in classical mechanics]; this book exercised a pro-found influence upon me in this regard when I was a student. I see Mach's greatness in his incorruptible skepticism and independence; in my younger years, however, Mach's epistemological position also influenced me very greatly, a position which today appears to me to be essentially untenable. (p. 21)

The influence of Mach's radical empiricism in psychology comes mainly through William James. James is described by Hilgard (1987) as a phenom-enologist whose preference was to stay with immediate experience. Hilgard says that James is "one who accepts naturalistic observations in their totality, without the requirement of analysis into simpler components: a description of experience free of suppositions about it" (p. 61). James (1912/1976) defined radical empiricism as follows: "To be radical, an empiricism must neither admit into its constructions any element that is not directly experi-enced, nor exclude from them any element that is directly experienced" (p. 22). James's conception of legitimate sources of experience included the paranormal, mysticism, and religion (Taylor, 1996).

One of the most influential applications of radical empiricism to psychology came through operant psychology in the writings of B. F. Skinner. In his influential paper, "Are Theories of Learning Necessary?" Skinner (1950) eschewed the use of theory, by which he meant "explanation of an observed fact which appeals to events taking place somewhere else, at some other level of observation, described in different terms, and measured, if at all, in different dimensions" (p. 193). Operant psychologists suggest that the task of the scientist is to describe functional relationships between variables and nothing more. Any attempt to provide an explanation for the functional relationship is regarded as unscientific and metaphysical.

Another strain of radical empiricism in psychology is to be found in various phenomenologies. As described by Turner (1965),

> In general terms, phenomenology is that empiricistic philosophy which asserts that the givens of experience are configurational entities having a unique integrity of their own and are, therefore, not reducible to sense contents or to any other elemental structure. Stress is placed on uniqueness of events. Formalized science is suspect because of its abstractive character. (p. 60)

Some contemporary exponents of phenomenology are Kenneth Gergen and Jerome Bruner. The outstanding proponent of contemporary pragmatism of the type espoused by James is, as was previously indicated, Richard Rorty.

It may surprise some that the viewpoint of individuals such as Gergen and Bruner is closely related to that of another radical empiricist, Skinner. They all are descendants of such radical empiricists as Berkeley, Comte, Mach, and James and, as such, are concerned more with description than with explanation.

Logical Empiricism

Logical empiricism, also known as logical positivism, developed and became a dominant philosophic perspective in science and psychology in the first half of the 20th century. Although it has waned in popularity in recent decades, many consider it to continue to be an influential position in psychology (Bechtel, 1988; Smith, Harré, & Van Langenhove, 1995a, 1995b). The term *logical* is meant to reflect the use of symbolic logic to formalize scientific systems. The term *empiricism* is meant to emphasize the importance of experience in science. In contrast to radical empiricists, who emphasize uninterpreted experience, the logical empiricists fully embraced interpreting experience within theoretical systems. Logical empiricists emphasized the verifiability theory of meaning. According to this view, the meaning of a sentence is the set of conditions that show that this sentence is true.

The logical empiricists distinguished sharply between the context of discovery and the context of justification. The context of discovery included all those processes involved in the formation of an idea, concept, or hypothesis and need not in itself be justified. That is, the scientist was free to construct hypotheses or theories on any basis whatsoever. However, the context of justification had to follow logical rules. That is, hypotheses, theories, and the like had to be justified, employing the normal methodological canons of science. For the logical empiricists, the context of discovery belonged to the realm of psychology, and the context of justification belonged to the realm of the philosophy of science.

In putting forth the central concept of the verifiability theory of meaning, the logical empiricists were aware that they had not solved Hume's problem of induction. The problem of induction, of course, is that a general statement cannot be shown to be true on the basis of a finite number of observations. However, the logical empiricists did think that if a sufficient number of confirming observations were made, one could come closer and closer to the truth. This verificationist view was subsequently brought into serious question by Popper. Popper (1959) indicated that the number of implications of a theory or hypothesis is infinite, and so any number of finite observations does not increase the probability of a statement being true.

Falsificationism

Popper (1959), in rejecting the verification theory of meaning, suggested that for a scientific statement to be meaningful, it had to be falsifiable. The idea here is that although no number of particular instances will serve to indicate that some statement is true, that statement can be rejected on the basis of a single falsifying instance. For Popper, the ability of a statement to be falsified was the demarcation criterion between science and nonscience. Many psychologists today think of falsification as an indispensable feature of scientific theories.

Popper's falsification criterion ran into its own problems because, as many indicated, it was possible to evade the implications of a falsifying incident, and reasonably so, by appealing to a number of specific considerations. For example, the instrument from which the observation was made may have been inaccurate. A minor adjustment in assumptions might serve to make the statement consistent with the so-called falsifying observation. These and many other things could be done to evade the implications of falsification because falsification when dealing with empirical observations is hardly the same thing as falsification when dealing with logical statements.

Lakatos (1970, 1978) is widely recognized as having produced a version of falsificationism, which he calls sophisticated falsificationism, that avoids the problems in Popper's version of falsificationism, which has sometimes been called naive falsificationism (Kuhn, 1970a). Lakatos emphasizes evaluation of research programs rather than theories in isolation. Theories have a hard core, which consists of assumptions that are not themselves candidates for falsification, and a protective belt, which consists of auxiliary hypotheses that are candidates for falsification. Another major suggestion of Lakatos's is that falsification becomes a major factor in the evaluation of a theory or research program only when that theory or research program ceases to be progressive, that is, fails to generate new predictions. Gholson and Barker (1985) consider Lakatos's approach to science to be superior to that of Kuhn but inferior to that of Laudan, both of which are discussed later.

Thomas Kuhn's System and Its Relation to Relativism

In his monumental book, *The Structure of Scientific Revolutions,* Kuhn (1962) differentiated five stages in the development of a science: (a) immature science, (b) normal science, (c) a crisis stage, (d) a revolutionary stage, and (e) a stage in which the crisis is resolved. Immature science, which Kuhn hardly considers to be science in many respects, is practiced in the absence of a dominant paradigm. The next stage, normal science, requires the establishment of what Kuhn had called the paradigm. A paradigm consists of a disciplinary matrix (e.g., a common education of scientists) and exemplars (e.g., force = mass × acceleration). At any one time, science is dominated by a single paradigm. During this period, normal science is practiced. In the normal science period, scientists seek to articulate the implications of the paradigm and in no sense seek to falsify it. Ultimately, problems arise, and the adequacy of the paradigm begins to be questioned. This is the crisis point. Kuhn suggests that crises, when they appear, are quickly resolved, and a revolutionary new paradigm emerges. At this point, normal science begins again.

Kuhn's system is widely regarded as a type of relativism, one that has had great influence in psychology and the social sciences. According to Barnes (1982), a well-known relativist, it was Kuhn's "account of scientific revolutions, with its *explicit relativistic implications,* which ensured that Kuhn's work became widely known" (p. 55, emphasis added). Similarly, a number of prominent philosophers of science—for example, Couvalis, Laudan, Kitcher, and Shapere—regard Kuhn as a relativist. Curd and Cover (1998), after discussing a number of Kuhn's positions that lead to relativism, sum up the matter by saying, "According to Kuhn, judgments about scientific rationality and progress can only be made relative to paradigms. With good reason, then, Kuhn's overall position is aptly described as a version of relativism" (p. 219). This opinion is widely shared in the philosophy of science, if not in psychology and the social sciences.

There are some who do not regard Kuhn as a relativist, a prominent example being Bernstein (1983). Bernstein's view is that Kuhn attempted to steer a third course between complete relativism, on one hand, and complete objectivism, on the other hand. As evidence for his view, Bernstein points out in various instances that Kuhn suggested that scientific matters were settled to some extent on the basis of rational criteria. Although Bernstein's argument is reasonable up to a point, we think he is incorrect in the final analysis inasmuch as that Kuhn's position contradicts Bernstein's own definition of relativism. Bernstein defines relativism as follows:

> As I have characterized the relativist, his or her essential claim is that there can be no higher appeal than to a given conceptual scheme, language game, set of social practices, or historical epoch. There is a nonreducible plurality of such schemes, paradigms, and practices; there is no substantive overarching framework in which radically different and alternative schemes are commensurable—no universal standards that somehow stand outside of and above these competing alternatives. (pp. 11-12)

This definition of relativism, with which we agree, can plausibly be taken as indicative of Kuhn's view that all scientific decisions, whether concerned with data, theory, or methodology, ultimately depend on the paradigm in which they are embedded. Although many quotes from Kuhn would serve to make this point, a particularly telling one is as follows: "If, as I have already urged, there can be no scientifically or empirically neutral system of language or concepts, then the proposed construction of alternate tests and theories must proceed from within one or another paradigm-based tradition" (Kuhn, 1962, p. 145).

Relativism, as commonly used, is a term with distinct meanings. In an effort to be precise, Laudan (1996) described three distinct types of relativism: *Epistemic relativism* is the view that any theory can be rationally retained in the face of any conceivable evidence. *Metamethodological relativism* is the view that the standards for theory evaluation are mere conventions or matters of taste. *Linguistic relativism* is the view that the conceptual framework of one paradigm cannot be understood or made intelligible in the language of another. Kuhn's philosophy of science exhibits all three forms of relativism.

The epistemic relativism of Kuhn (1962) may be illustrated by his statement concerning the adherents of different paradigms:

> Though each may hope to convert the other to his way of seeing his science and its problems, neither may hope to prove his case. The competition between paradigms is not the sort of battle that can be resolved by proofs. (p. 147)

As for metamethodological relativism, Kuhn's position is that the standards for theory evaluation are mere conventions or matters of taste and that scientists are not aware of the rules and methods that guide their behavior. Kuhn has said of scientists that they "are little better than laymen at characterizing the established bases of their field, its legitimate problems and methods" (Kuhn, 1962, p. 47). Kuhn is strongly committed to linguistic relativism, so much so that he has said that the conceptual framework of one paradigm cannot be understood or made intelligible in the language of another.

Many relativists are under the impression that relativism is the only alternative to positivism. Laudan (1996), in his monumental treatment of the philosophy of science, has shown that relativism and positivism have much in common and that, indeed, relativism is the progeny of positivism.

Laudan's Version of Normative Naturalism

Naturalism, a point of view that has come to be adopted by a number of leading and influential philosophers of science (see, e.g., Giere, 1985; Kim, 1988), is defined by Callebaut (1993) as follows:

> Naturalism as a philosophic movement claims that whatever exists or happens in the world is susceptible to explanation by natural scientific methods; it denies that there is or could be anything which lies in principle beyond the scope of scientific explanation. Although naturalism is firmly rooted in the philosophic tradition (materialism, empiricism), a thoroughly naturalized philosophy of science is only being developed now. (p. xv)

Some early naturalists would include Quine and Kuhn. Kuhn (1962), of course, suggested that science could be understood by examining histories of scientists in action. He and others have suggested that sociology and psychology have a lot to contribute to the philosophy of science. Indeed, Giere (1985) has suggested that naturalism is "the only viable approach to the philosophy of science" (p. 331).

One of the problems with naturalism is that of deciding how to get from what scientists do (descriptive practice) to what norms they should follow (normative practice). Laudan's (1996) variety of naturalism is one that stresses that philosophy of science can be normative as well as naturalistic. Normative naturalism is "a view about the status of epistemology and philosophy of science; it is a meta-epistemology. It maintains that epistemology can discharge its traditional normative role and nonetheless claim a sensitivity to empirical evidence" (Laudan, 1996, p. 154). The fact that epistemology can be and should be influenced by empirical evidence is one of the more attractive features of Laudan's position.

Laudan's (1996) approach, unlike many other recent approaches, is neither a species of positivism nor of relativism. As Laudan has recently suggested, positivism and relativism, which are normally looked on as opposite ends of a continuum, have a great deal in common. Laudan may be profitably consulted for a description of the major tenets that are common to both positivism and various species of relativism, as can Earman (1993).

In what follows, we describe some of the major features of Laudan's (1996) epistemological position. Laudan's position, in our view, has many implications for psychology.

Underdetermination

Underdetermination will be treated at length in Chapter 9. For now, we note only the following. It is generally agreed that scientific theories are not logically entailed by their evidence and that a given body of evidence could logically support other theories: This is the only sense in which scientific theories have been shown to be underdetermined. However, relativists have gone on to make the strong claim that on a given body of evidence, an infinite number of theories can be constructed. As a logical proposition, this is true. The implicit argument contained in the relativists' view is that we must give our cognitive assent to any proposition that is logically possible. For example, it is logically possible that you exist only in the dream of some sleeping person. Do you have any reason to believe that?

Laudan (1996) suggests that all logically possible versions of a theory that follow from a given body of evidence may not be equally reasonable. That this is the case can be illustrated by considering an example from Sagan's (1995) recent book, *The Demon-Haunted World*. Sagan examines the proposition that "a fire-breathing dragon lives in my garage." He arranges various tests to determine the dragon's existence, for example, seeing whether footprints are left on the floor when it is covered by flour. No footprints are found. The result of Sagan's treatment is as follows: What conclusions are possible after other numerous and exhaustive tests of the proposition also prove negative? Of course, the possibility that a dragon resides in the garage is still logically tenable. But as Sagan concludes, it is more reasonable to believe that it does not. As Laudan has said, "the fact that a course of action is logically possible does not create the slightest presumption that such a course of action is rational" (p. 49).

Methodological Rules

Examples of methodological rules include the following: Propound only falsifiable theories, avoid ad hoc modifications, and construct only internally consistent theories. For Kuhn, the positivists, and Popper, methodological rules are matters of taste or convention, and methodological directives of the sort mentioned are not sufficient in themselves to dictate theory choice. Laudan does not think of methodological rules as conventions, as do Kuhn, Popper, and the positivists, nor does he conceive of them as descriptive statements, as do Quine and others. Rather, methodological directives are conceived of by Laudan as empirical statements that express means-ends relations. Methodological rules are things that may be useful but not true or false. That is, methodological rules are hypothetical imperatives. Thus, a rule of the form "one ought to do x" should be recast in the form "if one's goal is y, then one ought to do x." It follows that an adequate methodological rule is one that has worked well in the past; it is to be preferred over some other rule if it promotes its cognitive ends better than its rival.

Demarcation of Science and Nonscience

No one has yet provided a convincing demonstration that scientific knowledge can be clearly demarcated from other forms of knowledge. However, Laudan (1996) disagrees with the relativists as to what implication can be drawn from the lack of demarcation between scientific and other forms of knowledge. Relativists see this as a basis for thinking that all knowledge claims have equal cognitive significance. As Laudan sees it, the critical question is not whether scientific and other forms of knowledge differ, but rather questions such as the following: Under what conditions is a theory well confirmed? When can a theory be regarded as well tested? What characterizes cognitive progress?

What makes a belief well founded and what makes a belief scientific are two different questions. An answer to the first question may be within our reach, whereas an answer to the second question may not be. The matter that should occupy our attention is deciding when theories are well confirmed and well tested.

Cumulativity/Progressivity

It is generally accepted that successor theories do not solve all the problems of theories they displace, a matter treated at greater length in Chapter 9. Kuhn and other relativists infer from this that progress does not occur in science, that successor theories are not superior to but merely different from the theories they displace. Indeed, according to Kuhn (1962), successor theories may be in some senses inferior. Although Laudan (1996) accepts the proposition that successor theories are not in all respects superior to the theories they displace, he rejects the idea that we have no independent means of assessing progress in science. Laudan suggests that we evaluate theories as we do other aspects of life, in terms of a cost-benefit analysis. The idea is that although some current theory may be inferior to an earlier theory in some respects, it may on the whole be better when placed in a wider context. Thus, contemporary engineers possess techniques that are in many respects superior to those possessed by Egyptian engineers, yet the Egyptian engineers may have known better such things as how to move large stones.

But who would doubt that contemporary engineering is on the whole better than ancient Egyptian engineering?

To be considered progressive, a theory must solve two sorts of problems: conceptual and empirical. Laudan (1996) identifies four categories of conceptual problems. A theory has conceptual problems if it (a) is internally inconsistent or the postulated mechanisms are ambiguous, (b) makes assumptions about the world that are inconsistent with other widely accepted assumptions, (c) fails to use concepts contained in more general theories, or (d) violates principles of the research tradition to which it belongs. Laudan distinguishes between three sorts of empirical problems: potential problems, solved problems, and anomalous problems. Potential problems represent what we assume to be the case about the world but are not as yet explained. Solved problems are what we take to be the case about the world but that have been solved by one or another theory. Anomalous problems are actual problems that are solved by one or another theory but not by the theory in question. A problem is anomalous only if it has been solved by some rival theory.

According to this formulation, a theory is more adequate than a rival only in cases in which it has exhibited a greater problem-solving effectiveness than have its rivals. With this approach, one has to assess the number and weight of empirical problems a theory solves, the number and weight of its empirical anomalies, and the number and centrality of its conceptual difficulties.

Algorithm and Translation Theses

It is generally agreed that there is no algorithm—that is, definite set of rules—for judging theory appraisal. However, as we have seen earlier, our position is that theories can be judged as to their cognitive worth or progressivity in terms of their problem-solving capacity.

Lack of translation between two theories occurs, according to the positivists and the relativists, because the two theories have different languages. Thus, it is impossible to express the concepts of one theory in the language of the other. Laudan (1996) disagrees. Scientists who subscribe to radically different theories about the natural world may understand each other if they share certain metalevel goals. Where this is so, scientists may nevertheless be able to agree on the relative cognitive successes and failures of their respective theories.

Range of Cognitive Attitudes

Most philosophers of science believe that one's attitude toward a theory is one of either acceptance or rejection. Popper (1959), for example, believes that a theory is either falsified or not. Laudan (1996) suggests, on the contrary, that scientists may hold a whole range of cognitive attitudes toward theories, from acceptance to rejection and everything in between. For Kuhn (1962), it would be impossible for a scientist who adheres to one paradigm to work in another, if only because his or her understanding of the rival paradigm would be limited at best. Laudan, in contrast, allows that it is quite possible for a scientist to feel that some dominant paradigm or theory is well supported, yet to entertain some other theory or paradigm. For example, a scientist may note that the dominant and accepted theory in his or her specialization has become relatively stagnant and nonprogressive, but some upstart theory is progressive in the sense that it has a high rate of solving novel problems. That scientist may well choose to work with the upstart theory while being aware of the virtues of the dominant theory.

Laudan's Evaluation of Relativism

Laudan (1996), in common with other philosophers of science who accept naturalism (e.g., Kitcher, 1993; Shapere, 1984), suggests that the influence of the various forms of relativism has run its course. The relativism of Kuhn and Feyerabend and thus, by implication, the forms of relativism accepted by various contextualists have met serious challenges, which they appear to be unable to refute. In consequence, to use the terminology of Lakatos (1970, 1978), they have become nonprogressive programs. Laudan makes this point in no uncertain terms, stating,

> In my view, postpositivism [i.e., relativism] is an intellectual failure. The arguments on its behalf are dubious and question-begging. Still worse, it has sustained virtually no positive program of research. While attracting a few noisy adherents (especially among social scientists), postpositivism has exerted no perceptible impact on any of those natural sciences whose philosophy it purports to provide. Within philosophy itself, its chief practitioners—Kuhn, Feyerabend, and Quine—have done little in the past decade to extend or to consolidate its insights; indeed, both Quine and Kuhn (alarmed at the relativist lengths to which their avowed disciples are extending

their doctrines) have been soft-peddling many of the claims that once made the postpositivist approach seem revolutionary. (p. 5)

Laudan continues by saying that "postpositivism has run out of steam and that it now teeters on the brink of conceptual bankruptcy" (p. 5).

SUMMARY AND CONCLUSIONS

In Chapter 2, the issue of whether the philosophy of science is irrelevant to the practice of science was considered, and reasons for rejecting that view were given. It was shown that early conceptions of science dating from Aristotle suggested that scientific knowledge was certain and that it identified causes. With Newton in the 17th century and the downfall of certainty in the 18th century, the distinctive feature of science came to be seen as its methodology. Five major positions in the philosophy of science were identified: radical empiricism, logical empiricism, falsificationism, postpositivistic relativism, and normative naturalism. Normative naturalism was indicated to be a new and currently popular position being developed by some of the leading philosophers of science. The major figures in contextualism and in various postmodern relativisms seem to ignore the major new developments in the philosophy of science. Thus, it is ironic that these individuals often accuse mainstream psychology of following an outmoded philosophy of science while proclaiming themselves as on the cutting edge of epistemological considerations.

The Metaphilosophy of Stephen Pepper

*J*n 1942, Stephen Pepper published a book in which he suggested that most adequate philosophic positions invented by humans can be subsumed under one or another of four relatively adequate worldviews, each of which has its own distinctive root metaphor. One of those worldviews he called contextualism, a position that stems mainly from James's version of pragmatism and much less from the versions of pragmatism associated with Peirce and Dewey. Pepper's writings are often cited as the source of modern-day contextualism in psychology. Virtually all of the serious treatments of contextualism in psychology cite Pepper as the original source of the view. As one example, the characterization of Skinnerian behavior analysis as contextualistic originated in a review of Pepper's book (Hayes et al., 1988). Kantor's (1959) interbehavioral approach is cited by some as containing some of the essential tenets of contextualism, particularly as it has arisen in behavior analysis, as discussed in Morris (1982).

The other three worldviews described by Pepper (1942) are formism, organicism, and mechanism. Pepper states that each of the worldviews derives from a distinctive root metaphor that provides a different, coherent, and defensible way of interpreting the world. Unlike some others who have characterized each of these approaches as possibly constituting an adequate basis for science (Cooper, 1987; Gillespie, 1992), Pepper sees each of these worldviews as being adequate in its own distinctive domain, with only mechanism being the worldview of science. Understanding the unique features of contextualism, as seen by Pepper, requires comparison of it to the three other worldviews, which we will treat briefly prior to a more extensive discussion of contextualism as understood by Pepper. In what follows, we provide a description of Pepper's views, views that we do not necessarily accept or agree with.

THE FOUR WORLDVIEWS

Formism

The root metaphor of the worldview known as formism is similarity. Any class of objects or ideas is similar either because the members are the reflection of some independently existing norm (Plato) or because we can see in the particulars that all members of the class manifest the norm (Aristotle). For Plato, oak trees are oak trees because they participate in the norm for oak trees, whereas for Aristotle, all oak trees have a common essence. The truth criterion of formism is correspondence of the individual to the characteristics of the class. For example, this particular bird is a bird because it has the characteristics peculiar to the class of birds.

Organicism

For organicism, the root metaphor is the growing organism. Things are seen as developing toward certain ends, according to predetermined stages. Piaget's taxonomy of stages of cognitive development is one example of organicism within developmental psychology. The criterion of truth for organicism is coherence. Systems—as, for example, scientific theories— progress over time (i.e., develop) toward greater and greater inclusion or coherence. Thus, Newton's theory is superior to that of Anaximenes. Why? "Because, answers the organicist, it includes vastly more data, because these data are much more determinate, and because these determinate data are so closely integrated that in very large measure they are all mutually implicative" (Pepper, 1942, p. 300).

Pepper (1942) suggests that the principle of organicity can be stated in either of two ways:

> According to the first statement, an organic whole is such a system that every element within it implies every other. According to the second, it is such a system that an alteration or removal of any element would alter every other element or even destroy the whole system. (p. 300)

Although Pepper (1942) does not think that these two statements of organicism are exactly equivalent, he does feel that they are similar enough "to converge in the end upon the same fact" (pp. 299-300).

Mechanism

According to Pepper (1942), the root metaphor of the sort of mechanism associated with Newton is the machine. The parts of the machine are assumed to interact in a lawful manner to produce the functioning of the entire machine. For example, the earth revolves around the sun in a fixed pattern determined by the mutual gravitational attraction of the two bodies. Mechanism is regarded by many as the metaphor of science and of most contemporary psychology (e.g., Gillespie, 1992; Morris, 1988). Newton attempted to explain a variety of phenomena on the basis of a small set of laws. The truth criterion of mechanism is correspondence between hypothesis and experimental findings. This version of the correspondence criterion of truth is so well-known and widely accepted as to not require elaboration.

Pepper (1942) distinguished between two types of mechanism—discrete mechanism, identified with Newton, and consolidated mechanism, identified with Einstein. According to Pepper,

> Discrete mechanism thus leads to consolidated mechanism. The customary mechanistic picture of the world as groups of planetary systems, or as particles pushed up and down and back and forth in the production of apparent waves, or as particles in random motion in a box, gives way to a picture more in the nature of a crystal or gelatin with an intricately involved internal structure. In place of the discrete particle is the spatiotemporal path, and in place of the discrete laws of mechanics is a geometry, better, a geography. The

purpose of the cosmic geometry is simply to describe to use the unique structure of the spatiotemporal whole. (p. 212)

According to Pepper (1942), 18th- and 19th-century science was based on discrete mechanism, whereas contemporary science seems to be based on consolidated mechanism.

Contextualism

As described by Pepper (1942), the root metaphor underlying contextualism is the historic event. Historic events are complex and composed of a variety of interconnected and related activities with patterns that change continuously rather than remaining constant. By historic event, according to Pepper, the contextualist does not mean a past event that is dead and gone; rather, the contextualist means the historic event that is alive in its present context, the event as it is going on now. Such events, according to Pepper, "are like the incidents in the plot of a novel or drama. They are literally the incidents of life" (p. 233). Pepper states, "To give instances of this root metaphor in our language with the minimum risk of misunderstanding, we should use only verbs. It is doing, and enduring, and enjoying" (p. 232).

Contextualists suggest that disorder may arise at any time. Pepper (1942) stated,

> Disorder is a categorial [categorical] feature of contextualism, and so radically so that it must not even exclude order. . . . Change in this radical sense is denied by all other world theories. If such radical change is not a feature of the world, if there are unchangeable structures in nature like the forms of formism or the space-time structure of mechanism, then contextualism is false. (p. 234)

Moreover, according to Pepper (1942), "the ineradicable contextualistic categories may thus be said to be *change* and *novelty*" (p. 235).

What is a novel event, and what is a categorical one? Consider novelty first. Although no contextualist appears to have defined a novel event or a novelty in a clear, unambiguous manner (see Capaldi & Proctor, 1994, for a discussion of the difficulty involved in deciding whether an event is novel), the use of the concept in practice leaves no doubt as to what is intended: It is that prediction of any sort is impossible in principle. The use of the terms *novel* and *novelty* by philosophic contextualists corresponds to the definitions as given in *Merriam-Webster's New Collegiate Dictionary* (1987): A novel event is one that is "new and not resembling something formerly known or used," and novelty is something that has "the quality or state of being novel."

There are two ways in which novel events can occur in contextualism. First, the structures governing the forms phenomena take may change over time. Second, in what is called multilevel determination, a complex of variables (e.g., physical, chemical, biological, psychological, and sociological) from many levels may interact in such a way to produce one phenomenon today and a different and unique phenomenon tomorrow. Some contextualists emphasize the former type of novelty, some the latter, and some both.

Categorical is defined by the dictionary cited above as "absolute; unqualified." In other words, novelty is an unconditional feature of contextualism. So committed is the contextualist to novelty and change that it is denied that there are unchangeable structures in nature. As we have seen, Pepper (1942) said that if nature contains unchangeable structures, then contextualism is false. He also stated that "absolute permanence or immutability in any sense is, on this theory, a fiction" (p. 243). On the basis of the contextualistic worldview, the future may resemble the past for some limited period of time. But clearly, any suggestion that the future will always resemble the past is not permissible within contextualism and is not to be taken seriously.

Contextualism favors an operational theory of truth, which has three distinct specifications. One of these truth criteria is that of "successful working." In terms of this criterion, Pepper (1942) states, "Truth is utility or successful functioning, and that is the end of it" (p. 270). According to Pepper, the successful working criterion eschews hypothesis testing altogether. The truth is whatever works in a particular situation. For example, a rat finding its way to the goal box has solved a practical problem and thus has isolated the true path.

Pepper (1942) indicates, however, that successful working is neither the only nor the best truth criterion of contextualism. He states,

> The "successful working" theory excludes hypotheses from truth, yet hypotheses are prominent textures in contextualism, and they are the very textures to which usage implies truth and falsity. A contextualistic theory of truth that leaves hypotheses out of the

theory is not fitting common-sense truth as closely as possible into the contextualistic categories. In fact, the "successful working" theory is only a halfhearted contextualistic theory. (p. 272)

Pepper (1942) goes so far as to say that successful working is not only the narrowest of the truth criteria of pragmatism, but it is also "the one the enemies of pragmatism try to associate with it" (p. 269).

Pepper describes two other more adequate contextualistic truth criteria. The first of these is that of verification of hypotheses. "The slogan of this type of operationalism is that truth is verification. According to this formulation, it is not the successful act that is true, but the hypothesis that leads to the successful act" (Pepper, 1942, p. 272). The trial-and-error behavior of a rat in a maze would produce true and false judgments according to the successful working criterion, but not according to the verified hypothesis criterion. However, if the animal were entertaining some hypothesis as to the correct path, its judgments would be true or false.

A third truth criterion is qualitative confirmation, which, like the second criterion, emphasizes confirmation of hypotheses. However, it adds to this the view that "the body of hypotheses possessed by science and philosophy gives us a considerable amount of insight into the structure of nature" (Pepper, 1942, p. 278). Pepper does not elaborate on what he means by the structure of nature.

The role of analysis in contextualism also bears comment. First, any attempt to analyze a complex event into its elements is presumed to distort the event and possibly may be misleading. Second, all analyses are tentative in the sense that no event can be completely analyzed. In dealing with particular events, we may go from one event to another, and there is no stopping place. Third, an event may be analyzed from many points of view, depending on one's purposes. For a contextualist, there is no correct or incorrect analysis; analysis always proceeds from some point of view and serves some practical purpose. The significance of analysis lies in the purpose one is pursuing. This, of course, is a species of relativism.

So rich are the events of life that contextualists recognize that selecting one feature of them rather than another is arbitrary. One may start anywhere and end up anywhere. Pepper (1942) stated that for contextualistic approaches, "the universe has for these theories the general effect of multitudes of facts rather loosely scattered about and not necessarily determining each other to any considerable degree" (p. 143). In short, contextualism is considered to be a dispersive worldview—which is to say that facts fly off in all directions—and values scope over precision.

A SPECIFIC EXAMPLE OF
CONTEXTUALISM IN PRACTICE

Many psychologists who are not well versed in contextualism are not aware of what a contextualistic analysis might produce. This is because abstract descriptions of the preceding type do not adequately convey the true flavor of a contextualistic approach in practice. In what follows, we provide some sense of what this flavor is, using an example that shows how extremely dispersive contextualism can be. The example is based on a review by Jacob Heilbrunn (1994) in *The New Republic* of 10 books written by historians dealing with the question, "Who is to blame for the cold war?" Notice that our example here is a historical one that totally embodies the root metaphor of contextualism, which is the ongoing historical event in context.

Who started the cold war? The liberal orthodox view, represented by Arthur Schlesinger, Jr., is that the cold war was the response of free men to the cruelties of communist aggression. A contrary view, the realist orthodox view—voiced by Hans Morgenthau, George Kennan, and Walter Lippmann—is that Stalin, not communism, was responsible for the cold war. The earliest of a long line of revisionist views, which tend to blame the cold war on the United States rather than on communism or Stalin, was that of the Wisconsin school, led by William Appleman Williams. His view was that the cold war was a result of American economic imperialism. Williams believed that Roosevelt and Truman were to blame for the cold war. Later revisionists, such as Gar Alperovitz, however, blamed Truman and exonerated Roosevelt. Gabriel Kolko implicated Roosevelt again, suggesting that he had hopes of establishing American global dominance. Subsequently, John Lewis Gaddis blamed not only the Soviet Union, as had Schlesinger, and not only the United States—as had Williams, Kolko, and others—but he suggested that both the Soviet Union and the United States were responsible for the cold war. Gaddis then modified his view, suggesting that the Soviets were more to blame than the United States.

Melvin P. Leffler, who is currently among the most popular of the revisionists, has suggested a new form of revisionism. His view, in a nutshell, is that the cold war started not because the United States sought geopolitical domination for economic reasons, but rather because it sought economic domination for geopolitical reasons. According to Heilbrunn (1994), "It is a central contention of Leffler's book that the Truman administration deliberately inflated the Soviet threat in order to boost defense spending; and that this act precipitated a wasteful arms race" (p. 34).

Heilbrunn (1994) disagrees with Leffler and suggests that Truman officials were working in a crisis atmosphere and improvised policy as they went along. The view that policy was formulated in a piecemeal and pragmatic fashion was also suggested in a book by Wilson D. Miscamble. On this view, the cold war was not started by either the Soviet Union or United States but rather was a catastrophe that the two sides bungled into. However, according to H. W. Brands, the cold war was not started as a result of deliberate policy, nor was it an event that we bungled into; rather, it was the product of an unstable American psyche. Still another view was suggested by Edward Pressen, who ascribes the cold war to the machinations of the military, the CIA, and the FBI. On this view, political figures such as Roosevelt and Truman were dragged into the cold war by others. Still other points of view as to who started the cold war, of which we spare the reader, were suggested by Lebow and Stein, Nichols, and Walker, among others. Add to this that Heilbrunn, the reviewer, disagrees with most of the opinions expressed by the revisionist authors and further suggests that when the Russian historians have a go at the question of who caused the cold war, even more opinions will become available.

Notice that to justify each of the viewpoints expressed earlier, quite disparate sources of information would have to be used. For example, vastly different sorts of information would be used to blame the cold war on Roosevelt, or Truman, or Stalin, or communism, or the United States's thrust for economic hegemony or geopolitical hegemony, or the unstable American psyche, and so on. This extreme diversity of opinion, with facts flying off in all directions, is, of course, what contextualists expect when dealing with historical events in context and what is meant by dispersiveness.

CAN CONTEXTUALISM BE SCIENTIFIC?

It is ironic that contextualism, which has the historical event as its root metaphor, would be seen by some modern writers such as Hayes, Lerner, Morris, and others as not only an adequate approach to science but a better one than that commonly practiced. Unlike scientific claims, many historical hypotheses, such as those described earlier, are untestable. As Gross and Levitt (1994) have put it, the factual knowledge claims of historians are "often contaminated by unprovable and bootless speculation" (p. 12). One reason why many, but of course not all, historical hypotheses are untestable is that some of the events that form an integral part of the analysis are gone forever and cannot be recovered (e.g., what Truman's state of mind might have been). In addition, we cannot have control groups; for example, it would be illuminating to have everything as it was except putting Truman or Roosevelt in a different state of mind. A final impediment to testability worth mentioning is that in describing some event such as the start of the cold war, the historian is dealing literally with a multitude of interconnected and disparate events simultaneously (i.e., multilevel determination), and the historian, unlike the laboratory scientist, lacks the means to evaluate the separate contributions of the various factors. It might be noted that whether or not the historians who have contributed books concerning the issue of who started the cold war are contextualists, each nevertheless seems to think that he or she has written an adequate account of the cold war. The contextualists would agree to at least some extent with the analyses of all the historians, suggesting that there is no single true analysis but rather numerous true analyses depending on one's point of view, even if these analyses are incompatible. For example, McGuire (1983) has said, "Contextualism maintains that all theories (including even mutually contradictory ones) are correct" (p. 7). Again, we see that a contextualist advocates a strong form of relativism.

Based on a careful reading of Pepper (1942), our opinion is that he would agree with us that contextualism is not the proper worldview for science. It may seem ironic that we as noncontextualists have a better and more appropriate interpretation of Pepper in this regard than many self-styled contextualists. But, nevertheless, that is our reading of Pepper, and the following statements by him support our view. Figure 3.1, taken from Pepper, shows his view of how the various worldviews relate along several important dimensions. The figure suggests that formism and mechanism are similar in being analytic theories and that contextualism and organicism are similar in being synthetic theories. The figure also suggests that formism and contextualism are similar in being dispersive theories, which lack precision, and that mechanism and organicism are similar in being integrative theories, which lack scope. But note that nowhere in the figure does Pepper suggest that mechanism and contextualism are similar along either of these two major dimensions, that is, analytic versus synthetic and dispersive versus integrative. Combine that fact with the further fact that Pepper sees mechanism as being the basis of science, and it becomes completely inexplicable how someone

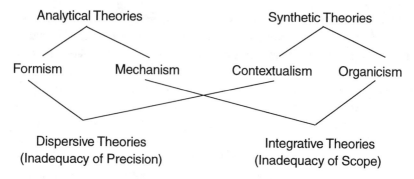

Figure 3.1. Pepper's (1942) Scheme for Classifying the Four Worldviews According to Their Analytic/Synthetic and Dispersive/Integrative Natures

who purports to represent Pepper can suggest that he or she sees contextualism as a proper basis for science.

Contextualism, as described by Pepper, is a nonanalytic, dispersive theory that also lacks precision. In our view, a system of this sort cannot possibly provide a basis for science. We are not the first to make this observation. For example, Overton (1984) has said that because of the dispersiveness of contextualism and the other dispersive worldview, formism, "whatever else their value, formism and contextualism as world views cannot form the basis for scientifically valid research programs—unless science were to abandon its attempt to establish an organized and systematic body of knowledge, which is unlikely" (p. 218). McCurry (1993), pointing out the inconsistency between science and a dispersive worldview such as contextualism, said, "Whether our goal is understanding, or prediction and control, we at present seem tied to an integrative need for order that is most clearly associated with mechanism and organicism" (p. 68). Similarly, Kendler (1986), taking note of the dispersiveness of modified contextualism, stated, "But for the scientist who seeks stable, natural laws that can be integrated into an organized system, adopting a contextualistic world view is not appropriate" (p. 90).

PEPPER WITH A PINCH OF PSALT

The heading for this section is taken from a commentary on contextualism by J. E. R. Staddon (1993), published in *The Behavior Analyst*. Staddon says,

"The whole Pepperian proposal strikes me as so outrageous, so outside any of the worldviews proposed by and for natural science, that it is rather difficult to criticize" (p. 245). Although we agree with Staddon, we nevertheless will attempt some criticism of Pepper's (1942) system in this section.

Just about all theoretical formulations and systems in science, including those of Darwin and Newton, have come under heavy criticism at one time or another. Therefore, it is surprising that, after having examined a number of articles and books written by contextualistically minded psychologists, we have found no contextualist who has quarreled with Pepper's (1942) division of all philosophic systems into formism, organicism, mechanism, and contextualism. Such seemingly uncritical acceptance seems more characteristic of religious than of scientific systems and does not seem entirely healthy to us.

Consider the proposition, universally accepted by contextualists, that the commonly accepted metaphor for science in general and psychology in particular is the machine. We have two quarrels with this proposition. First, even if one accepts the machine metaphor, and certainly it has been used within some areas of psychology, it does not imply that one literally thinks that all aspects of psychology are machine-like. Consider the metaphor, "The president is the captain of the ship of state." We do not literally think that the president is steering a ship. Rather, what we attempt to illuminate by this metaphor is that in forming governmental policy, the president must avoid making mistakes (i.e., avoid the reefs), that he must generate the best possible plan (steer a good course), that the final decision is his (as a captain is in charge of the ship), and so on. In other words, when using metaphors, we take them not literally but, excuse the term, metaphorically. As du Preez (1991) has indicated,

> What we ought to do is to attempt to explore the range and power of each metaphor as a heuristic device. Each opens up a set of problems, questions and possible answers. Each can be no more than a slice of the total. (p. 26)

Unfortunately, contextualists seem to take their metaphors literally.

Our second point is that, as the previous quote from du Preez (1991) implies, the machine metaphor is not the only popular metaphor within psychology. As du Preez has suggested, the foundational metaphor for some social psychology is theater (roles, actors, role distance, role relations, and scripts). Another popular metaphor in many areas of psychology is games.

TABLE 3.1 List of Memory Analogies

Spatial analogies with search

Wax tablet	Gramophone	Aviary
House	Rooms in a house	Switchboard
Purse	Leaky bucket or sieve	Junk box
Bottle	Computer program	Stores
Mystic writing pad	Workbench	Cow's stomach
Pushdown stack	Acid bath	Library
Dictionary	Keysort cards	Conveyor belt
Tape recorder	Subway map	Garbage can

Other spatial theories

Organization theory	Hierarchical networks	Associative networks

Other analogies

Muscle ("strength")	Construction of a dinosaur	Reconstruction
Levels of processing	Signal detection	Melodies on a piano
Tuning fork	Hologram	Lock and key

SOURCE: Adapted from Roediger (1980).

As other examples, the mind has been considered to be a blank slate to be written on by experience (Locke) or an active organizing space with a priori ideas and theories (Chomsky). Many other metaphors that are commonly used in psychology could be added to this list (see du Preez, 1991). Indeed, in the area of memory, dozens of metaphors have been employed, as may be seen in Table 3.1, which is adapted from an article by Roediger (1980).

Thus, characterizing science exclusively in terms of the machine metaphor is seriously restricted. There is a better way to characterize science. We prefer to think of science as an empirical, analytic endeavor that deals with closed as well as open systems (see Manicas & Secord, 1983, for a similar view). By a closed system, we mean one in which the ideal is to exclude from consideration all variables except those that we wish to examine. A prime example of a closed system is what scientists attempt to achieve in conducting experiments. Note that the empirical/analytic approach is useful no matter what the metaphor employed to characterize psychology—a machine, a stage, a game, and so on.

By an open system, we mean one in which significant variables not under the control of the investigator intrude to influence the phenomena of interest.

Open systems are to be found when examining behavior in real-world settings. One example of an open system is what contextualists mean by the term *multilevel context*. In a multilevel context, as previously indicated, behavior would be understood in terms of "atomic, molecular, chemical, biological, physical, psychological, community, social, societal, cultural, and historical variables, and so on" (Cicirelli, 1994, p. 32). For many contextualists, examining phenomena in closed systems distorts the phenomena or limits their generality to restricted if not artificial contexts.

As an illustration of the use of a multilevel analysis in an open system, consider the following example from Gillespie (1992), an advocate of a contextualistic approach to cognitive psychology. She uses a multilevel analysis in an attempt to reach a decision as to whether to send her daughter, Gemma, to kindergarten. Gillespie does so because she concludes that a better decision could be made by employing multilevel contextualistic categories rather than those normally associated with closed systems. She may be correct in this judgment. However, there is no alternative to Gillespie's approach because the problem of whether to send Gemma to kindergarten is not one that admits of a scientific answer. It is doubtful that we have general laws that apply to this particular case. Even if we had such laws, we could not apply them to Gemma because we know little of her social, cultural, and genetic background to which these laws would presumably apply. We also lack knowledge of the kinds of situations that Gemma might encounter in kindergarten. Is the teacher there to her liking? Will her classmates be friendly or unfriendly? The failure to have answers to these and many other questions precludes a scientific analysis of this and like examples of open systems.

It may be that in some open, multilevel systems, a contextualistic-interpretive approach is more useful than one based on information from closed systems. As one example, a contextualistic-interpretive analysis might provide a better basis for action than an empirical-analytic one in the case of Gemma. As another example, a contextualistic-interpretive approach to an open system might provide interesting hypotheses (context of discovery) that could then be subjected to empirical analysis in a closed system (context of justification). No doubt much useful science has been produced in just this way. Be this as it may, we see the distinction between open systems (in which interpretation may be practiced) and closed systems (in which variables may be isolated) as more fundamental than that between mechanism and contextualism, which are just two of the many metaphors that have been employed to facilitate understanding.

SUMMARY AND CONCLUSIONS

The popularity of contextualism in psychology stems mainly from a book written by Stephen Pepper in 1942. In that book, Pepper subsumed most major philosophic positions under what he regarded as four dominant worldviews: formism, organicism, mechanism, and contextualism. Each of these four views has a dominant metaphor. For formism it is similarity, for organicism it is the growing organism, for mechanism it is the machine, and for contextualism it is the historical act in context.

A specific example of contextualism in practice was provided that illustrated a major feature of contextualism identified by Pepper (1942)—namely, its dispersiveness. Mechanism, on the other hand, was considered by Pepper to be integrative. Pepper clearly identified mechanism as the dominant worldview appropriate for science. He did not suggest that contextualism could serve as a metatheory for science. Many of Pepper's followers, however, have suggested that contextualism provides a better basis for psychological science than does mechanism. Many others have concluded, however, that when contextualism is applied to science, it adopts many of the characteristics of mechanism, a position accepted by the authors. It was suggested that rather than viewing science as a machine, it is more appropriate to view it as primarily concerned with closed systems but useful also for understanding open systems. In contrast, contextualism, to the extent that it is appropriate, seems appropriate for open systems.

Philosophic Contextualism and Modified Contextualism Described

 ach variety of contextualism that has a different perspective can be seen as unique. For example, James (1907/1975) has said, "The pragmatist clings to facts and concreteness, observes truth as it works in particular cases, and generalizes. Truth for him becomes a class-name for all sorts of definite working-values in experience" (p. 61). For the purpose of this book, it is enough to describe and distinguish two broad categories of contextualism, one of which has two subcategories. Our purpose in this chapter is not to evaluate these two approaches to contextualism but merely to describe them in some detail. Following that, we will again highlight the ontological assumptions of contextualism, something neither Pepper (1942) nor any of his followers has done to any significant extent.

One wing of contextualism, philosophic contextualism, rejects mainstream psychology and sees its version of contextualism as being incompatible with practically any of the ways in which science is practiced. The other wing, modified contextualism, also rejects mainstream psychology. However, it sees itself as compatible with science and as offering a new, improved, and better way to conduct scientific psychology than that which stems from the orthodox and dominant worldview, mechanism, which is said to govern the scientific enterprise in psychology. We distinguish between two types of modified contextualism, developmental and functional.

PHILOSOPHIC CONTEXTUALISM IN PSYCHOLOGY

The proponents of philosophic contextualism include Jerome Bruner, James Deese, Ralph Rosnow, and Theodore Sarbin, among others. These philosophic contextualists argue strenuously that contextualism precludes approaching psychology from a conventionally accepted scientific perspective because they reject science, at least as applied to psychology. They reject science for two reasons: the acceptance of novelty and an emphasis on multilevel determination, with novelty being the more important of the reasons. This position is highly consistent with our understanding of contextualism as it was developed in philosophy.

The approach of the philosophic contextualists therefore demands a radically different sort of psychology, one that would involve transforming the field both substantively and methodologically. On one hand, they see many substantive approaches to psychology that occupy a position of central importance within the field (e.g., human information processing) as of little interest or value (see, e.g., Bruner, 1990; Gillespie, 1992). On the other hand, they advocate minimizing to one degree or another any procedure such as experimentation that leads to a restriction in the range of variables examined. The philosophic contextualists would replace such methods in part or in whole with a variety of other methods. Even more radically, they would abandon the search for lawful relations because in their view, none exist in psychology.

Rejecting Restriction of Variables

Philosophic contextualists see little value in any procedure that necessarily restricts the range of variables examined. A prime example of a procedure that does this is, of course, experimentation. From the standpoint of a philosophic contextualist, any phenomenon associated with the restricted set of variables is of little or no interest because when some new variable or variables are added to the restricted set, they may not merely modify the phenomenon quantitatively but change it qualitatively, that is, produce a novelty. In other words, the limited set may in no way provide information that is useful under a different set of conditions, no matter how minor the difference appears to be. This expectation of philosophic contextualists is the rule rather than the exception and contrasts radically with that of traditional science. Scientists assume that information gathered under one set of conditions may in one respect or another prove useful for understanding what may occur under a wider set of conditions. However, fundamental and qualitative alteration of phenomena is the normal expectation of the philosophic contextualist when some new variable is added to a variable set.

Note that the position espoused by the philosophic contextualists concerning the restriction of variables is diametrically opposed to that accepted by traditional scientists. For scientists, restriction of variables is necessary to establish causal relations, whereas for the philosophic contextualist, restriction leads to findings that are artificial, impoverished, and at best of limited usefulness.

Rejecting Lawfulness

Philosophic contextualists seem to be unanimous in rejecting the possibility of establishing lawful relations in most or all areas of psychology. The theme that runs through their statements on the impossibility of lawfulness is that phenomena fluctuate over time such that a given set of conditions will necessarily produce one outcome at one time and a different outcome at a later time.

Gergen (1973), in a highly influential article that often is praised by contextualists, rejected the possibility of discovering lawful relations in social psychology, as follows:

> It is the purpose of this paper to argue that social psychology is primarily an historical inquiry. Unlike the natural sciences, it deals with facts that are largely nonrepeatable and which fluctuate markedly over time. Principles of human interaction cannot readily be developed over time because the facts on which they are based do not generally remain stable. Knowledge cannot accumulate in the usual scientific sense because such knowledge does not generally transcend its historical boundaries. (p. 310)

In his later writings, Gergen has extended this position beyond social psychology to psychology in general, stating, "One might well argue that the scientist's claims to privileged knowledge have served as mystifying devices within the society more generally. Constructionism [which Gergen favors] offers no foundational rules of warrant and in this sense is relativistic" (Gergen, 1985, p. 273). Thus, we see that Gergen is quite explicit in describing his version of contextualism as a form of relativism.

Rosnow and Georgoudi (1986) explicitly reject the possibility of finding lawful relations in any branch of psychology, saying,

> The idea of contextualism intrinsically implies change and develop-
> ment as opposed to orderliness and stability (implied both by the
> mechanistic and organismic world views). Further, change is not
> something derivative but is basic or essential. . . . It is in this sense
> that contextualism implies that change is categorical and the search
> for absolute and immutable laws of behavior chimerical. (p. 15)

Hoffman and Nead (1983) suggest that the contextualist research strategy entails "rejection of the notion of 'universal law' " and "adoption of a notion of disorder" (p. 525). In a similar vein, Blank (1986) has proposed that contextualism implies that "universal, transhistorical laws of personal behavior are impossible and the search for them fruitless" (p. 107). Again, the position adopted by philosophic contextualists with respect to laws is diametrically opposed to that of conventionally accepted science. Far from rejecting lawfulness, scientists consider that one of the primary tasks of investigators is to search for and establish lawful relationships.

Accepting Novelty

Philosophic contextualists universally accept the idea that novel events will and must occur. As indicated by Rosnow and Georgoudi (1986) earlier, "Change is not something derivative but is basic or essential" (p. 15). Philosophic contextualists accept the reality of novelty in the here and now. In this respect, philosophic contextualists are true to Pepper (1942) in accepting that novelty is categorical within contextualism and is an ineradicable feature of that view.

Efran, Germer, and Lukens (1986) are explicit on this point, saying,

> Unlike some mechanistic positions, contextualism assumes that *novelty* (as seen by an observer) can spontaneously surface at any point; new action patterns do not need to await the extinction of older "habits". Patterns—like species—evolve, with new combinations or "mutations" emerging at all levels. (p. 177)

Regarding novelty, Crabb (1988) has commented,

> For the contextualist, though, this transitory nature of events means that when one goes in search of evidence relevant to a particular question, by the time such evidence is found, it is likely that the phenomenon—and the question—will have changed. (p. 29)

Deese (1993) says the following concerning novelty:

> My argument is that psychological events have multiple causes and reasons and that they combine . . . in unique configurations. Psychology is not like physics (which was our idol when I was a graduate student) but like history. History never repeats itself, but individual *features* of history occur again and again in unique combinations, as in a giant kaleidoscope. So it is with psychology. (p. 113)

Sarbin and McKechnie (1986) seem to have expressed best the view on novelty that necessarily follows from contextualism:

> It is precisely the capacity for novelty, for producing action and ideas and works that had not previously existed, that could not have been anticipated precisely from what had come before, which distinguishes the contextualist perspective. (p. 200)

Unlike philosophic contextualists, scientists do not assume that novelty is the ordinary condition. Of course, neither scientists nor anyone else can preclude the possibility that novelties may occur and that tomorrow may not resemble today. However, it is undeniable that scientists operate on the assumption that what is found today will hold tomorrow.

Rejecting Science

Not surprisingly, philosophic contextualists, who reject experimentation and the possibility of lawfulness and accept novelty, see little value in approaching psychology from a traditional scientific perspective. Essentially, philosophic contextualists see a scientific approach as irrelevant for better understanding psychology. They conclude that psychology should abandon the scientific approach to its subject matter. For example, Sarbin (1977) has predicted that psychology will gain more from literature than from the laboratory. He says of this view,

> I am painfully aware that this prediction has an antiscientific coloring. I say "painfully" because I have construed myself as scientist for almost 40 years. When I look at the achievements of science (rooted in mechanism) in such areas as deviance, hypnosis, and imaginings . . . and also language, moral development, teaching, and learning, I must admit that science may justifiably be called the false messiah—at least for problems that we identify as psychological. (p. 37)

Scheibe (1993) is also impressed with the potential contribution of drama to psychology. According to him, "A dramaturgical approach to psychology proposes that human life can be usefully analyzed from a theatrical point of view" (p. 191).

Deese (1996) is less than sanguine about the prospects of psychology being a science:

> When one surveys the progress psychology has made as a *science* in the last century's move toward maturity, one must conclude that the results are pretty meager for all of the investment that has been made. (p. 58)

Deese not only thinks that psychology has failed so far to make progress, but he also holds the conviction that the same will be in store for us in the future even if we try increasingly to "turn psychology into a rock-hard science in which knowledge is tested only by the toughest standards of prediction and control" (p. 61).

It is clear from what has been considered in this section, as well as in prior chapters, that philosophic contextualists reject the proposition that psychology can be conducted as a scientific enterprise, at least as science is normally understood. This stands in contrast to the viewpoint of most academic psychologists, who see science as being the major and indispensable means for advancing psychological knowledge and understanding.

MODIFIED CONTEXTUALISM
IN PSYCHOLOGY

The proponents of modified contextualism include Paul Baltes, Victor Cicirelli, Donald Ford, Steven Hayes, Vicky Lee, Richard Lerner, Edward Morris, and Hayne Reese, among others. Modified contextualists reject mainstream psychology as vehemently as their philosophic brethren. As merely one example, Lee (1988) has said, "It is time we abandon the sophistry of the pseudoscience that intellectual history has bequeathed to us in academic psychology" (p. 172). However, unlike the philosophic contextualists, all modified contextualists suggest that psychology can be a science but one that has a basis different from that currently employed in mainstream psychology.

Several rationales have been proposed for converting philosophic contextualism into modified contextualism. One that is particularly noteworthy because it has gained some general acceptance is that of Lerner and Kauffman (1985), who suggest that philosophic contextualism is too unconstrained to be useful (see also Hayes, 1993, for a similar position). They concluded that "a 'pure' contextualism [i.e., philosophic contextualism], in being completely dispersive would not be suitable for use as a philosophical model from which to derive a concept of development" (p. 319). However, they wished to retain certain features of contextualism, so that development may be studied from many different perspectives. To mitigate the extremely dispersive aspects of contextualism, Lerner and Kauffman proposed marrying it with organicism. This gives rise to a position, which they called developmental contextualism, that retains some dispersive aspects of contextualism and some predictive aspects of organicism. This position has been developed more fully by Ford and Lerner (1992), who later said, "If contextualism were to serve as a metamodel for developmental theory alternative to predetermined organicism/ dialectics, it could not do so in its 'pure' form" (p. 11). Others have made similar distinctions between philosophic and modified contextualism. For example, Cicirelli (1994) distinguishes between pure contextualism and quasi-contextualism, Hayes (1993) distinguishes descriptive contextualists (e.g., historians) from functional contextualists (e.g., behavior analysts), and Morris (1993b) distinguishes between the natural history and natural science versions of contextualism, with the latter but not the former entailing science.

The transformation of philosophic or "pure" contextualism into modified contextualism has produced what appears to be basic and fundamental differences between the two camps. The modified contextualists differ from the philosophic contextualists on each point raised in the previous section, as will be shown later.

Accepting Restriction of Variables

Modified contextualists, unlike philosophic contextualists, have accepted restrictions in the range of variables examined in at least two important ways. One is exemplified in a position expressed by Cicirelli (1994), who, as indicated earlier, distinguished between pure, philosophic contextualism and quasi-contextualism. He suggested that pure contextualism cannot form a basis for science, but quasi-contextualism can. Cicirelli stated his objection to philosophic contextualism as follows:

> In contrast to organicism, the direction of development in contextualism is not predetermined and does not have an end-point to development. . . . In pure contextualism, not only is there no end-point to development, but the direction of development is totally unpredictable. (pp. 33-34)

To correct this aspect of philosophic contextualism, Cicirelli recommended that we use quasi-contextualism, which "is conceptualized as if total predictability of development were the ideal" (p. 35) but with strategies used "that can predict to a certain degree the direction of development, while, of course, retaining a degree of unpredictability" (p. 35).

According to Cicirelli (1994), quasi-contextualism should employ the following strategy to restrict the range of variables examined:

> In carrying out research work, it would be overwhelming to include the total context if we were to attempt to collect data simultaneously on all the variables involved. . . . In practice, boundaries can be established to identify a subsystem of variables to be studied in

relation to a particular problem. First, we can identify the target variable, and then theorize as to the contextual variables that are most important in the particular situation. (pp. 35-36)

In suggesting that the range of variables can be restricted in this manner, Cicirelli (1994) is disagreeing rather starkly with a basic view of the philosophic contextualists. Remember, philosophic contextualists suggest that when some new variable is added to a prior set, no matter how broad or restricted that prior set, the new variable may modify the phenomenon of interest in a qualitative and unpredictable manner. It is fundamental to philosophic contextualism that when some new element is added to a situation, the situation may be radically altered. Thus, it seems clear that Cicirelli's proposal would be anathema to philosophic contextualists.

The second way in which modified contextualists have accepted a restriction in the range of variables examined is in their attitude toward experimentation itself. First, unlike philosophic contextualists, none of the modified contextualists appears to have criticized laboratory or experimental studies; in fact, they describe experimental methodology approvingly. Lee (1988) explicitly articulates a position that is in direct contradiction to that of philosophic contextualists:

> Some psychologists have difficulty accepting that the laboratory is an appropriate place to pursue psychological research. Laboratories are seen as artificial and as incapable of sustaining the full richness of the conduct outside them. Furthermore, the laboratory study of conduct is rejected because it leaves behind the interpersonal, social, and other realities of human lives. The relevance of the laboratory work to an understanding of conduct is questioned on these grounds which, in fact, turn out to be unconvincing. (p. 127)

Lee (1988) goes on to point out that the contrived nature of laboratory research is not unique to psychology but can be found in all fields, including physics. She states emphatically, "Laboratory research is essential in psychology if we want to develop a body of scientific knowledge" (p. 127).

Second, and even more directly, most if not all of the modified contextualists have actually conducted experimental investigations. Consider some examples. Cicirelli (1992) examined two groups of adult children, divided according to whether they had intact marriages or some form of marital disruption. Those with intact marriages reported giving significantly more help to their elderly parents than did their siblings, but those with disrupted marriages reported giving about the same amount of help as did their siblings. Jurden and Reese (1992) divided women into three groups on the basis of age and educational status and manipulated content familiarity and syntactic complexity of target propositions in short narratives. Among the findings was that intrusions in free recall were associated with higher content familiarity. Schneider and Morris (1992) trained rats such that a sequence of responses or individual responses were reinforced. Among their results was that in Experiment 2, the sequence of responses rather than individual responses more closely obeyed the well-known matching law. Smith, Staudinger, and Baltes (1994) examined wisdom ratings in clinicians as a function of age. Contrary to most studies of cognitive aging, young and older adults did not differ. Steele, Hayes, and Brownstein (1990) examined the effects of contingently reinforced versus noncontingently reinforced pretraining on subsequent rule discovery in undergraduates divided into three groups. Their results suggested that behavioral stereotypy might be due to repeated exposure to the task. All of these studies employed the experimental method, which of course by its nature places restrictions on the range of variables examined.

Accepting Lawfulness

There are two lines of evidence that modified contextualists accept lawful relations. First, unlike philosophic contextualists, no modified contextualist appears to have rejected lawful relationships. Second, some modified contextualists have accepted general positions that themselves assume lawfulness or have directly suggested that they seek lawful relationships. For example, a variety of modified contextualists accept the behavior-analytic approach to psychology (e.g., Biglan, 1993; Hayes et al., 1988; Morris, 1993b). Among these individuals is Lee (1988), who specifically rejects Gergen's (1973) contention that the historical character of psychology precludes general laws. In fact, Lee states, "Laws are central to what we mean by science" (p. 123).

According to Morris (1993b), the natural-science variety of contextualism, accepted by behavior analysts, seeks general laws and principles, a practice eschewed by the natural-history variety, which we call philosophic contextualism. Similarly, Hayes (1993) suggests that there are general principles of behavioral change, and the best way to test the utility of such principles is through controlled experimentation. As other examples, Lerner and Kauffman (1985) say, "A contextual perspective need not, should not, and typically does not . . . avoid the use of universalistic and thus constantly applicable principles of development" (p. 317), and Reese (1991) states, "The presently established empirical laws or principles can be used to predict findings and to explain failures to confirm predictions (as in any other world view)" (p. 207). It seems rather clear that modified contextualists, unlike philosophic contextualists, accept the possibility of establishing lawful relationships.

Ignoring or Minimizing Novelty

As we have seen, within philosophic contextualism, novelty is the normal condition, always to be expected and often actually occurring. This position, which is seen by philosophic contextualists as fundamental to their worldview, is rejected by modified contextualists. They have done so in one of two ways. Either they have expressed positions that restrict novelty, or they have more directly suggested that novelty is not to be expected. Cicirelli (1994) and Ford and Lerner (1992), as we saw earlier, recommend strategies that restrict the range of variables examined and thus the range of possible outcomes. In support of his position, Cicirelli has suggested that in many areas, change is so slow that novelty can be ignored except for the very long term. Although Ford and Lerner do not preclude the possibility that novel events may occur, they suggest, contrary to philosophic contextualists, that such events will not necessarily occur and only may happen.

Among the strongest proponents of the view that novelty can be disregarded within contextualism are Hayes et al. (1988) and Reese (1991). For example, Hayes et al. say, "The possibility of true novelty can be ignored" (p. 103). Reese (1991) has explicitly rejected novelty and done so in the following manner. He has suggested that novelty "exists only as a possibility and that contextualism is concerned with the concrete present, not with abstract possibilities" (p. 207). Clearly, talking about novelty as only an abstract possibility and as something that can be ignored is to disagree in no uncertain terms with the position that is most fundamental to philosophic contextualism. It might be noted that when one accepts the possibility of establishing lawful relations, as do the modified contextualists, it is hardly surprising that the possibility of novelty would be minimized or ignored, and necessarily so.

Accepting Science

As Deese (1993), Sarbin (1977), and others have suggested, psychology as science is an unattainable goal within philosophic contextualism. Contrary to this position, modified contextualists embrace the scientific approach with enthusiasm. For example, the recent volume edited by Hayes et al. (1993) is titled, revealingly, *Varieties of Scientific Contextualism.* There can be little doubt from an examination of such writings that the modified contextualists are attempting to develop a scientific approach to psychology that rectifies what they perceive as the weaknesses of mechanism as an approach to psychological science. This attitude is so pervasive in the writings of the modified contextualists that even a cursory examination of their works will reveal their attachment to what they regard as the new and improved way of doing science.

The following statements are examples of the attitude of a variety of modified contextualists to science. Lee (1988) states, "Taking behavior-in-context as psychology's subject matter allows contextualists to insist that psychology is an autonomous science" (p. 103). Reese (1991) has suggested that contextualism is "a legitimate model for the science" (p. 220) and goes on to say that modified contextualists who pursue a scientific approach do so "because they believe science is the best way to get temporarily effective answers" (p. 221). Hayes and Hayes (1989) say of the behavior-analytic approach to contextualism that "it is the only contextual position of which we are aware that has produced a robust experimental science" (p. 40). In agreement with Hayes and Hayes, Morris (1993b) asserts,

> One of the more fundamental distinctions between behavior analysis and other varieties of scientific contextualism is that behavior analysis takes itself to be a natural science of psychology, whereas other varieties assert the categorical impossibility of such a thing, that is, of a natural science of psychology. (p. 153)

Contrary to the sentiments expressed earlier by Hayes and Hayes (1989) and Morris (1993b), there are modified contextualists who are not behavior analysts but nevertheless think of themselves as scientists. Lerner and a variety of other developmental psychologists, such as Reese, clearly see themselves as both contextualistic and scientific. For example, Lerner (1985) has said,

This contextual view represents a "different drummer" for developmental psychology. Although as yet still playing relatively softly, the beat is steady, growing in intensity, and compelling. The 1980s may see more and more scientists begin to try to dance to the music. (p. 183)

Lerner's prediction turned out to be correct, inasmuch as modified contextualism has been described as the dominant metamodel in developmental psychology (e.g., Cicirelli, 1994).

Modified contextualism has been seen as a scientific approach to still other areas of psychology. For example, Biglan (1993) stated that his chapter "articulates a functional contextualist framework for the development of a science of community interventions" (p. 251). Social/personality psychology is another area that has been characterized as benefiting from a modified contextualistic approach. For example, Mancuso (1993) has argued that "psychological scientists, proceeding from a contemporary analysis of theory making, may assert a radical *constructivist/contextualist* position" (p. 111). Mancuso's intention is to devise "a contextualist based radical constructivism to frame our understanding of persons" (p. 115). As a final example, cognitive psychology, particularly the information-processing approach, has been seen as benefiting from a contextualistic approach to science. Gillespie (1992) opposes "the standard view of science in psychology," particularly in cognitive psychology, with that suggested by contextualism. She examines several research projects that she sees as deriving from contextualism and evaluates "what these new contextualist projects entail experimentally and theoretically in the study of perception, memory and categorization" (p. 62). It is clear that modified contextualists embrace science with an enthusiasm that would be difficult for a philosophic contextualist to understand, much less accept.

COMPARISON OF PHILOSOPHIC CONTEXTUALISM, MODIFIED CONTEXTUALISM, AND MAINSTREAM SCIENCE

Table 4.1 describes similarities and differences among philosophic contextualism, two categories of modified contextualism (developmental and functional), and mainstream science along five dimensions. Four of these

TABLE 4.1 Features of Philosophic Contextualism, Developmental Contextualism, Functional Contextualism, and Mainstream Science

Feature	Philosophic Contextualism	Developmental Contextualism	Functional Contextualism	Mainstream Science
Rejects restriction of variables	Yes	No	No	No
Rejects lawfulness	Yes	No	No	No
Accepts novelty	Yes	No	No	No
Rejects science	Yes	No	No	No
Accepts radical empiricism	Yes	No	Yes	No

dimensions were considered in this chapter, and the fifth, radical empiricism, was mentioned earlier in the book and will be treated at greater length in subsequent chapters. Considering the five dimensions, the philosophic contextualists and the functional contextualists are in agreement on only one: Both accept radical empiricism. The developmental contextualists differ from the philosophic contextualists along all five dimensions and from the functional contextualists only in not being radical empiricists. Both types of modified contextualists, but not philosophic contextualists, accept the value of procedures that restrict the range of variables examined. Philosophic contextualists, but not modified contextualists, reject the possibility of establishing lawful relationships. Philosophic contextualists, but not modified contextualists, accept the possibility that novelty may arise at any time. Philosophic contextualists, but not modified contextualists, reject science as it is conventionally understood. As the table indicates, the developmental contextualists and mainstream scientists are in agreement on all five dimensions, and functional contextualists differ from mainstream science only in accepting radical empiricism.

In an earlier article (Capaldi & Proctor, 1994), we argued that modified contextualists and mainstream scientists are similar in a variety of additional respects, which will be discussed in Chapters 6 and 7. Indeed, it is our view that modified contextualists have more in common with mainstream scientists than they do with philosophic contextualists in terms of the number of dimensions of agreement. However, the single dimension along which the functional contextualists and the philosophic contextualists agree—radical empiricism—is by far the most important single dimension. Indeed, radical empiricism appears to be the only factor of significance that unites the two camps.

For philosophic and functional contextualists, like their pragmatic forebears who embraced radical empiricism, experience is regarded as primary and is to be taken at face value. In short, radical empiricists claim that we should not attempt to describe experience at some other level. This commitment to radical empiricism is clearly shared by the functional contextualists—those such as Hayes and Morris, who take a behavior-analytic perspective. Other self-styled contextualists—for example, developmental contextualists such as Baltes and Lerner—may not in fact be contextualists if, as we believe, radical empiricism is the indispensable defining feature of contextualism. The attraction of contextualism to individuals such as Baltes and Lerner is that it permits, in their view, a greater emphasis on multilevel determination than does mainstream science. But a commitment to multilevel determination does not define contextualism. This has been made abundantly clear by Sarbin (1993), a philosophic contextualist, who said,

> Because of the vagaries of language usage, some psychologists subscribe to "contextualism" in a special way: they see contextualism as providing counsel to increase the number of dependent variables or to control for surrounding and accompanying stimulus events when offering an explanation of a phenomenon. In this respect, contextualism is employed as a corrective to the mechanistic practice of limiting the number of variables in a particular experimental program in order to render context-free the ultimate finding. This is a limited and perhaps trivial interpretation of contextualism. The root metaphor of the historical act implies more than looking at additional variables. The historical act calls for different categories of observation and explanation. (p. 53)

We are in strong agreement with Sarbin that a concern with multilevel determination is not sufficient to define one as a contextualist in any meaningful historical sense of that term (see Pepper, 1942). Thus, although developmental contextualists describe themselves as contextualists, strictly speaking they are not.

SUMMARY AND CONCLUSIONS

In Chapter 4, philosophic and modified contextualism were described, and the major proponents and positions of each were identified. It was indicated that philosophic contextualism rejects experimentation, lawfulness, and science as it is currently practiced while placing a heavy emphasis on novelty. Modified contextualism, on the other hand, accepts experimentation, lawfulness, and science and seeks to minimize novelty. A comparison of the various forms of contextualism and mainstream science along five significant dimensions (rejects restriction of variables, rejects lawfulness, accepts novelty, rejects science, accepts radical empiricism) indicated that modified contextualism is similar along more dimensions to mainstream psychology than it is to philosophic contextualism. The most significant defining characteristic of contextualism, which functional contextualists share with philosophic contextualists, is the acceptance of radical empiricism.

Philosophic Contextualism and Academic Psychology

A Comparison and Evaluation

*T*he aims and goals of philosophic contextualists are quite similar to those of other postmodernists. They think it is desirable to view knowledge as a social construction that is ephemeral and subject to constant change. An implication of this position, of course, is that establishing general lawful relations in psychology is neither possible nor desirable. Experimentation is seen, at least by most philosophic contextualists, as a relic of modernism, which is useless for obtaining knowledge and so should be consigned to the scrap heap of history. Those who do see a place for experimentation see that place as extremely limited, with experimentation being at the service of various nonexperimental methods. The emphasis in contextualism, as in postmodernism generally, is on what works in a practical manner of speaking. This attitude fosters an interest in applied problems and, of course, a total rejection of the kind of theorizing that is popular in mainstream, academic psychology. Finally, contextualists and postmodernists tend to see either a limited or nonexistent role for the psychology of the individual, emphasizing instead disciplines in which the focus is on social interaction, such as anthropology and sociology. All of these attitudes, to cite just a few sources, may be found in Gergen (1992), Kvale (1992b), and Polkinghorne (1992).

PHILOSOPHIC CONTEXTUALISM'S ONTOLOGY

The ontology of philosophic contextualism was succinctly and accurately stated by Pepper (1942) in the following quote:

> Contextualism is accordingly sometimes said to have a horizontal cosmology, in contrast to other views, which have a vertical cosmology. There is no top nor bottom to the contextualistic world. In formism or mechanism or organicism one has only to analyze in certain specific ways and one is bound, so it is believed, ultimately to get to the bottom of things or to the top of things. Contextualism justifies no such faith. There is no cosmological mode of analysis that guarantees the whole truth or an arrival at the ultimate nature of things. On the other hand, one does not need to hunt for a distant cosmological truth, since every present event gives it as fully as it can be given. (p. 251)

What Pepper (1942) is saying, essentially, is that contextualists are radical empiricists in the sense that there is no more basic reality beyond the reality that one observes. An ontology of this sort values describing experience and suggests that beyond the description, there is nothing more basic. For example, in examining two different cultures, the most that can and should be done is to describe them, their similarities, and their differences. Each culture is accepted on its own terms, and one cannot suggest that one represents a better reality than another because, essentially, there are no better realities. To put it differently, the contextualist, in examining cultures or anything else for that matter, would not seek to identify the underlying laws that make a culture what it is because there are no such underlying laws. In Pepper's terms, the cosmology is horizontal, rather than vertical. What you see is what you get, and that is the end of it. As Gergen, Gulerce, Lock, and Misra (1996) state,

> It is first essential that no single paradigm of psychological inquiry be granted preeminence. This is at once to honor the many traditions of Western psychology—empiricist, phenomenological, critical school, feminist, hermeneutic, social constructionist, and more—as well as those extant in other cultural traditions. At the same time, it

is to invite a certain humility. Should practitioners fail to appreciate the limitations necessarily inherent in their local paradigms and treat the alternatives as flawed inferiors, currently existing conflicts will not give way to productive dialogue. (p. 502)

Preferring description to causal explanation is universal among contextualists in the sense that it applies to any phenomenon that may come under investigation. Another way to understand this is to heed the words of James (1907/1975) that the pragmatist distrusts generalization of any sort and wishes always to describe the specific event and nothing more.

PHILOSOPHIC CONTEXTUALISM
AND METHODOLOGY

Because methods are a major wellspring of knowledge, it is appropriate to examine those that are recommended both in mainstream psychology and in philosophic contextualism.

Experimentation in Academic Psychology

The generally accepted assumption in academic psychology is that the methods we employ should produce knowledge that is as unequivocal as possible. The way to achieve such knowledge is through controlled observation. That is, one seeks to isolate the independent variables that are producing the phenomenon of interest. The ideal way to achieve such control, it is thought, is through conducting experiments that use procedures similar to those proposed by John Stuart Mill (e.g., the method of difference). The method of difference dictates that when, say, two groups are compared, they should differ in one respect and one respect only. Any difference in the results obtained can be attributed to the respect in which the groups differ. Of course, much useful knowledge has been obtained by means other than experimentation (e.g., by naturalistic observation), but observation is not thought of as an end point but as the starting point for more controlled study.

The results of our observations, controlled or otherwise, are thought to provide the basis for speculating about underlying processes giving rise to them. These speculations often go under the name of theory and provide the basis for further controlled observations. Sometimes the relation between independent and dependent variables is constant, so much so that the relation is called a law. A prime example is Weber's law. Most academic psychologists would agree that the normal procedures employed to generate knowledge have been successful, at least to a degree. Certainly, no one thinks that psychology has entered some sort of golden age, but neither do most academic psychologists think that their approach to matters has been a total failure. By and large, they think that progress has been made and will continue to be made (e.g., Pashler, 1998; Posner, 1982).

Contextualism and Rejection of Experimentation

Among postmodernists, by which we mean philosophic contextualists and their close allies, a different attitude prevails. There is a wholesale rejection of the sort of controlled observation that is popular among their academic colleagues. Experimentation is seen as providing information that is limited at best to the circumstances under which it is obtained. Worse, it is seen as not being relevant to the important questions of psychology. Often it is recommended that controlled observation be avoided entirely in favor of a variety of other methods that supply more valid and useful information. Along with the rejection of conventional methodology is the rejection of the fruits of that methodology—namely, the theory it produces. Such theory, like the methods themselves, is thought to be of limited usefulness at best and, at worst, of no value whatsoever.

Consider some of the attitudes toward conventional methodology expressed by various contextualists. Gergen (1985) expresses a general disdain for the usefulness of rigorous methods. He states,

> In large degree the sciences have been enchanted by the myth that the assiduous application of rigorous method will yield sound fact—as if empirical methodology were some form of meat grinder from which truth could be turned out like so many sausages. (pp. 272-273)

Sarbin (1993) recommends rejecting laboratory-based experimentation entirely, stating, "The methodological implications of the contextual approach . . . *require* the abandonment of the impoverished and artificial setting of the laboratory" (p. 56, emphasis added). Gergen and Gergen (1991), whose positions often find favor with philosophic contextualists, likewise reject experimentation, saying,

> We argue that not only are experimental attempts at "testing" general theoretical ideas wasteful of effort and resources, but that by engaging in reflexive techniques a scientist can learn more about a theoretical position in a brief period than research can ever "demonstrate." (p. 79)

Reflexive techniques, as described by Steier (1991), can be understood as "a bending back on itself" (p. 2). We describe a specific example of a reflexive technique, hypothetical data rotation, later in this chapter.

Jaeger and Rosnow (1988) similarly articulate the position that the role of experimentation within philosophic contextualism is necessarily limited. They state,

> Thus, while the experiment can play a role in describing certain relational patterns or identifying causal properties, by its limited and constraining nature it cannot accommodate the complexity of factors that simultaneously act upon or determine an event. Explanation of the event requires additional knowledge and information about its social, cultural, historical, and biographical context. Nor is the experiment well suited to describe the unfolding of an event and how the individual effects change in the course of the event. (p. 69)

From the jacket of *Rethinking Methods in Psychology,* edited by Smith et al. (1995a), is the following: "This accessible textbook introduces a range of key research methods that challenge psychology's traditional preoccupation with 'scientific' experiments." The word *challenge* in this quote hardly expresses the degree to which conventional methods are rejected by the editors and their contributors. This is made clear by a subsequent statement on the jacket, which states that "the recent widespread rejection of conventional theory and method has led to the evolution of different ways to gather and analyze data."

The word *rejection* in the above quote is to be taken literally because it is used again on the jacket of another book, *Discursive Psychology in Practice,* edited by Harré and Stearns (1995), Harré being common to the two books. This jacket says the following:

In the last decade many diverse streams of thought have come together in an international movement to reject the traditional view that a "scientific" psychology must rely on experimental methodology.

Underpinning this movement is the principle that the main characteristics of human life are best understood as produced through discourse. This "discursive" psychology has found adherents across the range of psychological disciplines and has ushered in a completely revised understanding of the subject.

An even more dolorous evaluation of current methodology recently was supplied by Gergen (1992), who is often cited with approval by many contextualists. Gergen says, in a section called "The Marginalization of Method,"

> Under modernism, methodology underwent a virtual apotheosis. Methodology was the means to truth and light, and thus to salvation. . . . Under postmodernism, however, methodology loses its coveted position. Under postmodernism, research methods in psychology are viewed, at worst, as misleading justificatory devices. They operate as truth warrants for a priori commitments to particular forms of value-saturated description. (p. 24)

Gergen is not only saying that the fruits of conventional methodology are worthless, but he also is saying that they are no more than confirmatory products of a prior set of prejudices. It is difficult to evade the inference that Gergen and, presumably, many of those who agree with him are more than contemptuous of mainstream psychology.

Bruner (1990), in a widely cited book, proclaims that Gergen is rightly in the forefront of the movement to undermine conventional methodology, which is his intention also. For example, Bruner says,

> Inside psychology there is a worried restlessness about the state of our discipline, and the beginning of a new search for a means of reformulating it. In spite of the prevailing ethos of "neat little studies," and of what Gordon Allport once called methodolatry, the great psychological questions are being raised once again. (p. xi)

Deese (1985), a prominent experimental psychologist who has recently come to accept contextualism, takes a more moderate view of experimentation than Harré, Gergen, and Bruner but nevertheless sees it as of limited usefulness. Deese believes that experiments in psychology are useful for demonstrational purposes but cannot be generalized across contexts. In one place, Deese states,

> The thousands of experiments performed in the mid years of the twentieth century attempting to study the validity of one or another theory of learning were, with few exceptions, a vast waste of time. Nothing was settled, and the experiments themselves uncovered almost nothing of intrinsic interest. (p. 107)

More recently, Deese (1996) has said of psychology that he came to realize that

> there was no principled way whereby one could generalize the results of one experiment to another or to the more general conditions to which the laboratory experiments were addressed. There were no rules by which one could declare some conditions to be so negligible in importance as to be safely ignored. (p. 57)

As a final example of the general rejection of conventional methodology, in a book called *Psychology and Postmodernism,* Kvale (1992a) says,

> Today, there are signs of a disintegration of the scientific foundations of modern psychology. Further, there is a growing boredom with current psychological knowledge, which currently appears to have less to say about the human situation than do the arts and humanities. (p. 10)

Contextualism and Alternative Methodologies

Given that conventional methodology is rejected, what do various philosophic contextualists and other postmodernists propose to put in its place? A number of diverse nonexperimental methods have been suggested, some of which are described later. The origin of these methods tends to be in literature, history, and European philosophy.

The origin of these methods in literature is illustrated by Polkinghorne (1990), who states,

The renewed psychology would operate more like a humanities discipline than like a natural science discipline, and the kind and validity of its conclusions would be more like the valid interpretations of literary expressions than like the valid conclusions of logical and mathematical deductions. (p. 112)

Polkinghorne is by no means alone in suggesting that literature provides the basis for a new approach to methodology. For example, the contextualist Sarbin (1977) has suggested,

The new scholars of personality will engage in a radical shift. Instead of looking upon 19th- and 20th-century natural sciences as models, they will explore the structure of identity and the means of identity transvaluation where these occurrences are most clearly presented— where the importance of context is continually confirmed—the world of literature, especially dramatistic literature. Shakespeare, Goethe, Thomas Mann, Kafka, Dostoevsky, O'Neill, Shaw, and Pirandello come immediately to mind as writers who could be perceived as authorities on identity shaping and on the contextual features that support the imputation or withdrawal of respect and esteem for role enactments. (p. 37)

More recently, Sarbin (1990) has suggested in connection with troubled persons that "understanding is more likely to be facilitated if we follow the lead of poets, dramatists, and biographers, and focus on the language of social relationships" (p. 281).

The origin of these methods in history is made clear by Deese (1993), who says,

The search for theories upon which we can build psychology is as futile as the search for theories upon which we can build human history. Marx, Spengler, Sorokin, and countless others have tried it, but it doesn't work. History, in the words of a modest contemporary historian is "narrative," and fortunately for us, Jerome Bruner has adopted the same stance for psychology. (p. 113)

Bruner (1990) has said that psychology should be cultural psychology, and "a cultural psychology is an interpretive psychology, in much the sense that history and anthropology and linguistics are interpretive disciplines" (p. 118). He suggests that we should strive not for causal explanations with predictive power but for plausible interpretations of human behavior.

The origin of these methods in European philosophy, particularly hermeneutics, is indicated by Van Langenhove (1995), who says, "Psychology can *only* become a well-established science if, epistemologically speaking, the hermeneutical model is adopted and if this model is applied in a proper ontological context" (p. 11, emphasis added). Of the hermeneutical approach, Dougher (1993) has said,

> At its most basic level, hermeneutics refers to interpretive methodologies as they are applied to the human domain. More broadly, hermeneutics refers to a collection of approaches that stand in opposition to the application of natural science methods to the study of human behavior and experience. . . . In particular, hermeneutics rejects the positivistic, ahistorical, objective, and empirical nature of the physical sciences. (p. 214)

In agreement with Dougher (1993), Woolfolk, Sass, and Messer (1988) state, "Within our account hermeneutics is a broad rubric that encompasses the view of thinkers who have attempted to provide cultural, philosophic, or methodological alternatives to the quantification, naturalism, objectivism, ahistoricism, and technism that have increasingly come to dominate the modern *Weltanschauung*" (p. 2).

Another influence of European philosophy on methodology is indicated by the widespread acceptance of the dialectical approach. According to Buss (1979), "Dialectic as a method involves the notion of a dialogue, where 'truth' is increasingly approximated through a clash of opinions, and conflict is resolved at higher levels of analysis" (p. 76). Georgoudi (1983) suggests that dialectic theory constitutes an important approach to social psychology, as well as to a variety of other areas such as cognitive development, changes in family structure over time, interpersonal attraction, and others. According to Reese (1993), dialectical materialism is actually a variety of contextualism.

A final example of European philosophy influencing methodological developments in psychology is provided by Giorgi (1995). He gives "theoretical and critical reasons for using phenomenological philosophy as an alternative philosophy of science in order to establish psychology as a human science rather than a natural science" (p. 42). According to Giorgi, the fundamental feature of phenomenology is to provide a new approach for psychology. This approach "requires nothing less than an objective grasp of the nonobjective or a rational understanding of the pararational" (p. 39).

Perhaps the most radical methodological recommendation comes from Gergen and Gergen (1991), who suggest that thought experiments should replace actual experiments entirely:

> One significant means toward such an end is through what may be termed *hypothetical data rotation.* As will be described, through this self-reflexive methodology investigators can force themselves to explicate the "known but unsaid." In the first step of this procedure, the investigator undertakes the traditional preparatory steps in generating an idea for a laboratory study. Theoretical preferences are singled out, hypotheses are formed, a research design is elaborated, and procedures (setting, subjects, etc.) are envisioned. However, at this juncture the standard research procedure is terminated. No funds are spent on equipment, subjects, data collection, data analysis, and the like. Rather, the researchers may lay out the research design and arrange the pattern of results in a matrix. At this point they are poised for the expansion of understanding. (p. 83)

CAN EXPERIMENTATION
BE REPLACED?

The major objections of philosophic contextualists and other postmodernists to traditional methodology, particularly experimentation, seem to be as follows. On one hand, they suggest that interpretive methods, such as narrative and hermeneutics, can supply meaningful data of the type required, but experimentation cannot. Such meaningful data often take the form of plausible interpretations, rather than causal explanations. On the other hand, in the opinion of philosophic contextualists, not only is experimentation unnecessary for the production of meaningful knowledge, but it has been employed to support whatever biases happen to prevail at a particular moment.

Our Evaluation of Alternative Methods

Our view of the usefulness of the sort of methods advocated by philosophic contextualists is somewhat different from theirs. Let it be understood at the outset that we in no way deny that the serious application of various postmodern methods may lead to important discoveries. Indeed, were that to occur, we would be among the first to strongly recommend the new methodology to others. However, in our view, the various methods recommended by postmodernists appear to be extremely limited in a variety of respects. Consider some examples. Narrative is of no use whatsoever in connection with infant humans or animal subjects. Indeed, it is not useful for understanding a variety of special adult human populations. For example, as is well known, amnesiacs may have no conscious memory of events and yet reveal by means other than verbal report that the event is recalled in some sense. There is the famous example of the patient who experienced a pinch whenever he shook Claparède's hand (see Reber, 1993, p. 18). Although having no conscious recollection of this experience, the patient ultimately came to refuse to shake hands.

A more serious criticism of narrative, hermeneutics, and interpretive methods in general is that they are subject to the whims of whatever assumptions the researcher may make. That is, when evaluating the meaning of, say, a narrative, one's interpretation will be influenced considerably by the sort of assumptions he or she entertains. Although this point has been made by many psychologists (e.g., Bransford, 1979), it has also been made by Stanley Fish, a professor of English who is often cited with approval by postmodernists (see, e.g., Gergen, 1992). Fish has suggested that in reading a particular literary work, the meaning of the text does not determine our assumptions about it, but rather our assumptions determine the meaning of the text. Fish (1980) says,

> I now believe that interpretation is the source of texts, facts, authors, and intentions. Or to put it another way, the entities that were once seen as competing for the right to constrain interpretation (text, reader, author) are now all seen to be the *products* of interpretation. (pp. 16-17)

To make Fish's view entirely clear, consider his further remarks:

When one interpretation wins out over another, it is not because the first has been shown to be in accordance with the facts but because it is from the perspective of its assumptions that the facts are now being specified. It is these assumptions, and not the facts they make possible, that are at stake in any critical dispute. (p. 340)

Bruner's (1990) point that we are to employ narrative and other similar methods to produce "plausible interpretations" faces two grave difficulties. First, as any schoolboy knows or should know, many things are plausible that have not the slightest basis in reality. This is a point that may not impress many postmodernists, given their ontological commitments. However, the point made by Fish should impress them because it suggests that slight changes in assumptions may result in dramatic changes in our interpretation of, say, a narrative, no matter whether it is the narrative of a real or a fictional person.

Other mistaken ideas of Bruner's (1990) are that psychology should be folk psychology—that is, the means by which persons organize their everyday or commonsense interactions with the world—and that it currently is not. That is, Bruner seems to think that folk psychology has been neglected by the mainstream and is benign. He does not seem to realize that a great deal of what social psychologists study, for example, is folk psychology and that its use has pitfalls. A prime example of folk psychology that has received an enormous amount of study in social psychology is attribution research (Fletcher, 1995). Fletcher, a widely published social psychologist who has thought deeply about folk psychology, says the following:

> The persuasive, taken-for-granted, feature of folk psychology is what makes it an inherently dangerous source for scientific psychology. My own impression is that folk psychology is built into scientific psychological theories in a more thoroughgoing fashion than is commonly realized by psychologists or cognitive scientists. Ideally, folk psychology should be incorporated into scientific formulations in the same way as any other theoretical or knowledge base—in a critical and disciplined fashion. (p. 97)

Experimentation Is Indispensable

Consider now the view of some postmodernists that experimentation can be dispensed with completely. It seems abundantly clear that at least some issues cannot be settled without reference to experimentation. It was appreciated long before the establishment of psychology as a science that experimentation was indispensable in the investigation of at least some psychological phenomena. Possibly the earliest use of experimentation in psychology was a test of Mesmer's idea that "animal magnetism" could cure disease. Mesmer claimed that the magnetic fluid was too subtle to be measured by any physical means. Thus, its effects on people had to be judged by other criteria. One of the effects was to produce in people being magnetized a convulsive state called the crisis. A commission of the French Academy of Sciences, presided over by Benjamin Franklin and including among its members the chemist Lavoisier, was appointed to test the powers of the magnetic fluid.

The commission conducted numerous experiments to evaluate the effects of magnetism on people. In one, for example, a woman (Mademoiselle B.), who previously had been shown to be sensitive to the animal magnetism procedure, was magnetized without her awareness by one of the commissioners located at close proximity but behind a paper screen. During an entire half hour of being magnetized without awareness, no convulsive state was produced. Immediately thereafter, the same procedure was performed, but with the commissioner in Mademoiselle B.'s sight, and a complete convulsive crisis occurred within minutes. When the commissioner indicated that he was taking steps to stop the crisis but continued the magnetization procedure, the crisis quickly dissipated. This and other experiments showed that the convulsive state was not produced when the participants were unaware of being magnetized but was produced when they were told they were being magnetized and were either not being magnetized or magnetized in an inappropriate way. The commission concluded on the basis of their experimental findings that "the animal magnetic fluid is capable of being perceived by none of our senses, and had no action either upon themselves or upon subjects of their many experiments. . . . The existence of the [magnetic] fluid is absolutely destitute of proof" (Franklin et al., 1784/1970, p. 126).

The first thing to note from this example is that controlled experiments established what seems to be two very important points: that the magnetic fluid is a fiction and that what people believe to be true can have a strong effect on their behavior—that is, people are suggestible. The second thing to note is that it would be extremely difficult, if not impossible, to establish the two points noted earlier by any of the methods recommended by postmodernists, such as narrative or hypothetical data rotation. Indeed, one supposes that if the individuals undergoing convulsions were asked, they would swear that they were being influenced by the magnetic fluid rather than by their own suggestibility. The third thing to note is that it seems impossible to accuse the commission of attempting to justify its own bias that the fluid is a fiction. First, the experiment they performed would have allowed the opposite finding, that is, that the magnetic field exists. Second, is there anyone today who believes with the advantage of hindsight that all of the diseases of the human condition can be cured by means of Mesmer's magnetism?

THE CHARACTER OF PSYCHOLOGY
UNDER PHILOSOPHIC CONTEXTUALISM

If philosophic contextualists were to prevail, what changes would occur in the discipline of psychology? Changes may be divided into two types, general and specific.

General Changes

In contrast to mainstream psychologists who value objectivity, philosophic contextualists and their close allies, such as social constructionists, glory in subjectivism. One of the clearest statements of the acceptance of subjectivism by philosophic contextualists is to be found in Guba (1990), who derives it both from his ontological and epistemological assumptions. Ontologically, according to Guba, "realities exist in the form of multiple mental constructions, socially and experientially based, local and specific, dependent for their form and content on the persons who hold them" (p. 27). Epistemologically, according to Guba, "Inquirer and inquired into are fused into a single (monistic) entity. Findings are literally the creation of the process of interaction between the two" (p. 27). Guba goes on to say,

> *Ontologically,* if there are always many interpretations that can be made in any inquiry, and if there is no foundational process by which the ultimate truth or falsity of these several constructions can be determined, there is no alternative but to take a position of *relativism.* . . . Realities are multiple, and they exist in people's minds. (p. 26).

"Epistemologically," Guba says,

> the constructivist chooses to take a *subjectivist position.* Subjectivity
> is not only forced on us by the human condition . . . but because it
> is the only means of unlocking the constructions held by individuals.
> If realities exist only in respondents' minds, subjective interaction
> seems to be the only way to access them. (p. 26)

Carrying this reasoning out to its logical conclusion results in a transformation of psychology that is thoroughgoing and fundamental.

First and foremost, psychology would be a social discipline with little or
no room for investigation of the individual person. This is because truth arises
out of the interactions of persons; thus, the psychology of any one individual
person is not merely of no interest but impossible. On this view, psychology
would take on the characteristics of anthropology or sociology. Taken to its
extreme, psychology as it is currently practiced would disappear entirely to
be replaced by the study of people in social interactions. One of the clearest
expressions of this point of view (but certainly not the only one) is to be found
in a chapter by Kvale (1992b), which is titled, appropriately enough, "Postmodern Psychology: A Contradiction in Terms?" Kvale suggests, "The science
of psychology may be out of touch with the current age" (p. 31) because the
terms *psychology* and *postmodernity* are incompatible, and thus "postmodern psychology is a contradiction in terms" (p. 31). This incompatibility arises
because "to understand human activity it is necessary to know the culture,
the social and historical situation, in which the activity takes place" (p. 31).

Shotter (1997) expresses a similar sentiment as follows:

> Once we allow people to be in continuous, living contact with each
> other, we can no longer sustain the idea of ourselves as being
> separate, self-contained entities or of our world as being an "exter-
> nal" world. Because, when a second living human being responds to
> the acts of a first and thus acts in a way that depends on his or her
> acts, then the activities of the second person cannot be accounted as
> wholly his or her own activity. (p. 816)

In agreement with this, Bruner (1990) has suggested, "It is man's participation
in culture and the realization of his mental powers *through* culture that makes

it impossible to construct a human psychology on the basis of the individual alone" (p. 12). Bruner quotes Geertz (1973), a cultural anthropologist, with approval as saying, "There is no such thing as a human nature independent of culture" (p. 49). Although we agree that it is important for psychology to consider culture, we do not think that it should be the exclusive concern.

Because the horizontal cosmology of the contextualist does not constrain observation, and because truth is determined by social interaction, accepted belief inevitably would be determined by what one considers to be politically appropriate. Under these conditions, good intentions or what are considered to be desirable outcomes inevitably will have a decisive impact on the content of belief. In short, under philosophic contextualism, politics would play a much larger role than it currently does in mainstream psychology.

Another general change in psychology would be replacing the concern with theory with the exclusive concern for application. Dispensing with theory would occur because, according to the philosophic contextualists, there are no universals to be found, and so it is useless to seek them. Application becomes important because philosophic contextualists are concerned with what works in a particular context. It follows from this that persons cannot be studied in themselves but only in relation to the culture in which they reside. As culture becomes important, vast areas of academic psychology become unimportant and trivial. Learning, as it is currently studied, with its emphasis on the individual, becomes superfluous, as do perception, cognition, problem solving, and all other areas as they are studied independent of a particular cultural context. To be specific, there are no laws of learning, memory, or cognition to be found, independent of the cultural context in which learning, memory, or cognition occurs. In short, if philosophic contextualism were to prevail, the field of psychology as it currently exists would not merely be transformed, but it would become unrecognizable.

Specific Changes

A quote from Harré (1993) contains some of the seeds of the more specific changes of the practice of psychology that would come about under the aegis of the philosophic contextualists:

> For adherents of the old paradigm coordinated behavior is the effect of causal processes, triggered by the stimuli to which the subjects are exposed. The job of the experimenter is to look for correlations between elementary stimuli and elementary behaviours, usually by

the use of statistical analyses to identify central tendencies. Individual people are the vehicle for causal processes. For adherents of the new paradigm coordinated behaviour is the product of the joint action of human agents acting intentionally according to local norms to accomplish certain projects. The job of the observer is to look for patterns of meaningful action by attending to the plans and intentions of the actors and the rules and conventions accepted as valid in their community, and which are known to the members. (p. 14)

One obvious change that would come about were philosophic contextualism to reign supreme is that we could close down all of the animal laboratories devoted to learning, cognitive neuroscience, or what have you. Philosophic contextualists and their allies equate psychology with the study of humans, preferably adult humans, and only humans. There are reasons for this, no doubt, major among them apparently being the belief that individuals are molded not merely by the culture they are in but more dramatically by the linguistic aspects of that culture, particularly their communication with each other. Such meaningful communication is probably not to be found in any nonhuman animal, including our closest relative, the chimpanzee.

Another change in the way psychology is currently practiced is that the emphasis on and the desirability of generalizing from one population to another would be drastically curtailed, if not wholly eschewed (Gergen et al., 1996). The tendency here would be to see all knowledge as local. For example, Harré (1993) has said,

> If one wants to know what knowledge and skill is required to create and maintain a friendship in India, it is almost wholly useless to transfer the conventions of friendship current in the American middle west to that distant subcontinent. (p. 24)

Contrary to Harré, somehow we denizens of the American Midwest have not found it too difficult to forge friendships with all sorts of foreigners, including Asians and Turks, among others. The reason for the emphasis on the local and on the nongeneralizability of knowledge, it seems, is to be found in the failure to postulate processes underlying the formation of friendships that operate similarly in all cultures.

Another change that would occur is what Geertz (1973) describes as the blurring of boundaries between disciplines. On this view, psychology is more like anthropology and literature than it is to the natural sciences. In a word,

one would thoroughly combine two or more areas that seem incompatible—
for example, "quantum theory in verse or biography in algebra" (Geertz,
1973, p. 20).

A further change would be to regard psychological phenomena as
transient, ever changing, and ephemeral. In these accounts, stability of
phenomena is eschewed. As Harré (1993) has said,

> Gergen (1973) has pointed out in a paper of considerable signifi-
> cance, what little evidence exists concerning the temporal stability
> of social formations and practices, personality-types, and so on,
> point to their remarkably ephemeral character. We are quite unjus-
> tified in supposing that the forms of microsocial action, and even
> perhaps the way individuals are related to these forms, that is their
> social psychology, are constant over time. All the evidence we have,
> slender though it is, suggests that social forms and individual cogni-
> tions of these forms are highly unstable and in rapid flux. (p. 139)

Still another change is the acceptance of plausible interpretations of
phenomena. The reason for this emphasis is that causal analysis is rejected
within these frameworks. Lacking causal analysis, one turns to plausibility.
This approach places a heavy emphasis on "understanding" phenomena,
rather than on prediction and control. As Harré and Gillet (1994) have
suggested, to understand human activity, it is necessary to enter into

> an empathic identification with the other that helps the observer
> make sense of what the other is doing. Such an approach to the
> understanding of behavior can be sensitive to the subtleties of the
> situation of the other in a way that an attempt to identify and isolate
> a surveyable number of objective independent variables cannot be.
> (p. 20)

Philosophic contextualists, as well as social constructionists, place heavy
emphasis on the works of Geertz, Rorty, and Vygotsky. An interesting idea
expressed by Vygotsky (1960) is that "any higher mental function was
external [and] social before it was internal" (p. 197). Thus, Vygotsky suggests
the primacy of social interactions.

In short, if philosophic contextualism were to prevail in psychology, the
changes it would produce would not only be numerous but also fundamental.
On one hand, many problems currently recognized as fundamental in psy-

chology would come to be ignored and neglected. On the other hand, psychology would come to concern itself with a variety of new issues that are not scientific in character, at least by any conventional standard.

SOME PROPOSED PRACTICAL
APPLICATIONS OF CONTEXTUALISM

Contextualists are not concerned merely with knowledge for its own sake but are primarily concerned with its application. We should not think, however, that in arriving at specific proposals for application, contextualists are in any more agreement among themselves than are mainstream psychologists. In this section, we describe ideas regarding applied issues that contextualists have in common and provide some specific proposals for application that they have made.

 Two major ideas that many contextualists hold in common are as follows. Knowledge is socially constructed and comes about as a function of negotiation among individuals interacting with their environment. The emphasis in practical situations is to see individuals as much more actively involved in the construction of such knowledge than is perhaps the case in mainstream psychology.

Prawat and Floden (1994) have described a specific proposal, which they see as stemming from contextualism, for modifying the educational curriculum. They identify themselves as postmodern social constructivists, which they see as a variety of contextualism stemming directly from the philosophy of Pepper (1942). An important assumption of social constructivism is that knowledge is a social product. Prawat and Floden reject what they consider to be the primary tenet of mechanism—"that learning is a process of acquiring accurate understanding of fixed entities and relationships that are thought to exist independently of human activity" (p. 41). Emergence of novelty, which is a key aspect of learning, is not handled well outside of contextualism, according to them. Students, they suggest, are in a complex, reciprocal relation with their environment, a relation that they describe as coimplicative. In the classroom, the teacher does not stand apart from the students but rather interacts with them. The teacher's role is to propose challenging questions to the students, which they criticize and evaluate. By interacting with one another, the students construct challenging alternatives to the teacher's

88 ♦ CONTEXTUALISM IN PSYCHOLOGICAL RESEARCH?

suggestions, and this process produces learning. According to Prawat and Floden, "The instruction is successful to the extent that students, as a group, are able to put together ideas that lead to further fruitful discussion" (p. 46).

An approach to clinical psychology in recent years stemming from contextualism is that of Sarbin (1990). Sarbin's approach recommends that we do away with the tendency to place individuals in diagnostic categories, such as schizophrenia. Sarbin proposes to treat individuals diagnosed as schizophrenic in the following way. The clinician attempts to perceive his or her patients as actors and performers. Within this general framework, the clinician's task is to determine what the person is trying to say or do, what goals he or she is attempting to reach, and what story the person is attempting to tell. The person is perceived as an agent trying, sometimes unsuccessfully, to maintain a coherent narrative in the face of a complex, unpredictable, and confusing world. The clinician's goal is to reconstruct the individual's self-narrative to enable him or her to deal more effectively with his or her environment. Understanding of the person's self-narrative, according to Sarbin, is more likely to be successful if the clinician follows the leads that stem from literary works of novelists and poets, rather than the scientific works that stem from mainstream psychology.

SUMMARY AND CONCLUSIONS

In Chapter 5, it was indicated that the aims of philosophic contextualists are those of postmodernists in general. Such contextualists seek a descriptive, rather than explanatory, science. They see psychology as a variety of cultural anthropology or sociology. Experimentation and lawfulness are rejected. Their epistemology is a horizontal one that embraces radical empiricism. In place of experimentation, which is the favored method of academic psychology, the philosophic contextualists propose a variety of alternative methodologies. These include narrative, hermeneutics, hypothetical data rotation, and ethnography. The view of science held by the philosophic contextualists is one that sees it as closer to literature than to the laboratory. In the chapter, we suggest that experimentation, although it may have its limitations for certain purposes, is indispensable for other purposes. Various limitations of the methods proposed by philosophic contextualists were discussed; that is, they are not applicable to infants, animals, psychotic persons, amnesiacs, and so on. Psychology under contextualism would become a branch of anthropology, with truth becoming a social creation established by interactions among individuals. Specific suggestions for applying philosophic contextualism to the practical problems of education and clinical psychology were described.

Developmental Contextualism and Academic Psychology

A Comparison and Evaluation

*M*odified contextualists differ from philosophic contextualists in advocating a scientific approach to psychology. Too, they see themselves as different from and superior to science as practiced in mainstream psychology. Any attempt to describe modified contextualism in general terms runs into a difficulty. That difficulty, simply put, is this. Although philosophic contextualists seem to hold similar beliefs in common, this is much less true of modified contextualists, who are much more varied in their beliefs. Despite this difficulty, it is sufficient to outline and evaluate the views of two major versions of modified contextualism: developmental contextualism and functional contextualism.

In this chapter, we will concentrate on describing in some detail the tenets of developmental contextualism and its methodological commitments; functional contextualism will be addressed in Chapter 7. Having examined the positions of developmental contextualists, we will contrast them with those of academic psychologists and evaluate their implications. We will suggest in this chapter that developmental contextualism and mainstream psychology have a great deal in common. The reasons for this are not difficult to isolate:

Developmental contextualism and mainstream psychology do not differ either in their ontological or epistemological assumptions (see Table 4.1).

ORIGINS OF DEVELOPMENTAL CONTEXTUALISM

In the early 1970s, Hayne Reese and Willis Overton published a series of papers in which they suggested that most work in developmental psychology had proceeded from mechanistic or organismic metatheories (Overton & Reese, 1973; Reese & Overton, 1970). They indicated that these were but two possible metatheories and that others should be explored. This led many developmentalists to explore alternative philosophical metatheories over the next two decades. As Ford and Lerner (1992) note, within developmental psychology, "there was considerable intellectual excitement in the 1970s and early 1980s about the scientific potential of models derived from these 'alternative' metamodels" (p. 5).

The search for alternatives focused primarily on varieties of contextualism. According to Ford and Lerner (1992),

> Indeed, it can be argued that the growing interest in contextualism metamodels . . . resulted in the recession of the mechanistic and (to a much lesser extent) the organismic models to the "back burner" of intellectual concern and empirical activity among developmentalists (Lerner, 1990). In their place, activity associated with the contextual metamodel moved to the cutting edge of the scientific study of human development. (p. 8)

The turning away of many developmentalists from organismic and mechanistic models to contextualistic models was in part motivated by a desire to account for the relative plasticity and multidirectionality of development. Contextualistic models seemed to some developmentalists "to hold more promise for leading to formulations that can integrate data about the plasticity and multidirectionality of and individual differences in developmental changes across the life span" (Ford & Lerner, 1992, p. 10).

Although the developmentalists interested in plasticity and multidirectionality thought that the worldview of contextualism held the most promise, they were aware that pure, philosophic contextualism is not very compatible with the goals of science. In Ford and Lerner's (1992) words,

> If philosophic contextualism were to be adopted as the metamodel for developmental theory, it would be able to deal with plasticity, multidirectionality, and individual differences—but only in the most radical of ways. The extreme dispersiveness of the contextual world view would mean that plasticity was infinite, that any direction of developmental change was possible, and that there were no necessary commonalities of human development. . . . Clearly these possibilities are counterfactual and, just as clearly, contextualism in its "pure" state—that is, as Pepper (1942) described it—cannot serve as an adequate metamodel for the study of human development (Lerner & Kauffman, 1985). (p. 10)

For this reason, the form of contextualism prominent in developmental psychology and developmental contextualism "is a modified view" (Ford & Lerner, 1992, p. 11).

TWO CENTRAL CHARACTERISTICS OF DEVELOPMENTAL CONTEXTUALISM

One of the two key characteristics of developmental contextualism is multilevel determination (Ford & Lerner, 1992). According to this idea, variables from multiple levels of organization are involved in all aspects of human life and development. As Ford and Lerner note, "Scientists adhering to virtually any theoretical viewpoint would probably agree with this view" (p. 55). But, they contend, most scientists would examine variables at only one level or adopt a reductionistic approach in which one level was considered most fundamental. In contrast,

> Developmental contextualists would reject both of these approaches as too limited. Instead they would adopt an interlevel-synthetic orientation in which variables from multiple levels are considered, including those reductionists might emphasize, but would emphasize the intralevel and interlevel patterning of variables. (p. 55)

In other words, the argument is that developmental contextualists would look more at the "total picture" of variables.

The second key characteristic of developmental contextualism is that variables from several levels of organization in human life exist in reciprocal relation. The basic idea is that variables at one level of organization are influenced by and influence variables at other levels. According to Ford and Lerner (1992), "Relations between levels of organization and not an isolated level per se become the key focus of developmental analysis, and *changing relations among levels constitutes the primary process of developmental change*" (p. 55). These authors argue that "combining the assumptions of multivariate, multilevel organization and dynamic interactionism leads to a key theoretical feature of developmental contextualism" (p. 58), which is its distinct position concerning the nature-nurture issue. They characterize this position as follows:

> Developmental contextualism proposes that variables from levels of organization associated with a person's biological or organismic characteristics (e.g., genes, tissues, or organ systems) dynamically interact with variables from contextual levels of organization (i.e., involving intrapersonal and extrapersonal variables), within which the biological characteristics are embedded. Therefore biological variables both influence and, reciprocally, are influenced by contextual ones. (pp. 58-59)

In short, neither biology nor context has primacy.

LESS CENTRAL CHARACTERISTICS OF DEVELOPMENTAL CONTEXTUALISM

Active Versus Passive Organism

Developmental contextualists consider that within mainstream psychology, organisms are seen as passive, which is to say that they respond only to outside stimulation and do not initiate activity themselves. For example, one of the reasons Baltes (1979) gives for why life span developmental psychologists adopt a contextualistic view, rather than a mechanistic or organismic view, is as follows: "As development unfolds, it becomes more and more apparent that individuals act on the environment and produce novel behavior outcomes, thereby making the active and selective nature of human beings of paramount importance" (p. 2). In a similar vein, Cicirelli (1994) has said,

> The core of the mechanistic model is the machine; man and the world are considered to be similar to or analogous to a machine. . . . A machine is basically passive or inactive. . . . To state that man is similar to a machine is to assert that man is basically passive. The individual does not initiate activity, behavior, or change; these are induced from the outside. (pp. 36-37)

The notion that developmental contextualists postulate an active organism, whereas so-called mechanists postulate a passive one, is simply a misunderstanding. That the organism is an active information processor has been advocated in any number of so-called mechanistic sources, a few of which we will cite here.

In a classic paper that deals with the problem of serial order behavior and whose influence in a variety of areas of psychology would be difficult to overestimate, Lashley (1951) indicated,

> My principal thesis today will be that input is never into a quiescent or static system, but always into a system which is already excited and organized. In the intact organism, behavior is the result of interaction of this background of excitation with input from any designated stimulus. Only when we can state the general characteristics of this background of excitation, can we understand the effects of a given input. (p. 112)

Similarly, Postman (1972), in characterizing the organizational approach to memory, said the following:

> One of the sources of appeal of the concept of organization is undoubtedly that it implies an active learner who imposes structure on the material to which he is exposed. The subject is credited with discovering and utilizing the systematic features introduced into the material by the experimenter, and also with inventing idiosyncratic bases of organization. (p. 18)

In a widely used textbook concerned with human memory, Klatzky (1980) described her approach as follows: "From the information-processing perspective adopted by this book . . . human memory is depicted as a continuously active system that receives, modifies, stores, retrieves, and acts upon information" (p. ix). More recently, in a textbook devoted to animal and human memory, Spear and Riccio (1994) state that there has been an "increasing realization that humans typically are active rather than passive processors of the information to be learned" (p. 13). Thus, from at least the early 1950s to the present, it has continuously been recognized that learners are active rather than passive in the processing of information.

Linear Causality Versus Mutual Causality

A characteristic attributed to mechanism and that has been accepted by developmental contextualists in general is unidirectional, linear causality. The idea here is that the mechanistic explanatory model is asymmetric, describing a one-way relation between independently defined causes and effects. Ford and Lerner (1992) reject this idea of causality in favor of what they call mutual causality. According to them,

> A typical view is that if A causes B, B cannot simultaneously cause A. In contrast the theory being presented in this book assumes not only that A and B simultaneously influence one another, but also that any change in A or B is a function of the organization of variables within which they are embedded. (p. 56)

The notion that mechanism is restricted to unidirectional, linear causality is simply mistaken. For example, Newton's third law of motion states the following: To every action there is always opposed an equal reaction, or the mutual actions of two bodies upon each other are always equal and directed toward contrary parts (Halliday & Resnick, 1966). How can such a serious misunderstanding of mechanism—that is, that causation is unidirectional—be explained? The likely reason has to do with the way that experimental research is normally conducted. In experimental arrangements, as a practical matter, scientists seek to examine the effects of independent variables on dependent variables. They are well aware, however, that effects occur in the reverse direction but ignore them not for epistemological or ontological reasons but for purely practical ones. If our reasoning here is correct, the contextualists have attributed to so-called mechanists beliefs they do not hold, mistaking strategic features for ontological ones.

Nonreductionism Versus Reductionism

Developmental contextualists consider that mechanists are reductionistic, unlike contextualists, who are not. For example, Lerner (1993) has suggested that although developmental contextualists consider that all variables from different organizational levels (e.g., biology, psychology, society, and history) have equal importance, other psychologists "would adopt a reductionistic orientation, seeking to study, or at least interpret, variables from multiple levels in terms of one level—a level conceived to be the core, constituent, or elemental level" (pp. 301-302).

The view that so-called mechanists are necessarily committed to reductionism is fallacious for at least two reasons. First, as Bechtel (1988) has indicated, within psychology in general and cognitive psychology in particular, there is a considerable difference of opinion as to whether reductionism is possible. Fodor (1974), for example, is an outspoken opponent of reductionism within cognitive psychology, contending that it is not possible to construct bridge laws equating terms in psychology with those of lower-level disciplines.

A second matter that Lerner's (1993) view overlooks is that even within mechanism, a major alternative approach to reductionism—interfield theory—has been proposed. Interfield theory is regarded by some as more realistic than reductionism. Bechtel (1988) indicates that interfield theories "do not attempt to derive one theory from another but rather seek to identify relationships between phenomena studied by the two different fields of inquiry" (p. 97). After describing a variety of mechanistic examples of interfield theory, Bechtel goes on to state the following:

> The mechanistic interfield theories sketched here open another possibility. This model can accommodate interaction between cognitive and neural inquiries without requiring reduction. It allows both analyses to inform each other in the attempt to develop an interfield theory, but does not require subsuming one explanation under another. (p. 107)

In agreement with the previously cited observations, Marr (1993), a noncontextualistic behavior analyst, has said,

Naive reductionism, wherein all phenomena at one level of analysis are fully accounted for by processes at a subadjacent level, and so forth, is not a view held by any modern perspective on mechanism, or, indeed, any scientific endeavor. The issues of reductionism, like those of mechanism, are very much more complex than are usually appreciated. (p. 61)

DEVELOPMENTAL CONTEXTUALISM COMPARED WITH ACADEMIC PSYCHOLOGY

Of course there is nothing wrong with the aim of developmental contextualists to study simultaneously the effects of a number of independent variables on some dependent variable, and much is to be said for doing so. Indeed, this approach may be a major and indispensable source of providing useful information regarding life span development. Many other areas of psychology are similarly situated. That is, such areas can benefit enormously from observing behavior in settings other than the laboratory: the classroom, the cockpit of the airplane, flight simulators, and the workplace. Areas of psychology that could ultimately benefit substantially from such observation include, in addition to developmental psychology, industrial-organizational psychology, educational psychology, engineering psychology, and all applied areas of psychology. Let us be clear that we have no objection to the developmental contextualists being concerned with multilevel determination and indeed believe that such a concern may lead to discoveries that would not be made otherwise.

One difference we have with the developmental contextualists is their assertion that dealing with multilevel determination is impermissible in what they call mechanism and what we are calling academic psychology. Academic psychology embraces any number of approaches to phenomena, spanning the continuum from casual observation, on one hand, to theory-generated experimental research, on the other hand. One of the egregious mistakes of Ford and Lerner (1992) is to suggest that so-called mechanistic psychology is concerned only with environmental variables (see their Table 1.1, p. 13) and is limited to the study of conditioning processes. A second error they make is to suggest that organicism, another worldview that is popular in developmental psychology, is concerned only with biological and behavioral variables. Accordingly, Ford and Lerner think it is necessary to describe developmental contextualism as a new approach that combines environmental, biological, and behavioral variables. This is not a necessary step because everything Ford and Lerner seek to gain by positing developmental contextualism (a combination of contextualism and organicism; see also Lerner & Kauffman, 1985) is already available to them in so-called mechanism.

These points, important as they are, are not unique to us and already have been made by other developmental psychologists. For example, Kendler (1986) has said,

> The version of contextualism and organicism presented by Lerner and Kauffman is so diluted as to lose the essence of their original meaning. In consequence, the concept of development they propose, which includes the notion of integrative levels, causal variables that interact differently at different times during the course of ontogeny, and probabilistic outcomes is more compatible with the mechanistic metatheory they eschew than with the contextualist and organismic ones they ostensibly espouse. (p. 80)

Similarly, Chandler (1993) has said, "By accident or propagandistic design, contextualism often wins converts for itself by claiming special virtues that are equally characteristic of quite different metatheoretical views" (p. 232).

Even if the above were not true, the difference between developmental contextualists and so-called mechanists is only a matter of emphasis and degree. For example, developmental contextualists do not eschew controlled experiments, and they accept the basic goals of academic psychology, prediction, and control. It is also important to recognize that although a concern with multilevel determination is an important starting point, it is by no means an ending point, and this observation is merely a matter of simple logic. If, for example, one finds a relationship between some behavior of teenagers and several simultaneously acting variables—parental control, teacher supervision, peer pressure, and hormonal factors—it would be sheer folly to be completely satisfied with establishing this relationship, as important as it might be. One would want to determine, for example, if any three of the four variables mentioned are responsible for the behavior in question. In short, one would want to go about making systematic observations of the sort recommended by so-called mechanists to isolate exactly those independent variables that are responsible for the dependent variable of concern. Another step that developmental contextualists would take, which is completely compatible with the so-called mechanistic approach to science, is to devise a theory that would explain the facts available to them.

The difference between developmental contextualists and so-called mechanists is at most a matter of degree. There are some areas in psychology in which it is less profitable to study phenomena in complex environments, as the developmental contextualists recommend. In some respects, at least, these areas are well past that step and can go directly into the laboratory, if not for all problems, at least for many. They do not eschew complex environments as a matter of ontology but merely as a matter of strategy; that is, in the case of these areas, little theoretical advancement can be gained by studying phenomena outside the laboratory. Examples of the above areas would include those in which the authors of this book work, human performance and animal learning. Most theoretical alternatives in these areas can simply be evaluated better under controlled laboratory conditions than under more open conditions. In the two areas mentioned, an enormous number of theoretical propositions cannot feasibly be evaluated under any other than controlled laboratory conditions.

These proposals are by no means far-out or controversial. They are dictated as a simple matter of logic and describe a progression in science that has long been recognized. For example, as Hull (1943) said more than 50 years ago,

> As scientific investigations become more and more searching, it is discovered that the spontaneous happenings of nature are not adequate to permit the necessary observations. This leads to the setting up of special conditions which will bring about the desired events under circumstances favorable for such observations; thus experiments originate. But even in deliberate experiments it is often extraordinarily difficult to determine with which among a complex of antecedent conditions a given consequence is primarily associated; in this way arise a complex maze of control experiments and other technical procedures, the general principles of which are common to all sciences but the details of which are peculiar to each. (p. 2)

It is worth emphasizing that what we and Hull have suggested is in no way related to a specific epistemology or ontology that one might embrace but is merely a matter of straightforward logic. What is being said is that the aim is to isolate the precise variables that are responsible for a phenomenon. Even those who eschew theory, such as the functional contextualists, recommend establishing the precise functional relationships that exist among phenomena.

In our opinion, developmental contextualism, although it does have some unique features, would not modify psychology as it is currently practiced in any fundamental sense. Essentially, psychology under developmental contextualism would differ in degree but not in kind from psychology as currently practiced in the academy. Indeed, in the final analysis, we think that developmental contextualists would eventually engage in the same sorts of scientific practices as so-called mechanistic psychologists. Specifically, we think that as developmental contextualists come to understand some particular phenomenon better and better, they would turn to hypothesis testing under more controlled conditions, even running highly controlled experiments.

What developmental contextualism lends itself to is examining phenomena under a broader set of conditions than is characteristic of academic psychology. Examples of this include the following. A developmental contextualist might be interested in the relationships among siblings—for example, how well they like each other, who is dominant and who is submissive, what sorts of obligations they feel that they have toward their parents, and so on. As another example, because developmental contextualists believe (as do the rest of us) that there are genetic-environmental interactions, they would want to examine development in several different environments. Baltes (1987) suggests that developmental psychologists should study wisdom, but wisdom should be studied under conditions that have a high degree of real-life complexity. As these examples suggest, developmental contextualists would seek to study the phenomena of interest under both a wider range of conditions (e.g., in the family as a whole) than is normally used in academic psychology and under a more varied set of conditions (e.g., examining persons in several different environments).

Having examined what we consider to be the major differences between developmental contextualism and so-called mechanism, we are in a position to detail what the similarities between these approaches might be. We think, as indicated, that ultimately developmental contextualists would bring the sort of problems suggested earlier into laboratory conditions. Because they are not radical empiricists, they would entertain hypotheses, seek general laws and overarching theories, and would be similar to so-called mechanists in a variety of other particulars. For example, it appears to us that developmental contextualists would have no hesitancy in employing data from nonhuman species if they thought it was appropriate to do so.

There currently exists substantial reason for believing that fundamentally developmental contextualists, insofar as they differ from so-called mechanists, do so only in degree. As a prime example of what we have in mind here, consider that Ford and Lerner (1992), in their influential book, *Developmental Systems Theory,* provide a figure (see Figure 6.1) titled, "A Simplified Prototypical Representation of a Person as a Self-Constructing Living System." What is significant about this figure is that it can be taken for a prototypical representation of an information-processing system, no different from that which might be offered by any red-blooded cognitive psychologist steeped in the assumptions of academic psychology. In truth, their figure, whatever its value may be—and we do not question its value—is not different in any significant respect from literally hundreds of similar models that have been supplied by academic psychologists.

We see nothing wrong with the emphasis of developmental contextualists on studying phenomena under wider and more varying conditions than is usual in academic psychology; indeed, we think that there might be much of value in it. There are many examples in the history of science in which phenomena studied under more general sets of conditions have had a substantial beneficial impact on the field of study as a whole. We see no reason why the same would not be true with respect to developmental contextualism.

If we would have any criticism of developmental contextualists, it is not in what they are doing or not doing but in the manner in which they represent what they are doing or not doing. On one hand, by representing themselves as embodying an approach that is fundamentally different from so-called mechanistic psychology, developmental contextualists risk erecting an artificial divide between themselves and others. One consequence of this might be that they would pay less attention to academic psychology (and vice versa) than is optimal for either approach. On the other hand, by identifying themselves with contextualism, developmental contextualists may give the false impression that they hold in common ideas and principles similar to those characteristic of functional and philosophic contextualism. In doing so, they engage in the dangerous game of giving rise to the misguided perception that they hold ideas, which they do not in fact hold—ideas that are inimical to their position.

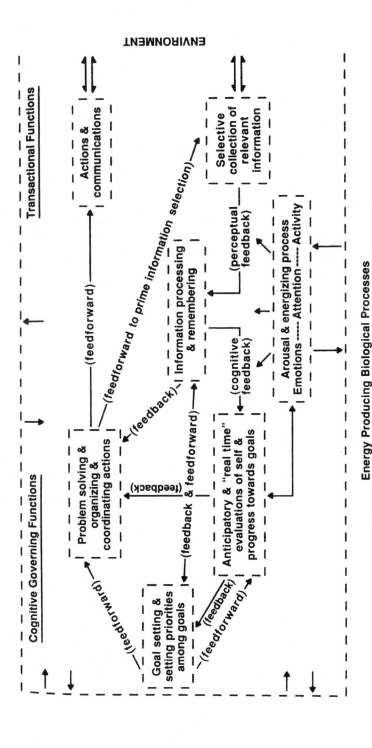

Figure 6.1. A Simplified Prototypical Representation of a Person as a Self-Constructing Living System.
SOURCE: Ford & Lerner (1992), p. 169.

103

SUMMARY AND CONCLUSIONS

In this chapter, we indicated that there are two forms of modified contextualism, one of which is developmental contextualism. Two key ideas underlie developmental contextualism: multilevel determination and the reciprocal relationship between several levels of organization in human life. Some less central characteristics of developmental contextualism are the postulation of an active organism, mutual causality, and nonreductionism. We suggested that although developmental contextualism has some unique features, it does not differ from mainstream psychology in any fundamental sense. To the extent that there is a difference, the developmental contextualists would examine phenomena under a broader range of conditions than is characteristic of mainstream psychology.

Functional Contextualism and Academic Psychology

A Comparison and Evaluation

*M*odified contextualism has emerged recently within the behavior-analytic, operant conditioning tradition associated with B. F. Skinner. Hayne Reese has again been a leader in this movement, along with Steven and Linda Hayes (Hayes et al., 1988). Hayes (1993) has described this variant of contextualism as functional contextualism.

The move to characterize behavior analysis as following a contextual worldview is intriguing for several reasons. For one, Skinner himself did not seem to regard his views as contextualistic. For another, most philosophic contextualists regard behavior analysis as the epitome of a mechanistic approach, and most developmental contextualists also characterize behavior analysis in that manner. For example, Reese and Overton (1970), in their early treatment of metatheories, said, with respect to behavior-analytic approaches to development, "The paradigm of the behaviorists is, of course, mechanistic" (p. 122), and more recently, Ford and Lerner (1992) stated, "Mechanism is illustrated by behavior analytic theory" (p. 4). In addition, there is considerable debate within the behavior-analytic community as to whether contextualism or mechanism is the worldview that most closely characterizes behavior analysis (Marr, 1993; Shull & Lawrence, 1993). For example, Marr (1993) states of behavior analysis that "the overall approach has, and continues to fit into, an already established mechanistic framework with a long evolutionary history" (p. 64). Moreover, it could be argued that functional contextualism is in effect an attempt to stem what appears to be the advance of behavior analysis into mainstream psychology. As Smith (1994) has noted, few operant psychologists today appear to be radical behaviorists in the sense described by Skinner (1950), and the push for contextualism in behavior analysis seems to reflect a desire to return to a radical empiricist ontology.

Finally, most psychologists would perceive contextualists such as Bruner and Gergen as holding views that are distinctly opposed to those of Skinner and his followers, a perception that is understandable but inaccurate in many respects. For example, Skinner (1950), in his often-cited paper "Are Theories of Learning Necessary?" rejects interpretations of behavior that appeal to processes at other than a behavioral level. Similarly, Gergen (1985, 1988) has suggested that in considering action, we should not explain it in terms of some underlying process at some other ontological level. The reason for this similarity in viewpoints between Skinner and Gergen, as is perhaps clear, is the common acceptance of radical empiricism. The radical empiricism of both Skinner and Gergen is evident from the following quotes, which suggest that behavior is primary and that any interpretation of behavior at some other ontological level is impermissible. Johnston and Pennypacker (1980), followers of Skinner, say of the Skinnerian approach,

> The behavioral scientist is concerned with what an organism can actually be observed doing, not with the existence of hypothetical agencies inside the organism that might be thought to cause or give purpose to what the organism is doing. (p. 15)

Similarly, Gergen (1988) says,

> Let us confront each other's actions directly. Let us consider the possibility that human actions are what they are and not an array of cryptic indicators of yet some other ontological realm. (p. 45)

As with the developmental contextualists, those who advocate a contextualistic approach to behavior analysis recognize that contextualism in its philosophic form does not provide a good basis for scientific research. For example, Hayes (1993) suggests that it is difficult to build a progressive science on what we have called philosophic contextualism. This difficulty arises, according to Hayes, because the goal of philosophic contextualism is to construct a holistic, personal account of experience for which no interpretation is ultimate or final. Because the goals of behavior analysis are prediction and control of behavior, clearly philosophic contextualism will not suffice.

Although Hayes acknowledges that some aspects of behavior analysis are more representative of mechanism than of contextualism, he argues that "the core of behavior analytic thinking (and all that is extraordinary or novel about it) is contextualistic" (Hayes & Hayes, 1989, p. 40). The most basic reason for this assertion is Hayes's (1986) opinion that "radical behaviorism is a most thoroughgoing form of 'contextualism'; it takes the 'act in context' as its root metaphor" (p. 40).

Hayes (1993) characterizes functional contextualism as follows:

> A functional contextualist in the world of psychology, approaches the study of a whole organism interacting in and with a historical and situational context much as an engineer and as a physicist interested in engineering. . . . Functional contextualists have an interest in both applied psychology on the one hand, and theory of behavior change on the other. An analysis is constructed that points to features of the historical strands and current context of a psychological action that can effectively guide the behavior of the scientist/ engineer. The functional contextualist readily admits that he or she cannot escape the effects of personal history and that no interpretation is ultimate or final, but knowledge can be shared and practical when principles emerge that effectively guide the actions of other analysts. Because the best way to test the general utility of principles that involve behavior change is controlled experimentation, this method is often embraced. While generally applicable rules of action are sought, the functional contextualist accepts the possibility of randomness. Thus, the preference for comprehensive principles is not an ontological statement but an intensely practical one. (p. 24)

Hayes and Hayes (1989) make the last point more directly, stating that "behavior analysis assumes that events are stable and open to direct investigation only because it works to do so with regard to behavior analytic goals, namely, prediction and control" (p. 37).

Following a contextualistic approach of the type outlined by Hayes (1993), psychological science would focus on functional relationships between variables—specifically on contingencies of reinforcement, with particular emphasis on the relationships as they occur in applied settings. Hayes (1988) states, "Psychology is most directly concerned with units of analysis that are observable at the level of the whole organism interacting with a context. Their strength occurs and is assessed within an individual across time" (p. 14). Biglan and Hayes (1996) suggest that psychologists might contribute more to the prevention and treatment of important behavioral problems by adopting functional contextualism, which seeks "the development of an organized system of empirically based concepts and rules that allow behavioral phenomena to be predicted and influenced [i.e., controlled] with precision" (p. 50). They note that the goal of prediction and control of behavior "would lead to less emphasis on studies of correlations among organismic events or constructs, and indeed on correlational research in general" (pp. 50-51) and more emphasis on experimentation. The strategy, according to Biglan and Hayes, would be to build generalizations from analyses of unique cases.

Morris (1991) proposes extending functional contextualism to the study of cognition, with the general idea being that "cognition is action in context—not a mechanistic process that resides in a separate realm" (p. 125). According to him,

> At an empirical level, exactly what a contextualistic research programme might entail cannot at this time be said, but "theory"-building would probably be simple and more cumulative; increased attention would be given to contingencies and context, and the activity of the person "cognizing" (e.g., remembering, problem-solving) would become more explicit. (p. 125)

Morris (1991) seems to have said, in a rather complicated way, that in studying cognition, he wishes to study behavior and only behavior.

CHARACTERISTICS OF FUNCTIONAL CONTEXTUALISM

Hayes et al. (1988) and Morris (1988, 1991, 1993a, 1993b) have described a number of features of the behavior-analytic approach that render it a contextualistic system—in particular, functional contextualism. Some of the features of functional contextualism overlap with those already mentioned under developmental contextualism. These are viewing the organism as active rather than passive and postulating mutual causality and nonreductionism. It will be remembered that our view is that these three characteristics also can be found in mainstream psychology. Thus, as was the case with developmental contextualism, these three characteristics do not differentiate functional contextualism from mainstream psychology.

Some other characteristics of functional contextualism that supposedly differentiate it from mainstream psychology have been described by Hayes et al. (1988) and by Morris (1991, 1993a, 1993b). We describe and evaluate those characteristics next.

The Concept of the Operant

According to Hayes et al. (1988), contained in contextualism is a view of behavior that is compatible with the concept of the operant, as it has been developed in behavior analysis. Therefore, the operant has several major characteristics that Hayes et al. see as particularly compatible with contextualism.

Operant Is a Functional Category

Among the most important of these is the idea that responses share members in an operant class to the extent that they produce common effects on the environment. For example, each of the following behaviors would be classified as a similar form of an operant. The rat might depress a bar with either its left paw, its right paw, its nose, or its backside. All of these constitute the same operant because they have the same effect on the environment, that is, depressing the bar.

It is perfectly absurd and beyond understanding to suggest, as Hayes et al. (1988) have, that functional contextualism is unique in its assertion that responses share membership in an operant class to the extent that they produce common effects on the environment. Although some psychologists may identify the animal as learning particular and specific behaviors, the idea that responses share membership in an operant class to the extent that they produce common effects on the environment has long been recognized by many psychologists. Indeed, it was examined experimentally by Muenzinger (1928) prior to the time it was emphasized by behavior analysts. The well-known Muenzinger study was prominently mentioned by Tolman

(1932), a cognitive behaviorist, to illustrate the "multiple trackness" of behavior. In that study, guinea pigs given more than 1,000 acquisition trials used a variety of responses over the course of the experiment. Thus, the animal might use its left paw for a number of trials and then switch over to using its right paw, and then switch again to using its left paw.

Tolman (1932) cites another study by Muenzinger, Koerner, and Irey (1929) in which the experimenters limited the animals to the use of the right paw. However, even here, the animals showed considerable response variability. In Muenzinger et al.'s words,

> The right paw might be used with a firm and deliberate pressing down of the lever, or a bare touch on the lever, or a quick tap, or a succession of quick taps, or brushing or sliding over the lever, or circular movement partly around the lever, or a gentle placing of the paw on the lever with pressure after some time, or a crossing of the right paw over the left. (p. 427)

All of these behaviors were regarded by Tolman (1932) and Muenzinger et al. (1929) as equivalent, despite their physical differences.

Tolman's (1932) approach of emphasizing response equivalence continues to be influential on the contemporary scene. For example, Mackintosh (1974) specifies several theories of instrumental learning that "may be regarded as modern versions of the theory of learning advanced by Tolman (1932)" (p. 199). Mackintosh continues, "One of the most direct sources of support for such a theory is that provided by evidence of response equivalence" (p. 199). Mackintosh then goes on to cite many additional experimental examples of the sort of findings originally reported by Muenzinger et al. (1929).

The view that behavior can be characterized in terms of acts rather than specific movements has been so widely accepted that we find the contrary opinion expressed by Hayes et al. (1988) and Morris (1991) to be utterly without foundation. For example, Spence (1956), a leading stimulus-response (S-R) psychologist, said, "Certainly all of the responses involved in instrumental conditioning and selective learning situations would be classified as acts rather than movements, and contrary to common belief, even the responses employed in classical conditioning appear to fall in this category" (pp. 42-43). Moreover, Adams (1984), an expert in the area of motor learning, has suggested that although concern with the act is legitimate, so is concern with movement sequences. He has gone so far as to state that preoccupation with the act in both human and animal learning has had deleterious consequences for the understanding of movement sequences (see especially pages 3 and 4 of his article).

Verblike Quality of Behavior

Another characteristic of the operant to be found in contextualism is the emphasis on the verblike quality of behavior, that is, behavior as running, driving, and so on. This emphasis can be found in the quote attributed earlier to Morris (1991)—that in studying cognition, one studies "cognizing," and in studying memory, one studies "remembering," that is, behaviors.

The idea that among academic psychologists only functional contextualists are concerned with the verblike quality of behavior (Pepper, 1942, earlier suggested that philosophic contextualists were concerned with verbs) is easily refuted. For example, Tolman (1932) said,

> A rat running a maze; a cat getting out of a puzzle box; a man driving home to dinner; a child hiding from a stranger; a woman doing her washing or gossiping over the telephone; a pupil marking a mental-test sheet; a psychologist reciting a list of nonsense syllables; my friend and I telling one another our thoughts and feelings—*these are all behaviors.* (p. 8)

As may be seen, even for a cognitive behaviorist presumably on the opposite pole from behavior analysts in a variety of important respects, the operant need not be restricted to any particular class of behavior, and each of the behaviors described by Tolman (1932) emphasizes verblike interactions, no less than those described by Morris (1991) earlier. Would it be possible for any variety of behaviorism to ignore the verblike quality of behavioral interactions?

Contextualism and the Act

Hayes et al. (1988) assert that in contextualism, the context must be included in the analysis of the act, and this approach is unique to functional contextualism. In our view, this position is clearly fallacious. As one example, the importance of context has been recognized in a book on learning, titled *Context and Learning* (Balsam & Tomie, 1985), of which the following are among a small sample of the opinions expressed by the chapter authors. Balsam (1985) states, "At a logical and procedural level, all learning occurs in context" (p. 1). Similarly, Rescorla, Durlach, and Grau (1985) state, "Modern discussions of Pavlovian conditioning increasingly acknowledge the importance of the context in which learning and performance occur" (p. 23). Also, Medin and Reynolds (1985) state,

> The present chapter describes work where context is afforded a central status and where context effects are manifest as strengths as well as limitations. We aim to show that analyses of context can provide insights into some key problems associated with learning and memory research. (p. 323)

Clearly, the authors of these chapters, in common with other authors in the book, acknowledge the importance of context for understanding learning. An extended discussion of how a variety of modern learning theories deal with context may be found in Hall (1991).

The inclusion of context is hardly limited to learning theories. Context is also presumed to play a crucial role in perception, cognition, and memory. Jenkins (1979), a theorist widely recognized as emphasizing context in his approach to memory, goes so far as to say this of modern memory theory: "*Everyone* now knows that memory phenomena are much more complicated and contextually determined than we used to think they were" (p. 430, emphasis added). The importance attributed to context in memory research is illustrated by the wide variety of studies examining environmental, internal, and semantic context, many of which are reviewed in the book *Memory in Context: Context in Memory* (Davies & Thomson, 1988).

Consider now perception. One of the classic studies in the area is an experiment by Bruner and Minturn (1955), accomplished when Bruner's views were more compatible with academic psychology. In that study, an ambiguous character was read as a letter when presented along with letters and as a number when presented along with numbers. In other words, the perception of the stimulus was influenced by the context in which it was embedded. Another example is the phonemic restoration effect discovered by Warren (1970). He presented subjects with sentences such as the following, in which the asterisk indicates a phoneme replaced by a nonspeech sound:

It was found that the *eel was on the axle.

It was found that the *eel was on the shoe.

It was found that the *eel was on the orange.

It was found that the *eel was on the table.

Even though the disambiguating context occurred after the missing phoneme, subjects reported actually hearing for each of these four sentences *wheel, heel, peel,* and *meal,* respectively. Many other examples from other areas of psychology could be cited.

Although indicating that so-called mechanists deal with context, Hayes (1988) and Morris (1991) suggest that they do so differently from functional contextualists. For example, Hayes states, "For a mechanist, context is relevant, but it does not alter the nature of the act itself" (p. 11). Similarly, Morris suggests that in functional contextualism, unlike in mechanism, "context imbues behaviour with meaning; the meaning of behavior emerges from its context" (p. 136). We think that the view expressed by Hayes and Morris is far too broad. In some instances, contrary to Hayes and Morris, the possibility that context is simply another variable influencing behavior, albeit an important one, is justified. Baddeley (1982) has used the term *independent context* to refer to such instances. However, in other instances, context has more fundamental effects, but this is generally realized and accepted by all researchers. In these instances, which Baddeley has called *interactive context,* the meaning of behavior is determined by the context in which it occurs. For example, "fire" uttered in a theater has an entirely different meaning than "fire" uttered on the rifle range. Moreover, the phonemic restoration effect described earlier illustrates that context can alter the act of hearing itself. Wickens (1987) has made a similar distinction, referring to context alpha and context beta.

The Role of the Scientist in Scientific Analysis

Hayes et al. (1988) suggest that contextualists "believe that scientists cannot stand apart from the world under analysis; they are, rather, a part of that world" (p. 103). Moreover, contextualists suggest that science is not directed "toward the attainment of ultimate knowledge" (p. 103). These propositions are accepted by behavior analysts, according to Hayes et al.

Depending on what Hayes et al. (1988) mean here, and what that is is not at all clear, these positions put them perilously close to the social constructionists. If they are recommending social constructionism, then the emphasis on prediction and control should be dropped or modified.

The Possibility of Novelty

Novelty, as we have seen, is a fundamental, ineradicable feature of philosophic contextualism (see Pepper, 1942, p. 235). What is the role of novelty in functional contextualism? Hayes et al. (1988) note that "this aspect of contextualism does not have obvious parallels in behavior analysis" (p. 103). As for novelty itself, as we saw in Chapter 4, Hayes et al. (1988) and Reese (1991) have suggested that the possibility of novelty can be ignored within functional contextualism. Leaving aside that it is difficult to understand how this position is compatible with contextualism, it is clearly evident that this is still another position similar to that to be found in so-called mechanism.

Truth Criterion

Both Hayes et al. (1988) and Morris (1988) argue that the truth criterion for contextualism is different from that espoused by mechanism and corresponds to that already employed by behavior analysis. This criterion is that of successful working, which "implies success with regard to the accomplishment of some potentially attainable goal" (Hayes et al., 1988, p. 102). In another article, Hayes (1988) states, "All events and all analyses are evaluated in terms of successful working" (p. 12). Hayes also says, "More than anything else it is this truth criterion that shows the contextualistic qualities of behavior analysis" (p. 11).

It seems to be true that functional contextualists, more than so-called mechanists, value successful working as a criterion of truth. Among academic psychologists, successful working is not considered to be very important, the emphasis being on the correspondence of hypothesis and data. However, as noted in Chapter 3, Pepper (1942) has suggested that hypothesis testing is not only an appropriate truth criterion for contextualism but also a better one than successful working (see p. 272 of Pepper's book).

COMPARISON OF FUNCTIONAL CONTEXTUALISM
TO ACADEMIC PSYCHOLOGY

If there were any doubt that functional contextualism is in agreement with so-called mechanism in accepting prediction and control as its goals and experimentation as its primary methodology, one could consult views expressed by Guba (1990), a constructivist and avowed relativist. He has said that the basic beliefs of positivism—which, as Guba uses the term, is closely identified with mechanism—include the following: "The ultimate aim of science is to predict and control natural phenomena" (p. 19). He goes on to say of positivism that "the most appropriate methodology is thus *empirical experimentalism,* or as close an approximation thereto as can be managed" (p. 19). Of course, prediction and control as goals and experimentation as the favored method are characteristic of functional contextualism. These goals and methods are precisely those recommended by so-called mechanism, as Guba has correctly recognized.

Extrapolation From Principles

A prime tendency of functional contextualism is to extrapolate from principles, isolated under highly restricted experimental conditions employing nonhuman subjects to human subjects, a characteristic it shares with mechanism. This is done in two principal ways. On one hand, there is application of these principles to human beings under particular conditions. A prime example would be to employ various principles of reinforcement in the attempt to modify human behavior, an approach that goes under the name of behavior modification (see, e.g., Kazdin, 1994). The various behavior modification techniques are too well-known to require elaboration here. A lesser-known but more ambitious application of behavioral principles to humans is found in the construction of entire society along these lines. Examples here are societies based on Skinner's (1948) novel, *Walden Two,* which, as the jacket of the book suggests, "provocatively pictures a society in which human problems are solved by a scientific technology of human conduct—and in which many of our contemporary values are obsolete." Societies modeled along the lines of Walden Two, such as Comunidad Los Horcones (1990) in Mexico, are considered to be scientifically shaped utopias (Newman, 1993). The belief that we are in a position to establish such utopias on the basis of known scientific principles is not widely shared outside of functional contextualist circles.

Interpretive Schemes

A second prominent feature in functional contextualism but generally eschewed by mainstream psychologists is the use of interpretive schemes. The idea here is to take some important aspect of human behavior—such as communication between humans, called verbal behavior—and to supply some plausible interpretation of it in terms of behavioristic principles (e.g., reinforcement contingencies). Two of Skinner's most controversial books, *Beyond Freedom and Dignity* (1971) and *Verbal Behavior* (1957), were interpretations of this nature. Skinner (1973) is explicit on this point, stating, "*Beyond Freedom and Dignity* does not use a scientific analysis of behavior for prediction and control. The science lies behind the book rather than in it. It is used merely for purposes of interpretation" (p. 260). Likewise,

> My *Verbal Behavior* was an exercise in interpretation. In it, I pointed to similarities between the contingencies of reinforcement that have been analyzed with much greater precision in the laboratory. The account is, I believe, more plausible than those proposed, without benefit of laboratory experience. (p. 261)

Elsewhere, Skinner (1988) characterized *Verbal Behavior* as "an interpretation, not an explanation, and is merely useful, not true or false" (p. 364).

In short, many if not all accounts of human action emanating from the Skinnerian camp are plausible interpretations, the variety of explanation that Bruner (1990) and other philosophic contextualists favor over prediction and control. A major feature that distinguishes this form of interpretation from that which might be employed in philosophic contextualism is that, whereas philosophic contextualists might consider a variety of different interpretations plausible, within the functional contextualist framework, interpretation is constrained by a single set of principles. That is, there are not multiple frameworks for interpretation but a single framework.

As we have seen, functional contextualists are similar to so-called mechanists in accepting experimentation as a primary method, seeing prediction and control as the object of their efforts, and attempting to establish lawful relationships. They differ from academic psychologists in eschewing theory and placing a much heavier emphasis on applied psychology and interpretive schemes. For example, Hayes (1993), a leading functional contextualist, suggests that psychology should be modeled on engineering. According to Hayes, "Engineers have little use for knowledge in the abstract" (p. 24). How better could the concern of the functional contextualists with application and their disdain for abstraction be expressed? Ironically, many who are not particularly friendly to operant psychology criticize it for being concerned with application and engineering rather than science, a charge often denied within the operant community.

Radical Empiricism

The central characteristic that distinguishes functional contextualism from mechanism is its emphasis on radical empiricism. Radical empiricism is not a characteristic of academic psychology, nor is it a generally accepted point of view in any of the so-called hard sciences such as physics and chemistry. On this basis, functional contextualism seems to be contextualistic only in its radical empiricism. Whereas academic psychology embraces theory, functional contextualists eschew theory in the sense meant by Skinner (1950). According to Skinner, behavior should be described only in terms of behavior and not in terms of events taking place elsewhere in some other system (e.g., in the nervous system). Although eschewing theory, functional contextualists would attempt to establish functional relationships among variables and seek even more general lawful relationships. Functional contextualists in the Skinnerian tradition do not look favorably on hypothesis-testing research, particularly research that examines differences between two or more groups, preferring instead to examine the behavior of single individuals under various conditions such as different schedules of reinforcement.

We are in agreement in this regard with Blackman (1993), who states,

> For exponents of functional analysis, a description of a functionally important set of environmental principles would provide the explanation of the behavioral effects of drugs, without the need for assuming "underlying" processes or responses. Thus, behavioral effects of drugs emerge from a functional analysis not as appendages to some other (underlying) events but instead as phenomena of scientific interest in their own right, explicable, at least in part, contextually, in terms of environmental principles acting upon behaving organisms. It is in this sense that one can detect a growing emphasis on contextualistic explanations in behavioral pharmacology. (p. 238)

Blackman (1993) elaborates on this point further, stating,

> Behavior analysis is unusual in experimental science in that it emphasizes the explanatory power of demonstrated functional relationships between dependent and independent variables. To that extent, behavior analysis can be fairly described as contextualistic, and thereby claim welcome but often-neglected points of contact with other intellectual traditions, such as social constructionism and symbolic interactionism. (p. 238)

In other words, the radical empiricism of behavior analysis links it to the traditions associated with philosophic contextualism. What functional contextualism has done, essentially, is to marry an essential feature of contextualism with a plethora of features of so-called mechanism.

Do Contextualism and Mechanism Marry Well?

Pepper (1942) long ago warned of the tendency of contextualists to effect such a marriage and the danger and futility of doing so. Pepper noted,

> There is also a very strong tendency for mechanism and contextualism to combine. Many pragmatists and some mechanists exhibit this combination in various proportions. The two theories are in many ways complementary. Mechanism gives a basis and a substance to contextualistic analyses, and contextualism gives a life and reality to mechanistic syntheses. Each is threatened with inadequacy just where the other seems to be strong. *Yet, mixed, the two sets of categories do not work happily, and the damage they do to each other's interpretations does not seem to me in any way to compensate for the added richness.* (p. 147, emphasis added)

Pepper goes on to say,

> Contextualism is constantly threatened with evidences for permanent structures in nature. It is constantly on the verge of falling back upon underlying mechanistic structures, or of resolving into the overarching implicit integrations of organicism. Its recourse in these emergencies is always to hurry back to the given event, and to emphasize the change and novelty that is immediately felt there, so

that sometimes it seems to be headed for an utter skepticism. But it avoids this impasse by vigorously asserting the reality of the structure of the given event, the historic event as it actually goes on. (pp. 234-235)

In other words, what Pepper is saying is that when contextualists stray too far off the contextualistic path by adopting mechanistic structures, they become incoherent and can only rectify their incoherence by once again becoming philosophic contextualists. We agree completely with Pepper on this point: One who adopts some variety of contextualism that is not philosophic contextualism is taking an incoherent position.

SUMMARY AND CONCLUSIONS

In Chapter 7, we have indicated that functional contextualism, unlike philosophic contextualism but like developmental contextualism, sees itself as applicable to a type of science that is superior to that practiced in mainstream psychology. Functional contextualism is similar to mainstream psychology in that both emphasize prediction and control. We examined a number of characteristics of functional contextualism that, according to its proponents, differentiate it from mainstream psychology (e.g., the operant is a functional category). In most cases, we found that these characteristics were shared by mainstream psychology. Although functional contextualists embrace prediction and control, they reject theory as it is normally construed.

Functional contextualists, of which some of Skinner's followers are prime examples, favor extrapolating relationships gathered under highly controlled conditions to real-life situations; a prime example here is the application of behavioral principles to a real society, as illustrated by Skinner's (1948) novel, *Walden Two*. Functional contextualists also favor interpretive schemes, which may be characterized as the attempt to apply plausible interpretations of real-world behaviors in terms of behavioral principles such as reinforcement contingencies. The major difference between functional contextualists and mainstream psychologists, as we see it, is that functional contextualists embrace radical empiricism whereas mainstream psychologists do not.

Are Mainstream Psychology and the Various Contextualisms in Competition, and Should They Be?

*W*e begin this chapter by describing in quite explicit terms what our position or bias, if you will, is relative to competition between points of view. It is our belief that in science and intellectual matters in general, one seldom if ever accepts a point of view in the absence of examining its competitors along relevant dimensions. This generalization applies to specific theories scientists may propose, as well as to metatheories. One examines a view, makes judgments about it, evaluates its strengths and weaknesses, and comes to some conclusion but not before going through the same steps with various other relevant points of view. An implication of our position is that in selecting a theory, metatheory, or any other intellectual product, one does not do so on an absolute basis but on a relative basis. We select or settle for the best available among the alternatives.

There should be nothing surprising in the selection criterion described above with reference to intellectual products. We go through similar processes, or at least should go through such processes, in making other kinds of decisions in real life. For example, we seek to buy the best automobile that is available within our resources. Should less be expected when "buying" intellectual products than when buying consumer products? We think not, and our assumption here will be evident throughout this chapter.

The three forms of contextualism that we have identified—developmental, functional, and philosophic—stand in quite different relations to mainstream psychology. Thus, they compete or do not compete with it in different ways. Accordingly, we shall consider separately the competitive relation between each of these types of contextualism and mainstream psychology. Identifying the type of competition is important because it will determine the extent of the consideration one view will accord the other.

DEVELOPMENTAL CONTEXTUALISM

The sense in which developmental contextualists are in competition with mainstream psychology is no different from the sense in which any specific point of view within mainstream psychology is in competition with some other point of view. Some specific theory within developmental contextualism may be in competition with some theory emanating from another point of view within mainstream psychology, and the two would be evaluated according to the same criteria as applied to any other two theories within mainstream psychology. Thus, we see nothing unique about the competitive position of developmental contextualism vis-à-vis mainstream psychology.

The reasons for this conclusion have been previously mentioned and will only be considered in passing here. In our view, developmental contextualism is not really a variety of the worldview contextualism, despite its name; it shares many fundamental features with mainstream psychology. Developmental contextualists value experimentation and lawfulness, seek meaningful theories, and by no means embrace radical empiricism. If there is a difference between developmental contextualism and mainstream psychology, it consists simply of this: Developmental contextualists, if anything, place a heavier emphasis on multilevel determination and practical application than do many mainstream psychologists.

FUNCTIONAL CONTEXTUALISM

In what sense are functional contextualists in competition with mainstream psychology? One answer to this has been given by Hayes et al. (1988):

> Behavior analysis has always had significant conflicts with other psychological perspectives. At their most fundamental level, these conflicts are often philosophical, concerning such issues as the nature of the human and the purposes of science. What are *these* conflicts? What if anything can we do about them? Can we resolve them? (p. 97)

Hayes et al. go on to say that functional contextualism should avoid conflict and interaction with mainstream psychology or mechanism because the two views are fundamentally incompatible and have little to offer each other.

Contrary to the opinion of Hayes et al. (1988) and other functional contextualists, it is our opinion that they are, like developmental contextualists, in competition with mainstream psychologists in a variety of respects. Consider some major respects in which functional contextualism and mainstream psychology are in competition, as indicated by Catania (1984), a behavior analyst, in a textbook on learning. In comparing behavior analysis and cognitive psychology, Catania notes,

> Although these two psychological orientations differ in their languages and in the research problems that they emphasize, they have in common the reliance on experimental method, the anchoring of concepts to experimental manipulations and observations, and the assumption that our subject matter, however complex, is orderly and not capricious. (p. 9)

Each of these beliefs, as we have seen, is accepted by functional contextualists (e.g., Hayes et al., 1988; Morris, 1993b). In agreement with Catania (1984), we would emphasize that insofar as functional contextualism adopts prediction and control as its aims and seeks to establish these aims by the use of experimental method, often but not always on animal subjects alone, it is necessarily and inescapably in competition with mainstream psychology. In fact, Hayes (1993) admits as much when he suggests that all approaches having the same goal should be evaluated in terms of how well each reaches that goal, a position that seems in contradiction with that adopted in Hayes et al. (1988). According to Hayes (1993),

> It is not enough to show that your activities move in the direction of a goal. If one truly values the goal, then one values efficiency in reaching it. Thus, we must be concerned with the *relative* performance of various courses of action. (p. 21)

Relative performance of competing views must be taken into account not only because functional contextualists share important goals with mainstream psychologists—that is, prediction and control of behavior—but also because workers within the behavior-analytic framework are concerned with phenomena that come under scrutiny within mainstream psychology. An obvious example here is so-called conditioned or secondary reinforcement. If mainstream psychology advances our understanding of secondary reinforcement to a greater extent than does behavior analysis, then on that basis, mainstream psychology would be the superior approach. Of course, the opposite would apply if behavior analysis did a better job of explaining secondary reinforcement than did mainstream psychology.

The example cited in connection with secondary reinforcement could be multiplied many times over. For example, all theories of learning, including contextualistic ones, attempt to explain how reinforcements such as food and water affect behavior. The behavior-analytic approach to reinforcement is in terms of functional relationships; that is, behavior followed by reinforcement becomes more probable. One of the newest and most successful mainstream theories of how reinforcement operates is in terms of relative deprivation (Allison, 1989). That is, to make something reinforcing, the organism must receive less of it than it normally requires. Let us say that when we compare the functional position with the relative deprivation hypothesis, one leads to a variety of confirmed predictions that are inexplicable in terms of the other. It is beyond comprehension that someone would suggest that these two views, which share the goals of prediction and control of behavior, cannot be reasonably evaluated with respect to each other and the experimental findings. It is impossible, it seems to us, to say that two approaches are not in competition when both employ prediction and control of behavior as their aim, attempt to achieve that aim through experimentation, and, moreover, in many instances investigate the same phenomena.

To be sure, there are methodological differences between behavior analysis and mainstream psychology. Behavior analysts tend to prefer single-subject designs, a procedure mainstream psychologists use less but will employ under a particular set of favorable conditions, for example, in an attempt to make someone an expert at a particular task (e.g., Chase & Ericsson, 1981) and in psychophysical investigations (e.g., Koenderink, Kappers, Pollick, & Kawato, 1997). Also, mainstream psychologists tend to emphasize statistical analysis to a greater extent than do behavior analysts. But behavior analysts do not completely eschew statistics. Although these and other methodological differences between behavior analysis and mainstream psychology are real, we suggest that in the larger scheme of things, the differences are not particularly large or important.

Another area in which functional contextualism and mainstream psychology are necessarily in competition is in matters of practical application. A rather well-known example of this is available from the recent past. The dispute between Skinner (1957), who advanced a behavioristic analysis of verbal behavior, and Chomsky (1959), a linguist whose views were essential to the founding of psycholinguistics, is well known. For example, Slobin (1971), a psycholinguist, after reviewing many of the arguments between Skinner's approach to verbal behavior and that of the psycholinguists, which were clearly in competition, said the following:

> Much more remains to be said about the important debate between learning theory [by which Slobin means behavior analysis] and cognitive psychology on the role of innate and acquired factors in language development. A forthcoming book [by Slobin] presents a range of theoretical arguments on all sides. (p. 61)

Another example of how functional contextualism necessarily comes into conflict with mainstream psychology when it ventures into practical areas is available from clinical psychology. An article by Hayes and Hayes (1992) described how contextualistic behavior analysis might be applied to clinical problems and their associated cognitive processes. Alford (1993), in an examination of the article by Hayes and Hayes, chided them for not comparing their approach with noncontextualistic approaches. Alford said, "Since cognitive therapy has been shown to successfully address cognitive processes . . . it would have been informative to compare the approach advanced by Hayes and Hayes (1992) with the theoretical perspective of Beck and associates" (p. 201).

Another area in which functional contextualism and mainstream psychology are in competition is theory. A few words must be said concerning what behavior analysis considers to be theory. Skinner (1950) rejected explaining behavior in terms of three kinds of learning theories, which he called physiological, mental, and conceptual. Skinner did, however, embrace one kind of theory when he said the following:

> This does not exclude the possibility of theory in another sense. Beyond the collection of uniform relationships lies the need for a formal representation of the data reduced to a minimal number of terms. A theoretical construction may yield greater generality than any assemblage of facts. But such a construction will not refer to another dimensional system and will not, therefore, fall within our present definition. It will not stand in the way of our search for functional relations because it will arise only after relevant variables have been found and studied. Though it may be difficult to understand, it will not be easily misunderstood, and it will have none of the objectionable effects of the theories here considered. (pp. 215-216)

A theory of the sort that Skinner is talking about here, one that would be embraced by the functional contextualists as well, must necessarily find itself in conflict with the physiological, mental, or conceptual theories advanced by mainstream psychologists for two reasons already mentioned. First, the sort of theory favored by Skinner and the functional contextualists has as its aim prediction and control and therefore must necessarily compete with mainstream theories having the same aim. Second, those mainstream theories and the theories that Skinner and his allies among the functional contextualists favor deal with the same phenomena. Although a great deal of hullabaloo has been attached to the rejection of mental events by behavior analysts, we think that much, if not most, of this hullabaloo is undeserved or, if you will, makes a mountain out of a molehill. If behavior analysts want to write theories eschewing mental events, the proper approach would seem to require of them less talk and more theory building than currently seems to be the case. In the final analysis, any theory that a behavior analyst proffers will not stand or fall on whether it includes mental events. But it will stand or fall on whether it is better at prediction and control than other available theories.

What is the upshot of our analysis? It is simply this. For all the differences that functional contextualists profess to see between themselves and mainstream psychologists, at the end of the day they are not in principle different from their mainstream colleagues in terms of methodological approach or in how practical solutions to problems and theoretical statements must be evaluated. Like it or not—and we shall see that the functional contextualists do not like it—they are tied necessarily to competition with mainstream psychology. It is true that they do not welcome such competition or even agree that it exists, but it is clear to us that it exists in considerable measure along a variety of dimensions. In fact, as we see it, the differences that functional contextualists see between themselves and mainstream psychology are highly exaggerated and overblown (see Capaldi & Proctor, 1994). Ontological aspects of functional contextualism are considered later in connection with philosophic contextualism because both accept radical empiricism.

PHILOSOPHIC CONTEXTUALISM

Ontologically, the philosophic contextualists, as well as the functional contextualists, are in competition with mainstream psychology. Philosophic contextualists are also in competition with mainstream psychology epistemologically. Because philosophic contextualists accept neither the ontology nor the epistemology of mainstream psychology, the two approaches necessarily fail to make contact at the level of either theory or phenomena. After all, if one believes that facts are created rather than discovered or that what passes for factual information is better derived from literature than from the laboratory, then one has neither much to offer mainstream psychology nor much to gain from it. Under these conditions, the two approaches will take as little note of each other as the proverbial two ships that pass in the night. Mainstream psychologists value data, particularly data gathered under experimental conditions. Philosophic contextualists and their close allies, such as the social constructionists, have little use for experimental data. Inevitably, then, the two approaches have little to say to each other.

Philosophic contextualists often complain that they fail to get a fair hearing from mainstream psychology. Mainstream psychologists could make the same claim, inasmuch as philosophic contextualists reject their work out of hand. For example, Gergen and Harré reject mainstream social psychology, and as Harré (1993) has complained, mainstream social psychologists return the favor. Unless matters change considerably, which unfortunately does not seem likely, this situation promises to continue indefinitely into the future. It is the case that philosophic contextualists, having little use for experimental data, reject the theories that mainstream psychologists erect to explain those data. On the other hand, mainstream psychologists are not too much impressed by uncontrolled data (e.g., data that arise either from literature or from agreement among interested parties) and so ignore any theoretical interpretations erected on such data.

The unfortunate aspect of the great divide that separates philosophic contextualism and mainstream psychology is that they may continue to have in the future as little effect on each other as they have in the past. It is our opinion, mentioned earlier, that one theoretical position will have an effect on another only insofar as the two are in competition. If they are not in competition, each will ignore the other. Our prognosis for the future is that, as in the past, philosophic contextualism and its close allies will have little impact on mainstream psychology, and this will be reciprocated by mainstream psychology. This is a bleak prognosis, and we arrive at it reluctantly. The two camps simply talk past each other, inasmuch as philosophic contextualists criticize mainstream psychology at ontological and epistemological levels, employing a language that mainstream psychologists do not wish to understand. The language of mainstream psychology is that of data, particularly experimental data, a language that philosophic contextualists in turn do not wish to understand.

As concerns ontology, the state of affairs that characterizes the relationship between philosophic contextualism and mainstream psychology also holds for functional contextualism. When functional contextualists or radical behaviorists criticize mainstream psychology, they usually do not do so in terms of specific theories or experimental outcomes. Instead, their criticisms center on ontological matters (e.g., Lee, 1988). These sorts of criticisms, like those of the philosophic contextualists, will have little impact on mainstream psychology because they are not based on specific interpretations of experimental data. It is interesting to note that the functional contextualists, like philosophic contextualists, feel they are ignored by mainstream psychology (e.g., Lee, 1988), as indeed in many respects they are.

SEPARATISM AND
ITS CONSEQUENCES

As indicated, many contextualists, in common with a variety of other individuals, have strongly recommended either directly or indirectly that the development of one's point of view should occur in isolation, without attempting to influence or be influenced by other perspectives. We shall call this position *separatism*. Separatism does not seem to be a feature of developmental contextualism, nor has it been advocated by developmental contextualists, so we will not consider them further.

Philosophic contextualists and social constructionists embrace separatism enthusiastically. For example, Sarbin (1993) has suggested that contextualists and traditional scientists see the world so differently that each has little to offer the other. Bruner, Gergen, and Shotter, as we have seen, have rejected traditional psychology in no uncompromising terms and see little or no value in it. In several volumes edited by Harré and colleagues (Harré & Stearns, 1995; Smith et al., 1995a, 1995b), he and some if not most of the contributors to those volumes have similarly rejected major aspects of traditional psychology: its philosophic underpinning, its methods, and its specific theories. Among this group, the tendency is not to make an overt case for separatism but rather to suggest its desirability indirectly by essentially dismissing central aspects of mainstream psychology.

An overt case for separatism has been made by the functional contextualists (e.g., Hayes et al., 1988; Morris, 1993b). The strongest, clearest, most vociferous statement of separatism by functional contextualists is that of Hayes et al. (1988), who claim to be expressing Pepper's (1942) belief, with which they agree. According to them, different worldviews "cannot compete directly" (p. 98). Moreover, as regards conflicts between worldviews, Hayes et al. state, "According to Pepper, world views are orthogonal to each other and therefore cannot conflict. Apparent conflicts are really pseudoconflicts. . . . These kinds of conflicts are illegitimate and cannot be resolved; they can only be recognized" (p. 105). Worldviews, they maintain, must and should develop in isolation from each other. Must, because effective communication between different worldviews is impossible. And should, because conceptual confusion arises from the mixing of metaphors.

Hayes et al. (1988) state, "Using the categories of one world view to analyze and criticize another is illegitimate and inherently useless" (p. 98). In another place, Hayes (1988) says, "Pepper claimed that it is illegitimate to criticize one world view in terms of the categorical concepts of another" (p. 12). That, in Hayes's (1988) opinion, there is little to be gained from either competing with or criticizing mechanistic positions or attending to their criticisms is clear from the following statement: "The only true intellectual allies and adversaries of a given specific position will always be found within a given world view" (p. 13). Hayes and Hayes (1992) state, in connection with mechanistic and contextualistic versions of radical behaviorism, "The two positions are incompatible, and the differences cannot be resolved by way of a compromise" (p. 231). Hayes et al. see value in separatism because they think (a) that effective communication across worldviews is impossible (linguistic relativism), (b) conceptual confusion arises from the mixing of metaphors, and (c) it is impossible to judge adequately one worldview employing the standards or criteria of another worldview (methodological relativism).

There are four problems with separatism, as outlined by the functional contextualists: Contrary to Hayes et al. (1988), separatism is not consistent with Pepper's (1942) analysis of worldviews. Moreover, separatism is not consistent with the way science has developed in the past, whether we are speaking of psychology or physics. Separatism, in the view of many (see, e.g., Popper, 1970), is a species of anti-intellectualism. Finally, separatism in psychology is indefensible if one accepts prediction and control of behavior as the goal of psychological science, as do Hayes et al. and the functional contextualists in general.

Pepper's Position on Separatism

A major weakness of the separatist position espoused by Hayes et al. (1988) is that they have misinterpreted Pepper's (1942) position on the competition between worldviews, although we must admit that Pepper is to some extent ambiguous on this score. Consider the following statements from Pepper:

> It is illegitimate to disparage the factual interpretations of one world hypothesis in terms of the categories of another—if both hypotheses are equally adequate. (p. 98)

> It is the cognitive obligation of a world theory to interpret the danda [a type of corroboration] and categories of other world theories in terms of its own categories. (p. 100)

We need all world hypotheses, so far as they are adequate, for mutual comparison and correction of interpretive bias. (p. 101)

When we say that world theories are mutually exclusive, we do not mean that they stand apart from one another like so many isolated posts. Each theory is well aware of the others, criticizes and interprets them, and entirely includes them within its scope. (p. 104)

Pepper's (1942) entire treatment of this issue seems to suggest that the worldviews are in a constant state of growth and healthy competition. How can our interpretation of Pepper on the relation between worldviews be reconciled with that of Hayes et al. (1988)? In our view, Pepper discouraged criticizing the fundamental assumptions of one worldview in terms of the fundamental assumptions of another worldview, much as one might criticize an ethical system from a scientific viewpoint. Clearly, criticism of this sort is not particularly useful. Pepper did not intend, however, to discourage criticizing what we shall call the products of a particular worldview from some other standpoint. Examples of products include such things as some particular theoretical formulation that is developed from within a worldview (e.g., Hull's [1943] mechanistic S-R theory) or some particular methodology that stems from a worldview (e.g., factor analysis or statistics in general). Our interpretation of Pepper is that such products of worldviews are fair game for competition, conflict, and criticism (see Gillespie, 1992, for a contextualist who agrees with our view on competition between contextualistic and mechanistic systems). In our opinion, then, Pepper encouraged rather than discouraged meaningful dialogue between individuals who ascribe to different worldviews concerning the products of those views.

The History of Science and Separatism

In our opinion, the origin of separatism may not be with Pepper (1942) but with Kuhn (1962). That is, we think it possible that Hayes et al. (1988) came to their separatist interpretation of Pepper at least in part as a result of reading Kuhn, whose separatist ideas have been widely accepted in psychology, as is well known. An earlier statement by Reese, one of the coauthors of the Hayes et al. article, directly implicates Kuhn as a basis for the separatist interpretation, as we contend here. Reese and Overton (1970) state, "According to Kuhn (1962) and Pepper (1942), differences between world views are irreconcilable, and even prevent full communication" (p. 121). Kuhn accepts separatism because different paradigms are incommensurable as a result of linguistic and methodological relativism. Kuhn believed that at any one time in a mature science, there is a single dominant paradigm. A paradigm has its own language, its own methodological standards, and its own set of unique problems. As a result, adherents of different paradigms are unable to understand or communicate with each other. In Kuhn's view, scientific paradigms are so different from each other that it cannot be said that one is superior to another.

Kuhn's (1962) reading of the history of science was challenged by Lakatos (1970) and Laudan (1977, 1984, 1996), who suggested that it is usual at any given time for several different paradigms (research programs, in Lakatos's terminology, and research traditions, in Laudan's terminology) to be in competition. Laudan has gone so far as to suggest that one never accepts a theory or a paradigm in isolation, a view also espoused by Lakatos. Acceptance of a theory or paradigm always involves comparing it as to its logical and empirical adequacy with its various rivals. In a highly provocative article, Gholson and Barker (1985) provide numerous examples from physics and psychology that are consistent with the competing paradigms view of Lakatos and Laudan. We briefly cite some of their major historical evidence here:

Themes of plurality, fruitful exchanges among programs, and the role of demonstrated progress in program replacement are also illustrated by the historical events surrounding the eventual success of Einstein's program. At least five research programs were involved in the Einsteinian revolution. First, of course, was the Newtonian program, which in the late 19th century was challenged by a program championed by Lorentz (Zahar, 1976). Lorentz's program took electromagnetism to be more fundamental than mechanics. A second rival, championed by Ostwald and Mach, attempted to develop a purely phenomenological physics, taking energy as a basic concept and dispensing with theoretical entities like atoms, ions, and molecules (Holt, 1977). These three programs were succeeded by the Einsteinian program involving the relativity theories, and by the quantum physics program that led through the early theories of Bohr, to the theories of Heisenberg, Schrodinger, and Dirac. (p. 758)

Note that Mach (1906/1959), who entertained views similar in some respects to those of current-day functional contextualists, proposed an alternative to the so-called mechanistic programs of Newton and Einstein. As we pointed out previously, the phenomenological approach to physics championed by Mach, which may be considered a precursor of pragmatism and thus of contextualism, was soundly defeated by the ascendancy of Einstein's theory. If the view of Hayes et al. (1988) had been accepted by Mach and other phenomenologists, they would not have competed with Newton and Einstein, as they did, but would have gone their own merry way.

Gholson and Barker (1985), like Laudan (1996), consider that behaviorism was a research program or paradigm with various competing theories. The paramount behavioristic theories, of course, were theories of learning. Gholson and Barker show how these theories developed in competition with each other and, as a result of that competition, were enriched. In addition, they describe how the various behavioristic theories of learning were enriched by and in turn enriched various cognitive approaches to learning (e.g., Harlow's [1950] error factor theory). The point here, as in the physics example, is contra Kuhn (1962) that research programs have not developed in isolation and, as a result of the competition between them, have been made the better for it.

Separatism, Counterproductivity, and Anti-Intellectualism

Regardless of whether our interpretation of Pepper (1942) or that of Hayes et al. (1988) is correct, we would suggest a third reason for rejecting their position that contextualistic systems should develop in isolation from other formulations, such as mechanistic behavior analysis and cognitive psychology: It is a course of action that seems counterproductive. As Abelson (1995) has indicated,

> In any discipline aspiring to excellence in its research methods, the long-run consequences of measures designed to protect against criticism will be the accretion of a body of practices that become habitualized in its methodology. Today's complaint becomes tomorrow's precaution. . . . *Criticism is the mother of methodology.* This is a major feature of my thesis that argument is intrinsic to statistical and conceptual analysis of research outcomes, and is good for the health of science. (p. 198)

Another drawback of not engaging in dialogue with others over specific interpretive and methodological differences is that one invites the charge of being unreasonable, if not anti-intellectual. No scientific approach that is seen as being either unreasonable or anti-intellectual will be able to exercise influence beyond its own boundaries. This surely is not an end to be desired even if, furthermore, more adequate arguments than have been supplied so far should ultimately reveal some portions of psychology to be contextualistic. The prominent philosopher of science, Karl Popper (1970), dubbed the idea that adherents to different paradigms are unable to communicate with each other as the myth of the framework. Popper goes on to say, "The Myth of the Framework is, in our time, the central bulwark of irrationalism" (p. 56).

We recognize that it is always difficult for people of different persuasions to communicate with each other, but we do not see this problem as an insurmountable one. On the problem inherent in such communication, we agree with Popper (1970), who has commented as follows:

> I do admit that at any moment we are prisoners caught in the framework of our theories; our expectations; our past experiences; our language. But we are prisoners in a Pickwickian sense; if we try, we can break out of our framework at any time. Admittedly, we shall find ourselves again in a framework, but it will be a better and roomier one; and we can at any moment break out of it again. The central point is that a critical discussion and a comparison of the various frameworks is always possible. . . . The difficulty of discussion between people brought up in different frameworks is to be admitted. But nothing is more fruitful than such a discussion. (pp. 56-57)

Laudan (1996) is another prominent philosopher of science whose position with respect to separatism is similar to that of Popper (1970). Laudan notes that separatism is a position of recent vintage. The logical positivists accepted separatism because, as they saw it, different theories have different languages and therefore cannot communicate with each other directly. Prior to the logical positivists, all philosophies of science accepted that although different theories had different vocabularies, they did not have different languages. Thus, it was always possible to make clear the ideas of one theory within the context of another theory. The denial of this idea, which originated with the logical positivists, came to be accepted uncritically by various relativists such as Kuhn.

Laudan (1996) states that even if theories are separated by a language gap, communication is still possible because

> the fact (if it is a fact) that scientists who subscribe to radically different theories about the natural world may not understand one another does not preclude the possibility that—if they share certain meta-level goals—they may nonetheless be able to agree on the relative cognitive successes and failures of their respective theories. (p. 12)

Finally, Longino (1998) provides cogent reasons why dialogue and criticism are necessary between individuals of different persuasions. Essentially, she suggests that in the absence of such dialogue, individuals will be unable to see past their own assumptions. She says,

> When, for instance, background assumptions are shared by all members of a community, they acquire an invisibility that renders them unavailable for criticism. They do not become visible until individuals who do not share the community's assumptions can provide alternative explanations of the phenomena without those assumptions, as, for example, Einstein could provide an alternative explanation of the Michelson-Morley interferometer experiment. Until such alternatives are available, community assumptions are transparent to their adherents. In addition, the substantive principles determining the standards of rationality within a research program or tradition are for the most part immune to criticism by means of those standards. (p. 184)

Prediction and Control in Contextualism

Laudan's (1996) point is that individuals from otherwise different perspectives who subscribe to certain metalevel goals are in a position to evaluate each other's theories. This point is applicable to functional contextualists who subscribe to the idea that science is concerned with the prediction and control of behavior (e.g., Biglan, 1995; Biglan & Hayes, 1996; Hayes et al., 1988; Morris, 1993b). As indicated earlier, prediction and control of behavior are the goals of virtually all academic psychologists. Whether a theory is of contextualist or noncontextualist origin is totally irrelevant. What matters is that alternative theories that speak to the same subject and also to the same methodological criteria can be evaluated with respect to those criteria.

SUMMARY AND CONCLUSIONS

In this chapter, we examined whether developmental, functional, and philosophic contextualism are or should be in competition with mainstream psychology. Developmental contextualism was seen as in competition with mainstream psychology in no sense that is unusual. Functional contextualism, on the other hand, seeks to separate itself from mainstream psychology, denies that it is or should be in competition with mainstream psychology, but in actuality is in competition. It was demonstrated that functional contextualism and mainstream psychology often examine the same phenomena—for example, what is the relationship between behavior and reinforcement? This competition necessarily arises because functional contextualism and mainstream psychology are concerned with the prediction and control of behavior. Other respects in which functional contextualism is in competition with mainstream psychology are in terms of the application of psychological principles to real-world phenomena and theory construction.

Philosophic contextualists, it was suggested, are in competition with mainstream psychology at the level of ontology and epistemology. They do not seem to be in competition at the empirical level because philosophic contextualists are so little concerned with developing empirical systems that compete with those of mainstream psychology. It was suggested that functional contextualism and philosophic contextualism should endeavor to compete with mainstream psychology at the empirical level, as well as at the epistemological and ontological levels. In the absence of such competition, it was suggested, functional and philosophic contextualism will not acquire a wider audience because views are accepted or rejected only on the basis of comparing them with other views. Kuhn's (1962) and Pepper's (1942) views on separatism were discussed and critically evaluated.

Underdetermination, Incommensurability, and Relativism

*U*nderdetermination has been without a doubt one of the more influential concepts in the philosophy of science over the past 40 years—most particularly as the philosophy of science is understood and employed in the social sciences. Indeed, in the social sciences, underdetermination is something of a cliché. Underdetermination is the view that a given body of evidence does not uniquely determine any particular theoretical position. To put the matter a little differently, underdetermination suggests that an infinite number of theories is logically compatible with any particular body of evidence. Underdetermination has led to two central positions adopted by contextualists and social constructionists—namely, relativism and the idea that progress does not occur in science inasmuch as no theory is better than another; that is, theories are merely different from each other.

Incommensurability is the idea that it is impossible for individuals who ascribe to different theories to communicate effectively with each other. The basis of this idea is that each theory has a particular language that does not translate well, if at all, into the language of a rival theory. As we will show later, incommensurability was accepted by relativists and nonrelativists alike.

It is the purpose of this chapter to describe underdetermination and incommensurability in detail and to show that they are seriously mistaken notions. If this is the case, then the rationale for social constructionism, particularly for philosophic contextualism, is undermined.

Underdetermination and incommensurability as points of view originally arose in the philosophy of science. Although underdetermination has many sources, sources to which we will refer soon, undoubtedly the major impetus to accepting that doctrine in psychology and social sciences in general is the work of Kuhn (1962). Consider a sampling of some remarks by Kuhn:

An apparently arbitrary element, compounded of personal and historical accident, is always a formative ingredient of the beliefs espoused by a given scientific community at a given time. (1962, p. 4)

[The] issue of paradigm choice can never be unequivocally settled by logic and experiment alone. (1962, p. 93)

The proponents of competing paradigms practice their trades in different worlds. (1962, p. 149)

The transfer of allegiance from paradigm to paradigm is a conversion experience that cannot be forced. Lifelong resistance, particularly from those whose productive careers have committed them to an older tradition of normal science, is not a violation of scientific standards but an index to the nature of scientific research itself. (1962, p. 150)

Paradigm change cannot be justified by proof. (1962, p. 151)

All experiments can be challenged, either for their relevance or their accuracy. All theories can be modified by a variety of ad hoc adjustments without ceasing to be, in their main lines, the same theories. (1977, p. 281)

Every individual choice between competing theories depends on a mixture of objective and subjective factors, or of shared and individual criteria. (1977, p. 325)

When scientists must choose between competing theories, two men fully committed to the same list of criteria for choice may nevertheless reach different conclusions. (1977, p. 324)

A variety of other individuals, perhaps less well-known to social scientists, have championed the doctrine of underdetermination in one form or another. Among scientists and mathematicians, Poincaré and Duhem are best known for suggesting some form of underdetermination. Recently, Laudan (1996) has provided the following useful list of individuals associated with the doctrine of underdetermination:

Quine has claimed that theories are so radically underdetermined by the data that a scientist can, if he wishes, hold onto *any* theory he likes, "come what may." Lakatos and Feyerabend have taken the underdetermination of theories to justify the claim that the only difference between empirically successful and empirically unsuccessful theories lies in the talents and resources of their respective advocates (i.e., with sufficient ingenuity, more or less *any* theory can be made to look methodologically respectable). Boyd and Newton-Smith suggest that underdetermination poses several prima facie challenges to scientific realism. Hesse and Bloor have claimed that underdetermination shows the *necessity* for bringing noncognitive, social factors into play in examining the theory choices of scientists (on the grounds that methodological and evidential considerations alone are demonstrably insufficient to account for such choices). H. M. Collins, and several of his fellow sociologists of knowledge, have asserted that underdetermination lends credence to the view that the world does little if anything to shape or constrain our beliefs about it. Further afield, literary theorists like Derrida have utilized underdetermination as one part of the rationale for "deconstructionism" (in brief, the thesis that, since every text lends itself to a variety of interpretations and thus since texts underdetermine choice among those interpretations, texts have no determinate meaning). (p. 30)

Numerous examples could be supplied as well of psychologists who have accepted underdetermination. Rychlak (1981) has said, "No matter how much our tough-minded, empirical psychologist would like to claim that the empirical findings of his or her experiments are immutable facts, the truth is: *There are N (unlimited) potential theories to explain any fact pattern"* (pp. 26-27). Similarly, Slife and Williams (1995) stated,

> That experimentation cannot prove anything true has been known for a long time. . . . There are in principle an unlimited number of possible explanations for any experimental result. . . . This means, of course, that in addition to not *proving* a hypothesis, data cannot "tell" or "indicate" to the researcher which of many interpretations is correct. (p. 187)

It is clear from the quotes supplied above that Rychlak (1981) and Slife and Williams (1995) ascribe to a strong version of underdetermination and thus, by implication, relativism.

Interestingly, Phillips (1990), an individual who is not sympathetic to relativism, nevertheless accepts underdetermination. According to Phillips,

> Over the past few decades, it has become increasingly clear that scientific theories are "underdetermined" by nature; that is, whatever evidence is available (or possibly could be available) about nature, it is never sufficient to rule out the possibility that a much better theory might be devised to account for the phenomena that our presently accepted theory also explains. Or, to put it another way, a variety of rival theories or hypotheses can always be constructed that are equally compatible with whatever finite body of evidence is currently available. (p. 35)

LIMITATIONS OF UNDERDETERMINATION

Humean, or Logical, Underdetermination

There is a sense in which underdetermination is an acceptable thesis, but it is a trivial sense. Despite its triviality, it has been used mistakenly as the justification for other senses of underdetermination, which are not acceptable and are pernicious. The trivial sense in which underdetermination is acceptable can be traced to the philosopher David Hume. Hence, Laudan (1996) refers to this form of underdetermination as Humean underdetermination, which he defines as follows: "For any finite body of evidence, there are indefinitely many mutually contrary theories, each of which logically entails that evidence" (p. 31).

To justify underdetermination of scientific theories on the basis of Humean underdetermination is to commit oneself to the view that all logically consistent statements are equally acceptable empirically, which is pure nonsense. That is, to accept a so-called theory merely because it is logically consistent with a body of data would be madness. For example, it is logically possible that dinosaurs never existed and that the evidence for their existence has been planted by individuals who want to convince us of the reality of evolution. The problem with this formulation, of course, is that there is not a whit of evidence to support it, and there is a great deal of evidence difficult to reconcile with it. With respect to Humean underdetermination, Kitcher (1993), a philosopher of science, has said the following:

> The notion that theories are inevitably underdetermined by experience has become a philosophic commonplace. Scientists, however, sometimes greet this allegedly mundane point with incredulity. "It's hard enough," they complain, "to find *one* way of accommodating experience, let alone many." And these supposed ways of modifying the network of beliefs are changes that no reasonable—sane?—person would make. There may be a *logical* point here, but it has little to do with science. (p. 247)

Kitcher (1993) goes on to say, "The underdetermination thesis, in its usual guise, is a product of the underrepresentation of scientific practice" (p. 247). Or, as Laudan (1990) has said,

> The *compatibility* of a hypothesis with the available evidence offers no positive grounds for holding that the evidence thereby *supports* the hypothesis with which it is compatible. If the underdetermination thesis is to have any punch against the realist or anyone else, you have to make it stronger than the claim that infinitely many theories are compatible with any finite body of evidence. (p. 50)

Thus far, what we have demonstrated is that Humean underdetermination is not a sufficient justification for supposing that scientific theories are empirically underdetermined, although as we shall see, that is a common mistake. To summarize our major point: That something is logically possible in no way, shape, or form in and of itself suggests that that something is empirically reasonable or worthy of belief.

Quinean, or Empirical, Underdetermination

Quinean underdetermination, unlike Humean underdetermination, is not concerned with logic but with the so-called empirical underdetermination of theories. Quine (1970) says this about physical theory:

> Naturally it is underdetermined by past evidence; a future observation can conflict with it. Naturally it is underdetermined by past and future evidence combined, since some observable event that conflicts with it can happen to go unobserved. Moreover, many people will agree, far beyond all this, that physical theory is underdetermined even by all *possible* observations. (p. 179)

In his essay, "Two Dogmas of Empiricism," Quine (1953) states,

> Any statement can be held true come what may, if we make drastic adjustments elsewhere in the system. Even a statement very close to the periphery can be held true in the face of recalcitrant experience by pleading hallucination or by amending certain statements of the kind called logical laws. (p. 43)

Quine suggests, essentially, that if our pet theory is faced with an empirically uncomfortable result, there are a number of things we can do to preserve the theory, if not in its original form than in one that retains its fundamental essence. For example, Laudan (1996) has suggested that, according to Quine, if we are confronted with an apparent refutation of the claim that "there are brick houses on Elm Street," we may now assert, for example, that Elm Street now refers to Oak Street, "which adventitiously happens to have brick houses on it, thereby avoiding the force of the apparent refutation" (p. 35).

Another view of Quine's that we should understand before subjecting him to criticism is that he accepted what has come to be known as the Duhem thesis. Essentially, what this means is that in testing theories, we are not testing individual statements but whole groups or networks of statements. When a prediction differs from an observed result, it is not possible, according to this view, to localize the failure more specifically within the network of statements. In his "Two Dogmas of Empiricism," Quine (1953) asserts, "If this view is right, it is misleading to speak of the empirical content of an individual statement" (p. 43).

An extensive critical evaluation of Quine (1953) was undertaken by Laudan (1996), who observed that there is a difference between the following two statements.

1. One may hold onto any theory whatsoever in the face of any evidence whatsoever.
2. It is rational to hold onto any theory in the face of any evidence whatsoever.

If Quinean underdetermination is applicable to anything at all, it is the first statement. What seems not to have been realized, especially in the social sciences, is that nowhere has the second statement been justified by Quine (1953) or by anyone else. Unfortunately, it is not only social scientists who have confused the first statement with the second statement, but it is an error that Quine himself frequently commits. Scientifically, it is important that the second statement be demonstrated if Quinean underdetermination is to be taken seriously, something that has not been done to this point in time and may, in fact, not be possible.

Let us consider how reasonable the various Quinean gambits might be. In what sense is it reasonable to suggest that a theory is now saved by asserting that houses initially said to be on Elm Street are now on Oak Street? Very few people would be satisfied with a formulation of this sort, which seems little more than an ad hoc ploy. Scientists are universally skeptical when an individual attempts to rescue her or his theory by employing an ad hoc hypothesis. Thus, employing ad hoc formulations, particularly of the egregious sort recommended by Quine (1953), is useless not only in principle but in practice as well. Now, just imagine how pleading hallucination and suggesting that the laws of logic be changed to preserve a theory would go over in the relevant scientific community. Such suggestions would be greeted by laughter and derision. Our point here is that ploys of this sort are not only unreasonable but are not likely to prove effective as well.

As for testing systems of statements, rather than individual statements, Quine (1953) suggests that it is always possible to salvage one's theory by suitably modifying some auxiliary assumption. Again, this sounds fine logically, but it encounters several difficulties when subjected to scrutiny. There is a general point here and several specific ones. The general point is that there is no guarantee (nor has there been any demonstration) that the modified theory would be as empirically adequate as the original one. As one example, by throwing out one of our auxiliary assumptions, we lose whatever predictive and explanatory power was associated with that assumption. Second, we have no guarantee that the newly added auxiliary assumption will explain or predict very much more than the specific phenomenon that led to its incorporation. Third, we have no guarantee that the revised assumption will fit as coherently into the system of statements as the original assumption. Until these points are addressed adequately by some epistemological analysis, we have no reason to believe that replacing auxiliary assumptions of a system of statements will necessarily result in improvement in the theory. There is as much warrant for believing that changing auxiliary assumptions in the fashion described will reduce, rather than increase, the scientific adequacy of our theory.

IMPLICATIONS OF UNDERDETERMINATION

Relativism

It follows that if theories are underdetermined by the evidence, then, empirically speaking, no theory is better than another, which of course is the doctrine of epistemic relativism. To put it differently, underdetermination suggests that there are no empirical grounds for suggesting that one theory is better than another. Popper, the eminent philosopher of science, was one of the first to suggest that Kuhn is, for all practical purposes, a relativist. Popper (1970) said of Kuhn's arguments, "This is a widely accepted and indeed a fashionable thesis, the thesis of relativism" (p. 56).

Kuhn, in a variety of places, denied that he embraced relativism. However, a close reading of Kuhn fails to dispel the idea that Kuhn is indeed a relativist. On one hand, Kuhn would proclaim vociferously and at great length that he was not a relativist, citing a variety of arguments to that effect. But on the other hand, he would then go on to undercut the very arguments that he had previously made. The upshot is that Kuhn seems to be arguing with himself. As an example of this, Hoyningen-Huene (1993), in a highly sympathetic treatment of Kuhn's philosophy, says the following:

When Kuhn expresses the dissimilarity between comparative theory evaluation and rigorous proof by claiming that theory choice "can never be unequivocally settled by logic and experiment alone" [Kuhn, 1962, p. 94], he by no means wishes to assert that logic and empirical findings are irrelevant to theory choice. Of course, logic and experiment play an important role, but they don't have the power to determine a decision rigorously. (p. 244)

Here is an author who is attempting to explain Kuhn to a wider audience in the clearest terms possible and nevertheless provides a statement that can be read in two different ways—that Kuhn is not a relativist, yet he subscribes in effect to a relativistic position by suggesting that logic and experiment are deficient to determine a rigorous decision. Many instances could be cited in which Kuhn himself denies being a relativist and then goes on to accept relativistic positions. If one desires a clear expression of Kuhn's view on how paradigms clash, consider the following: "When paradigms enter, as they must, into a debate about paradigm choice, their role is necessarily circular. Each group uses its own paradigm to argue in that paradigm's defense" (Kuhn, 1962, p. 93). As Feyerabend (1970) has said of Kuhn, if he is not a relativist, he nevertheless can be treated as one.

Guba (1990), who is a constructivist, embraces the doctrine of under-determination of theory:

No theory can ever be fully tested because of the problem of induction. Observing one million white swans does not provide indisputable evidence for the assertion, "All swans are white." There are always a large number of theories that can, in principle, "explain" a given body of "facts." Thus no unequivocal explanation is ever possible. (p. 25)

Not surprisingly, Guba is a relativist. He defines relativism as follows: "Realities exist in the form of multiple mental constructions, socially and experientially based, local and specific, dependent on their form and content on the person who holds them" (p. 27). Guba, unlike Kuhn, is ready to accept the consequences of underdetermination—namely, that it leads to relativism and necessarily so.

Lack of Progress

Another consequence of underdetermination is that it leads to the idea that successive scientific theories do not show progress in the sense of improving but are merely different from each other. According to this formulation, Aristotle's physics is in no sense inferior to Einstein's physics; the two are merely different. For the logical positivists and Popper, to conclude that a later theory is better than an earlier theory, it is necessary to show that the later theory explains all that the earlier theory explained plus other matters beside. It is generally agreed that progress in this sense does not occur (Laudan, 1996). Lack of progress in the sense described allows those who embrace some form of relativism to suggest that progress of any sort does not occur.

Kuhn (1962), of course, is one of the major figures responsible for the idea that when paradigms change, the change is neither for the better nor the worse. Kuhn says, "No paradigm ever solves all of the problems it defines, and since no two paradigms leave all the same problems unsolved, paradigm debate always involves the question: Which problems is it more significant to have solved" (p. 110)? Kuhn thinks that a legitimate answer to this problem is unavailable. In Kuhn's view, a successor paradigm may encompass both gains and losses relative to the preceding paradigm.

Kuhn's (1962) opinion regarding the lack of progress is also evident in the following quote:

> These characteristic shifts in the scientific community's conception of its legitimate problems and standards would have less significance to this essay's thesis if one could suppose that they always occurred from some methodologically lower to some higher type. In that case their effects, too, would seem cumulative. No wonder that some historians have argued that the history of science records a continuing increase in the maturity and refinements in man's conception of the nature of science. Yet the case for cumulative development for science's problems and standards is even harder to make than the case for the cumulation of theories. (p. 108)

Kuhn's idea is that science is like evolution. In his words, "My view of scientific development is fundamentally evolutionary" (Kuhn, 1970b, p. 264). In neither evolution nor science is there a goal; thus, there can be no progress toward a goal. Kuhn (1962) says,

The *Origin of Species* recognized no goal set by either God or nature. Instead, natural selection, operating in the given environment and with the actual organisms presently at hand, was responsible for the gradual but steady emergence of more elaborate, further articulated, and vastly more specialized organisms. Even such marvelously adapted organs as the eye and hand of man—organs whose design had previously provided powerful arguments for the existence of a supreme artificer and an advance plan—were products of a process that moved steadily *from* primitive beginnings but *toward* no goal. (p. 171)

Kuhn (1962) indicates, in comparing scientific progress to evolution, "The analogy that relates the evolution of organisms to the evolution of scientific ideas can easily be pushed too far. But with respect to the issues of this closing section it is very nearly perfect" (p. 171). In his closing section, Kuhn deals with the topic of progress through revolutions.

In Kuhn's (1962) view, as well as Popper's (1970) view, scientific theories are judged as progressive insofar as they solve all the problems of their predecessors, as well as certain significant new problems. This is known as the cumulativity thesis, and as indicated earlier, it is generally agreed that cumulativity in this sense is not characteristic of scientific theories. The cumulativity thesis is not the only unrealistic yardstick that has been offered to measure progress in science. One obvious candidate is that science leads us closer and closer to the truth. We cannot know whether science is getting us closer to the truth because we do not know what the truth is. Laudan (1996) makes the quite reasonable point that in measuring progress in science, we should select goals that are cognitively achievable. His candidate for a cognitively achievable goal is the ability of a theory to solve more problems than its predecessor.

As mentioned in Chapter 2, to be considered progressive, a theory must solve both conceptual and empirical problems. Laudan's (1996) emphasis on conceptual problems is unique among philosophers of science and has been discussed extensively by Gholson and Barker (1985). Conceptual problems exist if a theory (a) is internally inconsistent or the postulated mechanisms are ambiguous, (b) makes assumptions about the world that are inconsistent with other widely accepted assumptions, (c) fails to use concepts contained in more general theories, or (d) violates principles of the research tradition to which it belongs (see Gholson & Barker, 1985, for an extensive discussion of research traditions). Laudan identifies three sorts of empirical problems:

potential problems, solved problems, and anomalous problems. Potential problems represent what is assumed to be the case about the world but is not as yet explained. Solved problems are what we assume to be true about the world that have been solved by another theory. Anomalous problems are actual problems that have been solved by a rival theory but not by the theory in question.

Laudan (1996) suggests, "One theory is more adequate (i.e., more acceptable) than a rival just in case the former has exhibited a greater problem-solving effectiveness than the latter" (p. 84). As indicated, one assesses the number and weight of empirical problems a theory solves, the number and weight of its empirical anomalies, and the number and centrality of its conceptual difficulties. The problem-solving effectiveness of a theory cannot be judged in isolation. History shows that theories are always in competition with each other (see Gholson & Barker, 1985). The fact that a particular theory solves many problems is not to be taken to suggest that the theory is acceptable. It is only when we compare the problem-solving capacity of a theory relative to its rivals that the judgment as to which theory is to be retained is warranted.

INCOMMENSURABILITY

Incommensurability, the idea that it is difficult for individuals who ascribe to different theories to communicate effectively with each other, has been accepted by positivists and relativists alike. To the positivist, a theory consists of a formal uninterpreted calculus composed of syntactical rules. The formal calculus is given an interpretation that spells out the truth conditions in the theory's language. On this view, every theory is seen as formulatable as a formal language, and the positivist program was to discover translations between the theoretical and observational languages of rival theories. This task proved to be impossible. As Laudan (1996) has remarked, "Absent a neutral observation language, and absent translation manuals for rival theoretical languages, scientific communication between rival conceptual schemes became the first casualty of postpositivism" (p. 9). It became a casualty because postpositivists such as Kuhn and Feyerabend accepted the positivists' view on what was necessary for communication to occur between rival theories.

For example, Kuhn (1970b) has said,

The point-by-point comparison of two successive theories demands
a language into which at least the empirical consequences of both
can be translated without loss or change. That such a language lies
ready to hand has been widely assumed since at least the seventeenth
century when philosophers took the neutrality of pure sensation-
reports for granted and sought a "universal character" which would
display all languages for expressing them as one. Ideally the primitive
vocabulary of such a language would consist of sense-datum terms
plus syntactic connectives. . . . Feyerabend and I have argued at
length that no such vocabulary is available. In the transition from
one theory to the next words change their meanings or conditions
of applicability in subtle ways. . . . Successive theories are thus, we
say, incommensurable. (pp. 266-267)

Laudan (1996) rejects the idea that individuals who accept different
theories are unable to communicate with each other. He notes that prior to
the logical positivists, all philosophies of science accepted that different
theories had different vocabularies, but they did not have different languages.
Thus, it was always possible to make clear the ideas of one theory within the
context of another theory. Moreover, he is of the view that complete "translation" between competing theories is not necessary for rational evaluation.
The pragmatist in Laudan's (1990) dialogue stresses that "the explosive
potential of incommensurability can be quickly defused by pointing out that
the *wholesale translation* of the claims of one paradigm into the language of
its rivals *is not required to make rational choice between those rivals*" (p. 139).

The thesis of incommensurability is inextricably linked to the thesis of
empirical underdetermination. Because empirical underdetermination is not
a defensible position to hold, it is not surprising to find that the incommensurability thesis does not fare well either.

BACKING OFF FROM UNDERDETERMINATION
AND RELATIVISM

Both Kuhn and Quine have been challenged on their views of underdetermination and lack of progress in science. Both have backpedaled from these

positions—in Kuhn's case, suggesting that people have misinterpreted him and in Quine's case, suggesting that he has changed his mind. Given the responses of Kuhn and Quine to their critics, it is difficult to know what their final judgment may be with respect to underdetermination and incommensurability.

As for the lack of communication between theories, Kuhn (1970b) says in his "Reflections on My Critics,"

> I do not believe that it is ever total or beyond recourse. Where he [Feyerabend] talks of incommensurability *tout court,* I have regularly spoken also of partial communication, and I believe it can be improved upon to whatever extent circumstances may demand and patience permit. (p. 232)

If these statements cannot be taken to mean that communication between rival theories can be complete, what can they mean?

With respect to underdetermination, Kuhn (1970b) is similarly opaque. He says,

> My critics respond to my views on this subject with charges of irrationality, relativism, and the defence of mob rule. These are all labels which I categorically reject, even when they are used in my defence by Feyerabend. To say that, in matters of theory-choice, the force of logic and observation cannot in principle be compelling is neither to discard logic and observation nor to suggest that there are not good reasons for favoring one theory over another. (p. 234)

Kuhn (1970b) goes on to say, "It is emphatically *not* my view that 'adoption of a new scientific theory is an intuitive or mystical affair, a matter for psychological description rather than logical or methodological codification' " (p. 261).

Given these statements, Kuhn's position on underdetermination and various other matters is at best unclear. We are certainly not the first to suggest this, as Shapere (1984) has said,

> Kuhn appears to have retreated from his earlier position in just those respects in which it was most suggestive, important, and influential, and to have retained aspects which many have felt were the most objectionable feature of his earlier view. Finally, the consistency of what he has retained with his apparent departures from his former

view is certainly open to question. And it is far from being unambig-
uously clear what his current view is. He wants to say that there are
paradigm-independent considerations which constitute rational
bases for introducing and accepting new paradigms; but his use of
the term "reasons" is vitiated by his considering them to be "values,"
so that he seems not to have gotten beyond his former view after all.
He seems to want to say that there is progress in science; but all
grounds of assessment again turn out to be "values," and we are left
with the same old relativism. And he seems unwilling to abandon
"incommensurability," while trying, unsuccessfully, to assert that
communication and comparison are possible. (p. 56)

Quine's views on underdetermination have changed considerably since
his well-known "Two Dogmas of Empiricism" (1953). Gibson (1982), who
has provided a detailed exposition of Quine's philosophy, a work that Quine
endorses, has said the following:

Recently Quine has raised some doubts about the intelligibility of
the underdetermination thesis. He has concluded that in its full
generality the thesis of underdetermination is untenable, and that a
more modest version of the underdetermination thesis is tenable but
vague. (p. 85)

Quine has revised his position on underdetermination in a 1975 article.
In that article, Quine says of underdetermination, "The doctrine is plausible
insofar as it is intelligible, but it is less readily intelligible than it may seem"
(p. 313). Quine's position seems to be that underdetermination, insofar as it
applies to anything, applies to global theories of the sort that Pepper would
call worldviews, rather than to specific scientific theories. In short, Quine's
more recent position on underdetermination is one with which many scientists could agree and that gives no solace to relativists.

STATUS OF RELATIVISM

The primary point of this chapter is that a convincing case for the strong
forms of underdetermination and incommensurability and the relativism that

they imply has not been made. One must look with caution to Kuhn or Quine for a defense of relativism because they both disavowed it in their later writings. That is, the unwillingness of Kuhn or Quine to defend strong versions of their positions should give one pause in accepting underdetermination, incommensurability, and relativism. Another reason for skepticism here is that the belief that most philosophers of science accept relativistic positions is seriously mistaken. Laudan, in his book *Science and Relativism* (1990), states in no uncertain terms,

> Strong forms of epistemic relativism derive scant support from a clearheaded understanding of the contemporary state of the art in philosophy of science. I am not alone in that conviction; most of my fellow philosophers of science would doubtless wholeheartedly concur. But that consensus within the discipline apparently cuts little ice with those outside it, who evidently believe that Kuhn or Quine or Feyerabend has discredited the traditional picture of scientific knowledge. (p. viii)

Laudan's book, written as a dialogue among an imagined but prototypical relativist, pragmatist, positivist, and realist, provides a purgative "for those who have already succumbed to the wiles of relativism, mistakenly believing it to be a philosophically coherent position" (p. x) and a prophylactic for those who have not.

Callebaut (1993) makes much the same point in his book, which is a dialogue among actual philosophers of science. He states,

> More recently the realism-constructivism controversy has superseded the older debate about the rationality or relativism of science; it occasions a majority of philosophers to defend some variety of realism against the anti-realism of contemporary empiricists in philosophy and increasingly also against the actual or presumed anti-realistic implications or presuppositions of the new sociological approaches to science studies. (p. xvi)

This commitment to some form of realism is apparent in the comments of Helen Longino, a philosopher who places emphasis on personal and social factors in the construction of knowledge. Says Longino, "We have to be committed to the *hope* that the descriptions [of science] are in some way really descriptive of the world" (quoted in Callebaut, 1993, p. 28). The necessity of committing to some variety of realism was stated forcefully by Santillana and Zilsel (1941):

> The scientist always searches for laws, but he wants to think in terms of things. These things must be real, that is, he must be able to believe in them. . . . Whatever the limitations and conventions attached to the words "true" or "real," it is clear that the thing which is the principle of explanation command at least provisional belief. (p. 13)

According to the assertions of the contextualists and their allies, they are "in tune" with contemporary views in the philosophy of science. However, and ironically, their emphases on relativism and constructivism are not widely accepted in the philosophy of science. As the realist in Laudan's (1990) dialogue notes,

> Relativism is self-referentially incoherent, and to boot it is predicated on several dubious epistemological theses—for instance, incommensurability, holism, and radical underdetermination. The relativist supposes that fallibilism, which we all accept, entails that all beliefs are equally well- or ill-founded. (p. 169)

An ironic consequence of adopting relativism is thus to undermine the very positions that one wishes to advance.

Certain paradoxes arise in connection with cultural relativism and incommensurability. As Quine (1975) has noted,

> Truth, says the cultural relativist, is culture-bound. But if it were, then he, within his own culture, ought to see his own culture-bound truth as absolute. He cannot proclaim cultural relativism without rising above it, and he cannot rise above it without giving it up. (pp. 327-328)

Consider another paradox that Laudan (1996) attributes to Shapere:

> Since genuinely incommensurable theories are not certifiably mutually inconsistent (and vice versa), the avowed incommensurability of rival perspectives makes it impossible to tell whether or where they disagree—or even whether they are rivals! (p. 10)

SUMMARY AND CONCLUSIONS

In this chapter, we considered two of the most influential topics in recent philosophy of science—underdetermination and incommensurability—and we examined the implications of underdetermination for progress in science. Underdetermination, put simply, is the view that a given body of evidence does not uniquely determine any particular theoretical position. Underdetermination is widely accepted by psychologists of various persuasions and by some philosophers of science, and it has been made popular within psychology by Kuhn. We examined major positions of underdetermination suggested by Kuhn, Quine, and others. We suggested that only one version of underdetermination is plausible at present, a version that in no way threatens rational choice among theories. The plausible version of underdetermination is called Humean underdetermination, and it suggests merely that any body of evidence is logically compatible with a variety of interpretations. It was indicated that there is a vast difference between saying that evidence is logically compatible with a theory and saying that such evidence supports the theory. A second version of underdetermination examined, Quinean underdetermination, suggests that one may hold on to any theory whatsoever on the basis of any evidence whatsoever. It was shown that the case has yet to be made that gambits of this sort are workable in practice.

Incommensurability is the view that different theories have different languages and thus have difficulty communicating with each other, difficulty that in some cases may be insurmountable. It was indicated that theories may differ not so much in the language that they possess but in their vocabularies, and thus it is perfectly possible for different theories to communicate with each other, albeit with some difficulty.

Underdetermination and incommensurability, it was indicated, lead to the idea that science does not progress. In addition, they lead to relativism. Objections to both relativism and the idea that science does not progress were noted. It was indicated that Kuhn and Quine, on being challenged with respect to incommensurability, underdetermination, relativism, and other ideas, backpedaled furiously, softening most of their earlier positions. Finally, it was suggested that although relativism is alive and well in the minds of social and behavioral scientists, it is not currently a popular position in the philosophy of science.

Downplaying Ontology

*I*t is our belief that, potentially at least, contextualism and social constructionism, on one hand, and mainstream psychology, on the other, have a
lot to offer each other. Although few others share this belief, it is obvious that
neither position is attempting to have nor is having much influence on the
other. Nevertheless, we accept as a basic proposition that adherents of each
position are desirous of extending their influence as much as possible over
the total field of psychology. That is, contextualists and social constructionists
would like to see their influence increase in mainstream psychology, and at
the same time mainstream psychologists would like to extend their influence
into newer domains. If we accept that each side is desirous of influencing the
other, then to accomplish this, certain strictures will have to be observed. Put
differently, certain rules of the game must be observed for effective communication between groups to occur and influence to grow. These rules are not
currently being observed, and in consequence, neither side is paying much
attention to the other. Ignoring the rules of the game is somewhat understandable on both sides.

Contextualists and social constructionists, as well as adherents of postmodernism in general, are attempting to displace mainstream psychology
from the stage. This attempt involves the presentation of a variety of novel
viewpoints that are neither accepted nor well understood within mainstream
psychology. It is perfectly understandable that postmodernists in general

would place a heavy emphasis on explicating and establishing their first principles. Dealing with fundamentals of this sort is entirely understandable when done by individuals who are on the outside looking in. However, this approach, for reasons given later, is not apt to meet with great success if the objective is to gain converts among mainstream psychologists.

Mainstream psychologists, unlike contextualists and their allies, are pretty much satisfied with the sort of fundamental considerations that govern their everyday scientific activity. Being satisfied, they are not apt to go looking for new principles to govern their work and, indeed, might show irritation at the suggestion that they should. We are not necessarily condoning this attitude but rather are simply describing it. As indicated, we think it best if both groups would pay more attention to each other.

An example of a level of comparison that prevails when postmodernists of various persuasions are comparing themselves with mainstream psychology, as well as how mainstream psychologists react to such comparisons, is well exemplified by the following statement by Lee (1988):

> The literature of criticism [of academic psychology] does not concern particular techniques and theories. Rather, it concerns the goals, methods, and achievements of psychology. More fully stated, it concerns what psychology is about, what it is trying to do, and how it proposes to do it, and how much progress it has made so far. . . . The literature of criticism does not enjoy favor in academic psychology. On the contrary, psychologists most often ignore it. (p. 1)

Although Lee thinks that mainstream psychologists are at fault for ignoring criticisms of the above sort, mainstream psychologists on their part would tend to upbraid Lee's form of argument because it ignores the specific theories and findings with which they are concerned. Mainstream psychologists by and large would like to know what the specific theoretical implications are of any line of argument. Finding none, they are inclined to disregard the argument as irrelevant. In agreement with our point, Laudan (1996) has suggested,

> Scientists' judgments as to the success of a scientific practice depend not on abstract epistemological and methodological matters but on palpably *pragmatic* ones. A science is successful just insofar as it manages to confer some measure of control of the subject matter under investigation on the practitioner who has mastered the prac-

tice. Thus, a medical practice is successful or not depending on the degree to which it gives its initiates the ability to predict and to alter the course of common diseases. An astronomical practice is successful to the extent that it enables one to anticipate future positions of planetary and celestial bodies. (pp. 148-149)

THE BASIC RULES OF THE GAME

Abstaining From Caricatures

In reading the postmodernist literature, we have been amazed at the dismissive, even contemptuous, attitude displayed toward mainstream psychology. We do not as often find in the literature equally dismissive attitudes by mainstream psychologists toward postmodernists. The simple reason for this is that insofar as the literature is concerned, mainstream psychologists ignore various postmodernist movements. But based on conversations with our mainstream colleagues, we can assure various postmodernists that the tendency toward denigration is reciprocated. Although rare, harsh dismissals and unflattering evaluations of the postmodern approach to psychology can be found. Stuart-Hamilton (1988) has said the following about the book, *Cognitive Psychology in Question,* by Costall and Still (1987):

> This book almost makes one envy the illiterate. Rarely has a work of such woolliness of thought, meandering prose, and gross self-congratulation appeared. . . . I have tried long and hard, but I cannot think of anything complementary (sic) about this book. If the authors wish to settle back into armchair psychology, as it seems, then they are at (usually comfortably tenured) liberty to do so. To snipe at mainstream cognitive psychology is fair, provided the target is accurately identified. But it rarely is. . . . If the authors are going to be muddle-headed, they might at least have the decency to be entertaining, but, alas, their prose styles are as dull and banal as their ideas. . . . In brief, cognitive psychology is never put in question, but the business sense of Harvester Press who published this appalling work is. (pp. 411-412)

In citing various and more numerous inaccurate descriptions of mainstream psychology by postmodernists, we are not attempting to be one-sided. Rather, the disproportionate volume of remarks by postmodernists simply reflects the greater volume of such comments to be found in the literature. We assure the reader that we do not approve of either side caricaturizing the other.

One common caricature is to classify mainstream psychologists as following a philosophy of positivism. As recent examples, Slife and Williams (1997) state, "Psychology has often been characterized as positivistic in its scientific outlook" (p. 118), and Van Langenhove (1995) says, "Most psychologists today have tacitly adopted a logical positivist methodology" (p. 14). This is an assessment with which these and other advocates of a postmodern approach agree. Typically, the argument then is made that because logical positivism is no longer accepted in the philosophy of science, mainstream psychology is following an outmoded philosophy. According to Callebaut (1993), the term *positivist* is often used in a pejorative sense. He states, "In some quarters, the word 'positivism' has become synonymous with 'whatever we don't like.' Even people who are otherwise wary of 'whiggish' interpretations of history are liable to oversimplify the philosophical past" (p. 19). In reaction to Callebaut's comment, David Hull replies, "The received view was very good, and those of us who criticize it are never fair to it. We present a parody of it and then knock it down; but that's the way the game is played" (quoted in Callebaut, 1993, p. 19). Callebaut later says, "People involved in empirical science studies often use the label 'positivism' in the sense of 'the bad guys' " (p. 28).

Another common caricature is to classify mainstream psychologists as mechanists (see, e.g., Hayes et al., 1988; Sarbin, 1993). Morris (1991) engages in such caricature and goes on to state that "for psychology mechanism is the wrong world-view of its subject matter, and always was" (p. 124). Morris's opinion is easy to understand because he has a limited and distorted view about what mainstream psychology is all about. For example, Morris (1991, 1993a) states that mechanists postulate a passive rather than an active organism, adhere to unidirectional and linear causality, are necessarily reductionists, are necessarily associationists, and believe that behavior change is little more than response weakness or strength. We have shown that none of these positions is necessarily characteristic of mainstream psychology, although each of these positions may have some adherents among mainstream psychologists.

Engage in Relevant Arguments

As indicated in the previous chapter, it is our view that individuals make decisions, including scientific decisions, on a comparative rather than an absolute basis. This is a view that is widely shared in the philosophy of science. For example, Kuhn (1962) has said, "Competition between segments of the scientific community is the only historical process that ever actually results in the rejection of one previously accepted theory or in the adoption of another" (p. 8). To be sure, there is a sense in which contextualists evaluate their approach relative to approaches existing in mainstream psychology. The problem here is that the type of comparisons engaged in are far too general and abstract to have any influence on mainstream psychologists. To be specific, such comparisons are often at the level of ontology or epistemology or methodology, rather than at a specific theoretical level concerned with empirical matters. It is true that, as Bechtel (1988) has indicated, "the evaluation of theories often depends on judging the coherence of their ontological assumptions. Theories that make inconsistent ontological assumptions, or ones that contemporary researchers find unacceptable, are criticized in much the same way as theories that make false empirical predictions" (p. 10).

Nevertheless, it seems to us that comparison at the level of specific empirical theories is unavoidable, regardless of whether one thinks psychology is a science or whatever one's view of science may be. As we have seen, Kuhn (1962) has suggested a similar position. And Bechtel (1988), who thinks that the resolution of ontological disputes is important, nevertheless does not see them as primary. According to Bechtel,

> The link between ontological issues and empirical inquiry stems from the fact that although ontological issues often play a role in developing a particular kind of research program, the ability of such a research program to produce a progressive tradition of theorizing often affects subsequent judgments about the adequacy of the ontological position underlying the program. (p. 11)

So, it behooves both mainstream psychologists and contextualists to engage in competition with each other at the empirical-theoretical level.

Although this competition could take many different forms, it necessarily must take some form that involves comparison along dimensions commonly suggested by individuals of various persuasions. We have in mind methods of the following sort for comparing theories. Theories are judged for their adequacy along dimensions such as accuracy, consistency, simplicity, scope, fruitfulness, plausibility, contribution to understanding, ability to predict and explain, empirical adequacy, truth, generation of specifiable interactions with the natural or experienced world, and reliability as a guide to action (see, e.g., Kuhn, 1977; Longino, 1998). It seems impossible to believe that a theory judged less adequate than another along all of these dimensions simultaneously would command the respect of any significant number of individuals. Accordingly, it seems reasonable to suggest that a theory stemming from philosophic contextualism would necessarily have to be superior to some mainstream theory along at least some of these dimensions, perhaps at least half.

As we have seen, the functional contextualists, who ascribe to prediction and control of behavior, are necessarily in competition with mainstream psychologists along these dimensions. It is not clear to us at present which of the many dimensions described earlier would be selected by philosophic contextualists as most representative of their approach. But it is clear to us that they cannot reject all of these dimensions and still claim to be superior in any respect whatsoever to mainstream psychology. As Longino (1998) has said of the sort of criteria we have listed earlier, "Standards do not provide a deterministic theory of theory choice. Nevertheless, it is the existence of standards that makes the individual members of a scientific community responsible to something besides themselves" (p. 182).

If we are correct, competition as described above is the only route to better establishing one's position. Such competition should be sought because, after all, members of both groups are concerned ultimately with the most adequate approach to psychology. A matter of that sort can only be judged by dealing with specific empirical issues according to some of the criteria suggested earlier and cannot be decided by appeals to matters of ontology, no matter how sophisticated these appeals may be.

Examples of comparing a contextualistic approach with a mainstream approach that are far too broad to have much impact in mainstream psychology include the following:

Postmodern thought is characterized by a loss of belief in an objective world and an incredulity toward meta-narratives of legitimation. With a delegitimation of global systems of thought, there is no foundation to secure a universal and objective *reality*. (Kvale, 1992b, p. 32)

Within psychology, universal laws of behavior have been sought by natural science-oriented schools such as behaviorism, whereas the uniqueness of the individual person has dominated humanistic psychology. In a postmodern approach the quest for universal knowledge, as well as the cult of the individually unique, is replaced by an emphasis on the heterogeneity and contextuality of knowledge, with a shift from generalization to contextualization. (Kvale, 1994, p. 232)

One way of highlighting the problem with academic psychology is to consider the limited epistemology to which it subscribes. Thus, while it is true that much psychological research has moved beyond the confines of the laboratory experiment, we would argue that the same positivist logic and empiricist impulse, which were at the heart of the behaviorist experimentation, are still central to the way psychological inquiry is conceived and conducted. . . . We would argue that an important and unfortunate consequence of the impoverished empiricist epistemology and privileging of method (indeed, one particular form of method) has been the neglect of a range of alternative conceptual foundations for psychological inquiry together with the prescribing of the type of questions psychology can address and the forms in which it is legitimate to ask them. (Smith et al., 1995b, p. 2)

General arguments of the sort exemplified by these quotes, whatever their intention, are not apt to have much, if any, influence on mainstream psychologists whose major priorities, as indicated, are empirical data and theory constructed on empirical data. What needs to be done to have such influence? It is not enough to suggest that one is collecting the "right sort" of data, whereas mainstream psychologists are not. No amount of praiseworthy comments about one's approach and no amount of scorn about the approach of mainstream psychologists will accomplish much of anything. What has to be done is this: One must show in a detailed, specific, and concrete manner that a particular approach offers this or that advantage over the particular approach employed in some mainstream theory. Lacking such comparison of this sort regarding specific psychological matters, the outcome is totally predictable: The work, no matter what its value may be, will be dismissed as irrelevant by mainstream psychologists.

In agreement with our point, Pashler and Carrier (1996), in a chapter evaluating the information-processing approach to psychology as it applies to memory, state,

> As with any scientific tradition, there is little to be gained in debating the merits and deficiencies of the information processing approach in the abstract. If analyzing memory at the information processing level allows one to make sense of the many important phenomena of memory, and leads to novel successful predictions, then it constitutes a useful scientific approach. If it cannot do these things, other approaches will need to replace it. (p. 4)

Although postmodernists should pay more attention to the empirical adequacy of theories as judged by simplicity, consistency, and so on, mainstream psychologists, for their part, should engage contextualists and their allies at the ontological, epistemological, and methodological levels. Far too many mainstream psychologists ascribe to some outmoded philosophy of science at a verbal level. Fortunately, and this is not generally appreciated by postmodernists, the way that mainstream psychologists practice science is better than their explicit articulation of it. Nevertheless, if mainstream psychologists paid more attention to the philosophy of science, it would be valuable in itself. Another benefit that might flow from this is that mainstream psychologists might engage various postmodernists in a dialogue and, consequently, might more likely influence their way of thinking. In addition, such an attempt by mainstream psychologists might result in postmodernists stating the arguments in favor of their position in more cogent terms. Our point here is that postmodernists, like anybody else, can benefit from reasoned opposition, something that is not generally available but that we have attempted to provide in this book.

Proper Evaluation of Methods

The proper approach to justifying methods, metamethodology, has a long and complex history in science itself and in the philosophy of science. As Laudan (1996) has noted,

Where methodology once enjoyed pride of place among philosophers of science, many are now skeptical about its prospects.
Feyerabend claims to have shown that every method is as good (and
thus as bad) as every other; Kuhn insists that methodological standards are too vague ever to determine choice between rival theories.
Popper generally treats methodological rules as conventions, between which no rational choice can be made. Lakatos goes so far as
to assert that the methodologist is in no position to give warranted
advice to contemporary scientists about which theories to reject or
accept, thereby robbing methodology of any prescriptive force.
Quine, Putnam, Hacking, and Rorty, for different reasons, hold that
the best we can do is to *describe* the methods used by natural
scientists, since there is no room for normative methodology which
is prescriptive in character. To cap things off, everyone in the field
is mindful of the fact that the two most influential programs in
20th-century epistemology, associated with the inductivists and the
Popperians respectively, have run into technical difficulties which
seem beyond their resources to surmount. (p. 125)

In light of these comments, is there available today a viable philosophy
of methodology that is a viable metamethodology? The answer to this
question is positive in terms of one of the major movements in contemporary
philosophy of science, naturalism (Callebaut, 1993). Quine (1953) is considered to be the father of naturalism, and Kuhn (1962), by emphasizing
the importance of history for science, is himself a naturalist. Naturalism is
the view that philosophic questions are to be decided in terms of the same
criteria employed to decide scientific questions, there being no sharp distinction between these approaches. Laudan's (1996) particular approach
to metamethodology is called normative naturalism. The position holds
that methods are amenable to matter-of-fact considerations while being
normative.

According to normative naturalism, methodological rules are hypothetical imperatives. For example, the methodological rule, "one ought to do x,"
should be recast in the form, "if one's goal is y, then one ought to do x."
Laudan (1996) gives the following example of a methodological rule refor-
mulated into a hypothetical imperative. Popper's familiar rule—"avoid
ad hoc hypotheses"—is more properly formulated as the rule, "if one wants
to develop theories that are very risky, then one ought to avoid ad hoc
hypotheses." Two points should be emphasized with regard to methodologi-

cal rules. First, every methodological rule may be recast as a hypothetical imperative. Second, the hypothetical imperative will link a recommended action to a goal or aim.

What are the criteria that go into the selection of methodologies? Laudan (1996) answers as follows:

> When we claim that a certain rule is methodologically sound, we are not committed to saying that the ends of science can be promoted *only* by following the rule in question; nor are we saying that the ends of science will always be furthered by following said rule. Rather, when we endorse a rule, we are asserting our belief that following that rule is more likely to realize one's goals than violating it will. What makes a rule acceptable as a rule is our belief that it represents the *best strategy* we can imagine for reaching a certain desired end. (p. 103)

According to normative naturalism, the aim of methodology is to discover the most effective strategy for investigating the natural world in the specific domain of interest.

It seems to us that contextualists and social constructionists such as Gergen and Bruner are, at least to some extent, normative naturalists. That is, they seem to accept some methods and to reject other methods on the basis of the promise or lack of promise that a particular method may have, in their view. If we are correct in this assessment, then individuals such as Gergen, Bruner, and Sarbin, among others, are inconsistent in their evaluation of methods. That is, they suggest that the methods they favor, such as hypothetical data rotation or narrative, have value while failing to recognize completely the value that other methods, such as experimentation, may have in other areas. The idea that experimentation is useless in psychology generally, in our opinion, is simply absurd. We are willing to grant that experimentation may not be a particularly useful method for some of the various phenomena of concern to contextualists and social constructionists. However, contextualists should not forget that their methods are judged by the same criteria according to which experimentation is judged. That is, contextualists must demonstrate that a particular method they favor is better for certain purposes than is some other method, which they may or may not favor.

It should be remembered, however, that establishing the usefulness of some method for certain purposes in no way necessarily implies that some other method is not useful for some other purpose or purposes. Contextualists, individually and collectively, often go too far—far too far—when they reject experimentation for any and all psychological purposes. With experimentation being employed so extensively and successfully in so many areas of psychology, it would trivialize our point here to cite specific examples. The general point that contextualists and social constructionists must recognize and accept is that mainstream psychologists are concerned with specific empirical questions that are best addressed by experimentation.

What normative naturalism says to contextualists and social constructionists, on one hand, and to mainstream psychologists, on the other hand, is that determining that one's specific methods are best for the goals one has in no way implies that the methods used by the other side are totally useless for their goals. These are separable issues.

GENERALIZABILITY

In contextualism and social constructionism, the capacity to generalize from one situation to another is seen as drastically limited, at best. Consider, for example, what Deese (1996) has to say on this point:

> Contextualism is the notion that all significant psychological judgments and actions are so determined, to the extent that they may be said to be determined at all, by such a unique concatenation of circumstances that they cannot be subject to the ordinary scientific canons of repeatability. That is to say any psychological event occurring on one occasion is so liable to depend on one or more conditions peculiar to the observation that it may not be generalizable to other situations. Nor is psychological theory sufficiently developed that we may over-come the limitations of particular contexts by appealing to a theory to tell us what conditions may be safely ignored. (p. 58)

Gergen et al. (1996) state,

> There is a resurgence of interest in approaching human action through more local modes of understanding, and issues of subjectivity, interpretation, and everyday understanding become in-

creasingly salient. This shift signals the possibility of developing more culturally grounded and locally useful forms of knowledge. It goes beyond the positivist position and proposes that knowledge claims in the human domain are relative to the setting in which they are developed. (p. 498)

As indicated in Chapter 1, according to Fosnot (1996), constructivism is a theory that "describes knowledge as temporary, developmental, nonobjective, internally constructed, and socially and culturally mediated" (p. ix). Harré (1993) states, "It has become a commonplace that much of what we take to be psychological is local, that it exists only within a culture and not across cultures" (p. 5). This point of view is reflected in what today is known as multiculturalism, which suggests that a culture can only be evaluated relative to its own terms and not relative to the terms of some other culture. Guba (1990) indicates, " 'Reality' exists only in the context of a mental framework (construct) for thinking about it . . . If 'reality' can be seen only through a theory window, it can equally be seen only through a value window. Many constructions are possible" (p. 25).

According to social constructionists and contextualists, experimentation is of limited usefulness because it is simply one of many possible contexts and, indeed, not the most illuminating of contexts. Sarbin (1993) is among those who think of experiments as not useful because of the limited contexts they provide. But Sarbin, as indicated earlier, being a true contextualist, disapproves of those who call themselves contextualists but who only increase the number of variables examined in a particular situation. For a contextualist such as Sarbin, any strategy that to any extent involves experimentation is regarded as ineffectual.

Harré (1993) rejects experimentation in the following terms:

The central thesis of social constructionism is the claim that most psychological phenomena are created in and have their primal being in social encounters. . . . I shall show, very briefly, how the traditional "experimental" methodology fails as a technique for revealing the act-action structures of the episodes of everyday life. (p. 95)

Later in his book, Harré makes the following comment: "Experimentation consists in attempting to explore the nature of the hidden mechanisms. It works well for molecules, not so well for quarks, and not well at all for thoughts" (p. 105).

Van Langenhove (1995) rejects experimentation as follows:

> Mainstream psychology today, be it psychometric or experimental psychology, is dominated by a Galtonian approach that has the following characteristics; groups of people are "investigated" (aggregated data); people are endowed with countable attributes; and people are subjected to questionnaires, tests or experiments. Many of the contributions in this volume [Smith et al., 1995b] challenge such an approach on *epistemological* grounds. (p. 18)

Contextualists and social constructionists commenting on the lack of generalizability from one culture to another or from an experimental situation to some other broader situation are making too strong a claim and one that, if taken literally, is indefensible. Whether generalization is feasible and permissible is not a matter that can be decided a priori. Permissible generalization is something that only can be established on the basis of experience. It is often the case that generalization appears permissible but turns out not to be. On the other hand, there are cases in which it appears that generalization is not permissible, but it turns out to be highly feasible. For example, Mendel's discoveries with garden peas turned out to be highly relevant for understanding the inheritance of characteristics not only in plants but in animals as well. As another example, Wilson (1998), in his best-selling book, *Consilience: The Unity of Knowledge*, states,

> The laws of physics are in fact so accurate as to transcend cultural differences. They boil down to mathematical formulae that cannot be given Chinese or Ethiopian or Mayan nuances. Nor do they cut any slack for masculinist or feminist variations. We may even reasonably suppose that any advanced extraterrestrial civilizations, if they possess nuclear power and can launch spacecraft, have discovered the same laws, such that their physics could be translated isomorphically, point to point, set to point, and point to set, into human notation. (p. 49)

Oftentimes, social constructionists, in particular, suggest that psychology, at least as they understand it, is a subject that is limited to human beings and only human beings; that is, findings from other species are not generalizable to human beings. However, it is a trivial matter to show that many phenomena isolated in animals can also be found in humans and, moreover, the phenomena in various species are established on the basis of highly similar or even identical variables. For example, the taste aversion phenomenon, which consists of animals avoiding specific foods that precede gastric illness, can be found in all manners of animals from birds to humans (Tarpy, 1997).

It is equally easy to show that a variety of psychological phenomena are invariant over cultures. One example is spatial stimulus-response compatibility effects (Hommel & Prinz, 1997; Proctor & Reeve, 1990). Basically, people have faster reaction times with a stimulus-response mapping in which stimulus locations and response locations correspond than with a mapping in which they do not. For example, if the stimulus alternatives are left and right lights, mapping the left light to a left keypress and the right light to a right keypress yields faster reaction times than does the opposite mapping. Such spatial compatibility effects are independent of culture. They have been investigated with subjects from many countries and cultures, yet it is rarely ever necessary to invoke cultural differences to explain empirical findings.

Although the topic of intelligence testing is considered controversial in some quarters, it should be noted that experts in the area itself are in substantial agreement on most points (Seligman, 1994; Snyderman & Rothman, 1988). One of the matters on which there is substantial agreement is that intelligence is of predictive usefulness in a wide variety of situations; that is, its predictive value is not limited to a narrow context. For example, Schmidt (1997) says of intelligence that

> the scientific and practical value of intelligence stems . . . from the many important real world things that intelligence predicts; for example, performance in elementary school, high school, college, and graduate school—and in all of the subjects studied therein. It also predicts occupational level attained after completing schooling, income, level of job performance within one's occupation, and many other things. (p. 488)

Although the examples of generalization cited earlier are not apt to be totally convincing to either contextualists or social constructionists, it is difficult to see how they could minimize the importance of the following examples. Each of these examples demonstrates significant commonality over cultures. The well-known sociologists of science—Barnes, Bloor, and Henry (1996), in their book, *Scientific Knowledge: A Sociological Analysis*—say the following about realism:

Some scientists are realists by philosophical inclination. More are realists in the sense that they are moved by explicitly realist forms of argument and persuasion. But all scientists are realists in the sense that they use realist strategies, *as indeed are all human beings in all cultures.* A number of examples of the use of realist strategies have already been considered in Chapter 1 [of Barnes et al.]. They show how perceptions and observations are interpreted as real (of the world) or artefactual (of the perceiving organ, instrument or apparatus), in ways which sustain a single coherent account of what exists in the world. (pp. 81-82, emphasis added)

Of course, the fact that realism is accepted by all people in all cultures does not in itself suggest that realism is the correct position. However, the observation by Barnes et al. (1996) certainly suggests that some extremely important assumptions are shared over cultures.

Rosenberg (1995), in his book, *Philosophy of Social Science,* describes a principle of folk psychology that is common to all cultures:

For any agent *x,* if *x* wants *d* and *x* believes that doing *a* is the best way for him to secure *d,* then *x* does *a.* (p. 37)

Now it is reasonable to believe that when entering into a negotiation, people in all cultures want to make the best deal possible. Given that this is true, Sagan (1995) provides us with a specific example of the principle of folk psychology suggested by Rosenberg:

The idea that critical thinking is the latest Western fad is silly. If you are buying a used car in Singapore or Bangkok—or a used chariot in ancient Susa or Rome—the same precautions will be useful as in Cambridge, Massachusetts. (p. 184)

As one further cross-cultural example, it is commonplace to suggest that nationalism is one of the strongest psychological forces in the world today.

These few and varied examples, many more of which could be provided, illustrate that high degrees of generalization are possible in psychology across different species, across different cultures, and across people engaged in a variety of different activities. The fact that generalization is possible in these circumstances is not something that was established a priori but rather is based on specific experience. It could not have been predicted ahead of time, nor could it have been precluded ahead of time. Experience is ultimately the only guide that informs us whether generalization is possible. The habit of contextualists and social constructionists to preclude on ontological grounds the possibility of generalization in a particular area, forever and for all time, is not defensible and/or sound scientific practice.

RANGE OF COGNITIVE ATTITUDES

In Kuhn's (1962) depiction of science, the displacement of one paradigm or theory by another is a monumental achievement, which he describes as akin to a conversion experience. This is because within a Kuhnian perspective, it is rare and almost impossible that a psychologist who adheres to one theory or paradigm will entertain—or even be capable of entertaining—another. Laudan (1996) offers a different point of view. From Laudan's perspective, it is commonplace and to be expected that a psychologist may work within several different theoretical frameworks. In the absence of the accept-reject dichotomy, so favored by Kuhn, the working psychologist who entertains a variety of attitudes toward theories is more or less easily persuaded to test the mettle of some newer, less established theory. We consider this to be one of the important differences between the approaches of Kuhn and Laudan. It more accurately describes how at least some psychologists work, and it is to be desired that psychologists approach the problems of their field in the open-minded manner suggested by Laudan. In effect, adopting Laudan's position, a psychologist may choose to work with one theory, even a less well-established theory, perhaps discovering in the process that it has a variety of advantages over its competitors. In our view, this is the way science is done.

It would appear that social constructionists and contextualists adhere more to Kuhn's point of view than to Laudan's, and we think that the reason for this is fairly clear. The tendency in those camps is to evaluate mainstream psychology in terms of their own ontological and epistemological categories. Because these are not the categories favored by mainstream psychology, the only result is the wholesale rejection of the field. As indicated earlier, we think that from a pragmatic point of view, this is an unsound strategy. Mainstream psychologists are apt to reject this method of evaluation not because of ontological or epistemological reasons but because it simply is not the way they operate. Within mainstream psychology, even wildly different ontological and epistemological approaches get a hearing. But the hearing is at the level of empirics. To put it bluntly, a mainstream psychologist is less interested in any abstract reasons one might have for accepting a particular ontology than he or she is in what the empirical consequences of that ontology might be. An example of what we have in mind is available from Sagan's (1995) recent book, *The Demon-Haunted World.*

In the book, Sagan (1995) is confronted with the belief of a person that a fire-breathing dragon resides in his garage, as described earlier in Chapter 2. It is our view that Sagan's ontology is such as to give low probability to the existence of fire-breathing dragons. Nevertheless, Sagan does not dismiss the claim of a fire-breathing dragon with logical, epistemological, or ontological arguments. Rather, as indicated previously, he goes about evaluating the claim empirically. Sagan suggests a series of tests to evaluate the possibility that a dragon resides in the garage. For example, he suggests putting flour on the floor of the garage so as to detect the footprints of the dragon. However, he is told that the test is not useful because the dragon floats in the air. Sagan suggests a number of other tests, all of which for one reason or another are deemed inappropriate. But Sagan does not let the matter rest there. Finding no positive evidence of a fire-breathing dragon, he then goes on to suggest that perhaps one should widen the investigation to include the possible reasons why the person is making such claims. If such good reasons are found and there is no evidence of a fire-breathing dragon, then Sagan suggests we have little reason to believe in the existence of the creature, although that possibility cannot be ruled out with certainty.

We suggest that there are good reasons for social constructionists and contextualists to abandon their exclusive concern with ontological and epistemological evaluation of rival approaches and to operate a bit more like Sagan. We think it would be marvelous if contextualists would examine and evaluate severely the empirical products of mainstream psychologists and, if finding them deficient in some respects, would so indicate. It would be even more marvelous if the deficient empirics were replaced by something better. There would seem to be two substantial reasons for operating in this manner. It would appear to be the way in which progress is made in science. Pragmatically, it would appear to be not only the best way but perhaps the only way for contextualists to extend their influence into mainstream psychology and to attract the attention of mainstream psychologists.

CONTEXTUALISM'S GREATEST FALLACY

Contextualists, social constructionists, and other postmodernists are of the opinion that in the absence of the proper ontological assumptions, nothing that is meaningful, either empirically or theoretically, can result. There are many examples of this fallacious reasoning, only one of which will be cited here. Lee (1988) suggests that psychology's first task is to establish categories through ontological analysis that "hold the promise of leading to a body of reliable and extraordinary knowledge" (p. 27). In the absence of establishing such categories, Lee suggests that little will be accomplished. She says,

> The first task of a pristine science is not to perform experiments and to elaborate mathematical theories. It is to identify the kinds (i.e., classes) of concrete particulars that constitute the special domain of the science. The enthusiastic pursuit of experimentation and mathematics without first dealing with this qualitative task is scientistic rather than scientific. (pp. 28-29)

Not everybody shares this opinion. For example, Laudan (1996) has said,

> We can, and often do, talk without contradiction about a certain sequence of events representing progress even though the final products of that sequence are far from what the actors intended. It is a cliché that actions have unintended consequences. Because they do, it can happen that those unintended consequences eventually come to be regarded as more worthwhile than the goals which the actors were originally striving for. (p. 139)

Even a cursory examination of the historical record will serve to show that great scientists often produced monumental accomplishments that not only had little to do with some of their more important ontological assumptions but were actually contrary to those assumptions. For example, Charles Darwin, whose contribution to psychology can hardly be overrated, in his book, *The Descent of Man and Selection in Relation to Sex* (1871/1981), exhibited a naïveté that would be uncharacteristic today. The reference here is to Darwin's uncritical use of anecdotes to ascribe higher mental capacities to animals. Newton, clearly one of the great scientists of all time, is reported to have spent as much time on alchemy as on physics. Ironically, Kepler, whose contributions to astronomy were monumental, was a devout believer in astrology. Pythagorous, who contributed substantially to geometry, was a mystic who believed in, among other things, the transmigration of souls. To cite one last example, Fechner, who attempted to solve the age-old problem of mind and body, produced a psychophysics that was and continues to be employed in experimental psychology for entirely different reasons. These few examples amply demonstrate that the relationship between one's background assumptions and the ultimate contribution that results with them is hardly as straightforward as the contextualists and their postmodern allies would have us believe. Contextualists would be well-advised to abandon the belief that good science can only result from a particular set of ontological propositions, those they favor, and to join in the scientific fray with the rest of us. If they do not join in the battle, then from the viewpoint of mainstream psychology, they are more apt to be classified as false prophets than as saviors of the field.

SUMMARY AND CONCLUSIONS

It was suggested that, potentially, contextualism and mainstream psychology have much to offer each other. However, before this potential may be transformed into actuality, certain rules of the game will have to be observed. It was noted that each side, when discussing the other, engages in what can only be called gross caricature. Each side must replace this with a more realistic appraisal of the other side if reciprocal influence is to be achieved. It was noted that each side, when discussing the other, does not always provide relevant arguments. For example, contextualists and social constructionists seem to judge mainstream psychology inadequate because of the specific ontological assumptions it employs. Social constructionists tend to favor nonexperimental methods and suggest in addition that experimentation as a method is sterile. Mainstream psychologists, on the other hand, tend to emphasize experimentation and downplay ontology. It was suggested that methods should be evaluated on the same basis as other empirical claims. This approach is known as naturalism. Social constructionists and contextualists tend to think that generalization from one species to another or from one culture to another is limited at best. We suggested that whether in a particular circumstance generalization is efficacious is an empirical matter that cannot be decided a priori. It was suggested that a prominent of feature of contextualism and other postmodern movements is to suggest that reasonable science is impossible in the absence of proper ontological assumptions. Specific historical examples to the contrary were cited, and it was recommended that this point of view be abandoned for a more reasonable one.

References

Abelson, R. P. (1995). *Statistics as principled argument*. Hillsdale, NJ: Lawrence Erlbaum.

Adams, J. A. (1984). Learning of movement sequences. *Psychological Bulletin, 96,* 3-28.

Alford, B. A. (1993). Contextualistic behaviorism, radical behaviorism, and cognitive therapy: A dialogue on clinical behavior therapy. *Behavior Therapist, 24,* 201-203.

Allison, J. (1989). The nature of reinforcement. In S. B. Klein & R. R. Mowrer (Eds.), *Contemporary learning theories* (pp. 13-39). Hillsdale, NJ: Lawrence Erlbaum.

Altman, I., & Rogoff, B. (1987). World views in psychology: Trait, interactional, organismic, and transactional. In B. Stokols & I. Altman (Eds.), *Handbook of environmental psychology* (pp. 7-40). New York: John Wiley.

Baddeley, A. D. (1982). Domains of recollection. *Psychological Review, 89,* 708-729.

Balsam, P. D. (1985). The functions of context in learning and performance. In P. D. Balsam & A. Tomie (Eds.), *Context and learning* (pp. 1-21). Hillsdale, NJ: Lawrence Erlbaum.

Balsam, P. D., & Tomie, A. (Eds.). (1985). *Context and learning*. Hillsdale, NJ: Lawrence Erlbaum.

Baltes, P. B. (1979, Summer). On the potential and limits of child development: Life-span developmental perspectives. *Society for Research in Child Development,* pp. 1-4.

Baltes, P. B. (1987). Theoretical propositions of life-span developmental psychology: On the dynamics between growth and decline. *Developmental Psychology, 23,* 611-626.

Barnes, B. (1982). *T. S. Kuhn and social science*. New York: Columbia University Press.

Barnes, B., Bloor, D., & Henry, J. (1996). *Scientific knowledge: A sociological analysis*. Chicago: University of Chicago Press.

Bechtel, W. (1988). *Philosophy of science: An overview for cognitive science*. Hillsdale, NJ: Lawrence Erlbaum.

Bernstein, R. J. (1983). *Beyond objectivism and relativism*. Philadelphia: University of Pennsylvania Press.

Biglan, A. (1993). A functional contextualist framework for community interventions. In S. C. Hayes, L. J. Hayes, H. W. Reese, & T. R. Sarbin (Eds.), *Varieties of scientific contextualism* (pp. 251-276). Reno, NV: Context Press.

Biglan, A. (1995). Choosing a paradigm to guide prevention research and practice. *Drugs & Society, 8,* 149-160.

Biglan, A., & Hayes, S. C. (1996). Should the behavioral sciences become more pragmatic? The case for functional contextualism in research on human behavior. *Applied & Preventative Psychology, 5,* 47-57.

Blackman, D. E. (1993). Mechanism and contextualism in behavioral pharmacology. *The Behavior Analyst, 16,* 237-239.

Blank, T. O. (1986). Contextual and relational perspectives on adult psychology. In R. L. Rosnow & M. Georgoudi (Eds.), *Contextualism and understanding in behavioral science: Implications for research and theory* (pp. 105-124). New York: Praeger.

Bransford, J. D. (1979). *Human cognition: Learning, understanding, and remembering.* Belmont, CA: Brooks/Cole.

Bruner, J. S. (1990). *Acts of meaning.* Cambridge, MA: Harvard University Press.

Bruner, J. S., & Minturn, A. L. (1955). Perceptual identification and perceptual organization. *Journal of General Psychology, 53,* 21-28.

Buss, A. R. (1979). *A dialectical psychology.* New York: Irvington.

Callebaut, W. (1993). *Taking the naturalistic turn or how the real philosophy of science is done.* Chicago: University of Chicago Press.

Capaldi, E. J., & Proctor, R. W. (1994). Contextualism: Is the act in context the appropriate metaphor for scientific psychology? *Psychonomic Bulletin & Review, 1,* 239-249.

Catania, A. C. (1984). *Learning* (2nd ed.). Englewood Cliffs, NJ: Prentice Hall.

Chaiklin, S. (1991). From theory to practice and back again: What does postmodern philosophy contribute to psychological science? In S. Kvale (Ed.), *Psychology and postmodernism* (pp. 194-208). Newbury Park, CA: Sage.

Chandler, M. J. (1993). Contextualism and the post-modern condition: Learning from Las Vegas. In S. C. Hayes, L. J. Hayes, H. W. Reese, & T. R. Sarbin (Eds.), *Varieties of scientific contextualism* (pp. 227-247). Reno, NV: Context Press.

Chase, W. G., & Ericsson, K. A. (1981). Skilled memory. In J. R. Anderson (Ed.), *Cognitive skills and their acquisition* (pp. 141-189). Hillsdale, NJ: Lawrence Erlbaum.

Chomsky, N. (1959). Review of B. F. Skinner's *Verbal Behavior. Language, 35,* 26-58.

Cicirelli, V. G. (1992). *Family caregiving: Autonomous and paternalistic decision making.* Newbury Park, CA: Sage.

Cicirelli, V. G. (1994). The individual in the family life cycle. In L. L'Abate (Ed.), *Handbook of developmental family psychology and psychopathology* (pp. 27-43). New York: John Wiley.

Comunidad Los Horcones. (1990). "Personocracy: A government based on the science of behavior analysis. *Revista Latinoamericana de Psicologia, 22,* 111-130.

Cooper, C. R. (1987). Conceptualizing research on adolescent development in the family: Four root metaphors. *Journal of Adolescent Research, 2,* 321-330.

Costall, A., & Still, A. (Eds.). (1987). *Cognitive psychology in question.* Brighton, UK: Harvester Wheatsheaf.

Crabb, P. B. (1988). A contextual psychology? The curious case of behavior-analytic theory. *Theoretical and Philosophical Psychology, 8,* 28-34.

Curd, M., & Cover, J. A. (Eds.). (1998). *Philosophy of science: The central issues.* New York: Norton.

Dampier, W. C. (1949). *A history of science and its relations with philosophy and religion* (4th ed.). Cambridge, UK: Cambridge University Press.

Darwin, C. (1981). *The descent of man and selection in relation to sex.* Princeton, NJ: Princeton University Press. (Original publication 1871)

Davies, G. M., & Thomson, D. M. (Eds.). (1988). *Memory in context: Context in memory.* Chichester, UK: Wiley.

Deese, J. (1985). *American freedom and the social sciences.* New York: Columbia University Press.

Deese, J. (1993). Human abilities versus intelligence. *Intelligence, 17,* 107-116.

Deese, J. (1996). Contextualism: Truth in advertising. *The General Psychologist, 32,* 56-61.

Dougher, M. J. (1993). Interpretive and hermeneutic research methods in the contextualist analysis of verbal behavior. In S. C. Hayes, L. J. Hayes, H. W. Reese, & T. R. Sarbin (Eds.), *Varieties of scientific contextualism* (pp. 211-221). Reno, NV: Context Press.

du Preez, P. (1991). *A science of mind.* San Diego, CA: Academic Press.

Earman, J. (1993). Carnap, Kuhn, and the philosophy of scientific methodology. In P. Horwich (Ed.), *World changes: Thomas Kuhn and the nature of science* (pp. 9-36). Cambridge: MIT Press.

Efran, J. S., Germer, C. K., & Lukens, M. D. (1986). Contextualism and psychotherapy. In R. L. Rosnow & M. Georgoudi (Eds.), *Contextualism and understanding in behavioral science: Implications for research and theory* (pp. 169-186). New York: Praeger.

Einstein, A. (1951). Autobiographical notes. In P. A. Schilpp (Ed.), *Albert Einstein: Philosopher-scientist* (pp. 1-95). New York: Tudor.

Feyerabend, P. (1970). Consolations for the specialist. In I. Lakatos & A. Musgrave (Eds.), *Criticism and the growth of knowledge* (pp. 197-230). New York: Cambridge University Press.

Fish, S. (1980). *Is there a text in this class?* Cambridge, MA: Harvard University Press.

Fletcher, G. (1995). *The scientific credibility of folk psychology.* Mahwah, NJ: Lawrence Erlbaum.

Fodor, J. A. (1974). Special sciences (or: Disunity of science as a working hypothesis). *Synthese, 28,* 97-115.

Ford, D. H., & Lerner, R. M. (1992). *Developmental systems theory: An integrative approach.* Newbury Park, CA: Sage.

Fosnot, C. T. (1996). Preface. In C. T. Fosnot (Ed.), *Constructivism: Theory, perspectives, and practice* (pp. ix-xi). New York: Teachers College Press.

Fox, N. J. (1993). *Postmodernism, sociology and health.* Buckingham, PA: Open University Press.

Franklin, B. et al. (1970). Rapport des commissaires chargés par le roi de l'examen du magnétisme animal (Report of the commissioners charged by the king to examine animal magnetism). In M. W. Tinterow (Ed.), *Foundations of hypnosis: From Mesmer to Freud* (pp. 82-128). Springfield, IL: Charles C Thomas. (Original work published 1784)

Geertz, C. (1973). *The interpretation of cultures.* New York: Basic Books.

Georgoudi, M. (1983). Modern dialectics in social psychology: A reappraisal. *European Journal of Social Psychology, 13,* 77-93.

Gergen, K. J. (1973). Social psychology as history. *Journal of Personality and Social Psychology, 26,* 309-320.

Gergen, K. J. (1985). The social constructionist movement in modern psychology. *American Psychologist, 40,* 266-275.

Gergen, K. J. (1988). If persons are texts. In S. Messer, L. Sass, & R. Woolfolk (Eds.), *Hermeneutics and psychological theory: Interpretive perspectives on personality, psychotherapy, and psychopathology* (pp. 28-51). New Brunswick, NJ: Rutgers University Press.

Gergen, K. J. (1992). Toward a postmodern psychology. In S. Kvale (Ed.), *Psychology and postmodernism* (pp. 17-30). Newbury Park, CA: Sage.

Gergen, K. J., & Gergen, M. M. (1991). Toward reflexive methodologies. In F. Steier (Ed.), *Research and reflexivity* (pp. 76-94). Newbury Park, CA: Sage.

Gergen, K. J., Gulerce, A., Lock, A., & Misra, G. (1996). Psychological science in cultural contexts. *American Psychologist, 51,* 496-503.

Gholson, B., & Barker, P. (1985). Kuhn, Lakatos, and Laudan: Applications in the history of physics and psychology. *American Psychologist, 40,* 755-769.

Gibson, R. F., Jr. (1982). *The philosophy of W. V. Quine: An expository essay.* Tampa: University of South Florida.

Giere, R. N. (1985). Philosophy of science naturalized. *Philosophy of Science, 52,* 331-356.

Gillespie, D. (1992). *The mind's we: Contextualism in cognitive psychology.* Carbondale: Southern Illinois University Press.

Giorgi, A. (1995). Phenomenological psychology. In J. A. Smith, R. Harré, & L. Van Langenhove (Eds.), *Rethinking psychology* (pp. 24-42). Thousand Oaks, CA: Sage.

Goodman, R. B. (Ed.). (1995). *Pragmatism: A contemporary reader.* New York: Routledge Kegan Paul.

Gross, P. R., & Levitt, N. (1994). *Higher superstition: The academic left and its quarrels with science.* Baltimore, MD: Johns Hopkins University Press.

Guba, E. G. (1990). The alternative paradigm dialog. In E. G. Guba (Ed.), *The paradigm dialog* (pp. 17-27). Newbury Park, CA: Sage.

Hall, G. (1991). *Perceptual and associative learning.* Oxford, UK: Clarendon.

Halliday, D., & Resnick, R. (1966). *Physics* (Parts I and II). New York: John Wiley.

Harlow, H. F. (1950). Analysis of discrimination learning by monkeys. *Journal of Experimental Psychology, 40,* 26-39.

Harré, R. (1990). Exploring the human *Umwlet'.* In R. Bhaskar (Ed.), *Harré and his critics.* Oxford, UK: Basil Blackwell.

Harré, R. (1993). *Social being* (2nd ed.). Oxford, UK: Basil Blackwell.

Harré, R., & Gillet, G. (1994). *The discursive mind.* Thousand Oaks, CA: Sage.

Harré, R., & Stearns, P. (Eds.). (1995). *Discursive psychology in practice.* Thousand Oaks, CA: Sage.

Hayes, S. C. (1986). Behavioral philosophy in the late 1980's. *Theoretical & Philosophical Psychology, 6,* 39-43.

Hayes, S. C. (1987). A contextual approach to therapeutic change. In N. Jacobson (Ed.), *Psychotherapists in clinical practice* (pp. 327-387). New York: Guilford.

Hayes, S. C. (1988). Contextualism and the next wave of behavioral psychology. *Behavior Analysis, 23,* 7-22.

Hayes, S. C. (1993). Analytic goals and the varieties of scientific contextualism. In S. C. Hayes, L. J. Hayes, H. W. Reese, & T. R. Sarbin (Eds.), *Varieties of scientific contextualism* (pp. 11-27). Reno, NV: Context Press.

Hayes, S. C., & Hayes, L. J. (1989). Is behavior analysis contextualistic? *Theoretical & Philosophical Psychology, 9,* 37-40.

Hayes, S. C., & Hayes, L. J. (1992). Some clinical implications of contextualistic behaviorism: The example of cognition. *Behavior Therapy, 23,* 225-249.

Hayes, S. C., Hayes, L. J., & Reese, H. W. (1988). Finding the philosophical core: A review of Stephen C. Pepper's world hypotheses: A study of evidence. *Journal of the Experimental Analysis of Behavior, 50,* 97-111.

Hayes, S. C., Hayes, L. J., Reese, H. W., & Sarbin, T. R. (Eds.). (1993). *Varieties of scientific contextualism.* Reno, NV: Context Press.

Heilbrunn, J. (1994). The revision thing: Who is to blame for the cold war? A new quarrel. *The New Republic, 211* (7), 31-39.

Hilgard, E. R. (1987). *Psychology in America: A historical survey.* San Diego, CA: Harcourt Brace Jovanovich.

Hoffman, R. R., & Nead, J. M. (1983). General contextualism, ecological science, and cognitive research. *Journal of Mind and Behavior, 4,* 507-560.

Holt, N. R. (1977). Wilhelm Ostwald's "The Bridge." *British Journal for the History of Science, 10,* 146-150.

Holton, G. (1988). *Thematic origins of scientific thought: Kepler to Einstein.* Cambridge, MA: Harvard University Press.

Hommel, B., & Prinz, W. (Eds.). (1997). *Theoretical issues in stimulus-response compatibility.* Amsterdam: North-Holland.

Hoyningen-Huene, P. (1993). *Reconstructing scientific revolutions: Thomas S. Kuhn's philosophy of science* (A. T. Levine, Trans.). Chicago: University of Chicago Press.

Hull, C. L. (1943). *Principles of behavior.* New York: Appleton-Century-Crofts.

Hume, D. (1993). *An enquiry concerning human understanding.* Indianapolis, IN: Hackett.

Jaeger, M. E., & Rosnow, R. L. (1988). Contextualism and its implications for psychological inquiry. *British Journal of Psychology, 79,* 63-75.

James, W. (1975). *Pragmatism: A new name for some old ways of thinking.* Cambridge, MA: Harvard University Press. (Original work published 1907)

James, W. (1976). *Essays in radical empiricism.* Cambridge, MA: Harvard University Press. (Original work published 1912)

Jenkins, J. J. (1979). Four points to remember: A tetrahedral model of memory experiments. In L. S. Cermak & F. I. M. Craik (Eds.), *Levels of processing in human memory* (pp. 429-446). Hillsdale, NJ: Lawrence Erlbaum.

John-Steiner, V. (1997). *Notebooks of the mind: Explorations of thinking* (Rev. ed.). New York: Oxford University Press.

Johnston, J. M., & Pennypacker, H. S. (1980). *Strategies and tactics of human behavioral research.* Hillsdale, NJ: Lawrence Erlbaum.

Jurden, F. H., & Reese, H. W. (1992). Educational context differences in prose recall in adulthood. *Journal of Genetic Psychology, 153,* 275-291.

Kantor, J. R. (1959). *Interbehavioral psychology.* Granville, OH: Principia Press.

Kazdin, A. E. (1994). *Behavior modification in applied settings.* Pacific Grove, CA: Brooks/Cole.

Kendler, T. S. (1986). World views and the concept of development: A reply to Lerner and Kauffman. *Developmental Review, 6,* 80-95.

Kim, J. (1988). What is "naturalized epistemology?" *Philosophical Perspectives, 2,* 381-405.

Kitcher, P. (1993). *The advancement of science: Science without legend, objectivity without illusion.* New York: Oxford University Press.

Klatzky, R. L. (1980). *Human memory: Structure and processes* (2nd ed.). San Francisco: W. H. Freeman.

Koenderink, J. J., Kappers, A. M. L., Pollick, F. E., & Kawato, M. (1997). Correspondence in pictorial space. *Perception & Psychophysics, 59,* 813-827.

Kuhn, T. S. (1962). *The structure of scientific revolutions.* Chicago: University of Chicago Press.

Kuhn, T. S. (1970a). Logic of discovery or psychology of research? In I. Lakatos & A. Musgrave (Eds.), *Criticism and the growth of knowledge* (pp. 1-23). New York: Cambridge University Press.

Kuhn, T. S. (1970b). Reflections on my critics. In I. Lakatos & A. Musgrave (Eds.), *Criticism and the growth of knowledge* (pp. 231-278). New York: Cambridge University Press.

Kuhn, T. S. (1977). *The essential tension: Selected studies in scientific tradition and change.* Chicago: University of Chicago Press.

Kvale, S. (1992a). Introduction: From archeology of the psyche to the architecture of cultural landscapes. In S. Kvale (Ed.), *Psychology and postmodernism* (pp. 1-16). Newbury Park, CA: Sage.

Kvale, S. (1992b). Postmodern psychology: A contradiction in terms? In S. Kvale (Ed.), *Psychology and postmodernism* (pp. 31-57). Newbury Park, CA: Sage.

Kvale, S. (1994). *InterViews: An introduction to qualitative research interviewing.* Thousand Oaks, CA: Sage.

Lachman, R., Lachman, J. L., & Butterfield, E. C. (1979). *Cognitive psychology and information processing: An introduction.* Hillsdale, NJ: Lawrence Erlbaum.

Lakatos, I. (1970). Falsification and the methodology of scientific research programmes. In I. Lakatos & A. Musgrave (Eds.), *Criticism and the growth of knowledge* (pp. 91-196). New York: Cambridge University Press.

Lakatos, I. (1978). *The methodology of scientific research programmes.* Cambridge, UK: Cambridge University Press.

Lashley, K. S. (1951). The problem of serial order in behavior. In L. A. Jeffress (Ed.), *Cerebral mechanisms in behavior: The Hixon symposium* (pp. 112-136). New York: John Wiley.

Laudan, L. (1977). *Progress and its problems.* Berkeley: University of California Press.

Laudan, L. (1984). *Science and its values: The aims of science and their roles in scientific debate.* Berkeley: University of California Press.

Laudan, L. (1990). *Science and relativism: Some key controversies in the philosophy of science.* Chicago: University of Chicago Press.

Laudan, L. (1996). *Beyond positivism and relativism: Theory, method, and evidence.* Boulder, CO: Westview.

Leahey, T. H. (1992). *A history of psychology* (3rd ed.). Englewood Cliffs, NJ: Prentice Hall.

Lee, V. L. (1988). *Beyond behaviorism.* Hillsdale, NJ: Lawrence Erlbaum.

Lerner, R. M. (1985). Individual and context in developmental psychology: Conceptual and theoretical issues. In J. Nesselroade & A. von Eye (Eds.), *Individual development and social change: Explanatory analysis* (pp. 155-187). New York: Academic Press.

Lerner, R. M. (1990). Weaving development into the fabric of personality and social psychology: On the significance of Bandura's *Social Foundations of Thought and Action. Psychological Inquiry, 1,* 92-95.

Lerner, R. M. (1993). Human development: A developmental contextual perspective. In S. C. Hayes, L. J. Hayes, H. W. Reese, & T. R. Sarbin (Eds.), *Varieties of scientific contextualism* (pp. 301-316). Reno, NV: Context Press.

Lerner, R. M., & Kauffman, M. B. (1985). The concept of development in contextualism. *Developmental Review, 5,* 309-333.

Liddle, H. A. (1987). Family psychology: The journal, the field. *Journal of Family Psychology, 1,* 5-22.

Longino, H. (1998). Values and objectivity. In M. Curd & J. A. Cover (Eds.), *Philosophy of science: The central issues* (pp. 170-191). New York: Norton.

Mach, E. (1959). *The analysis of sensations* (C. M. Williams, Trans.). New York: Dover. (Original work published 1906)

Mackintosh, N. J. (1974). *The psychology of animal learning.* New York: Academic Press.

Mancuso, J. C. (1993). Personal construct systems in the context of action. In S. C. Hayes, L. J. Hayes, H. W. Reese, & T. R. Sarbin (Eds.), *Varieties of scientific contextualism* (pp. 111-133). Reno, NV: Context Press.

Manicas, P. T., & Secord, P. F. (1983). Implications for psychology of the new philosophy of science. *American Psychologist, 38,* 399-413.

Marr, M. J. (1993). Contextualistic mechanism or mechanistic contextualism? The straw machine as tar baby. *The Behavior Analyst, 16,* 59-65.

McCurry, S. M. (1993). Discussion of Sarbin: Metaphor and method in the narratory principle. In S. C. Hayes, L. J. Hayes, H. W. Reese, & T. R. Sarbin (Eds.), *Varieties of scientific contextualism* (pp. 66-69). Reno, NV: Context Press.

McGuire, W. J. (1983). A contextualist theory of knowledge: Its implications for innovation and reform in psychological research. In L. Berkowitz (Ed.), *Advances in experimental social psychology* (Vol. 16, pp. 1-47). New York: Academic Press.

Medin, D. L., & Reynolds, T. J. (1985). Cue-context interactions in discrimination, categorization, and memory. In P. D. Balsam & A. Tomie (Eds.), *Context and learning* (pp. 323-356). Hillsdale, NJ: Lawrence Erlbaum.

Merriam-Webster's new collegiate dictionary (9th ed.). (1987). Springfield, MA: Merriam-Webster.

Morris, E. K. (1982). Some relationships between interbehavioral psychology and radical behaviorism. *Behaviorism, 10,* 187-216.

Morris, E. K. (1988). Contextualism: The world view of behavior analysis. *Journal of Experimental Child Psychology, 46,* 289-323.

Morris, E. K. (1991). The contextualism that is behavior analysis: An alternative to cognitive psychology. In A. Still & A. Costall (Eds.), *Against cognitivism: Alternative foundations for cognitive psychology* (pp. 123-149). Hempstead, UK: Harvester Wheatsheaf.

Morris, E. K. (1993a). Behavior analysis and mechanism: One is not the other. *The Behavior Analyst, 16,* 25-43.

Morris, E. K. (1993b). Contextualism, historiography, and the history of behavior analysis. In S. C. Hayes, L. J. Hayes, H. W. Reese, & T. R. Sarbin (Eds.), *Varieties of scientific contextualism* (pp. 137-165). Reno, NV: Context Press.

Muenzinger, K. F. (1928). Plasticity and mechanization of the problem box habit in guinea pigs. *Journal of Comparative Psychology, 8,* 45-69.

Muenzinger, K. F., Koerner, L., & Irey, E. (1929). Variability of an habitual movement in guinea pigs. *Journal of Comparative Psychology, 9,* 425-436.

Newman, B. (1993). Discriminating utopian from dystopian literature: Why is *Walden Two* considered a dystopia? *The Behavior Analyst, 16,* 167-175.

Nicolson, P. (1995). Feminism and psychology. In J. A. Smith, R. Harré, & L. Van Langenhove (Eds.), *Rethinking psychology* (pp. 122-142). Thousand Oaks, CA: Sage.

Overton, W. F. (1984). World views and their influence on psychological theory and research: Kuhn-Lakatos-Laudan. In H. W. Reese (Ed.), *Advances in child development and behavior* (Vol. 18, pp. 191-226). Orlando, FL: Academic Press.

Overton, W. F., & Reese, H. (1973). Models of development: Methodological implications. In J. R. Nesselroade & H. W. Reese (Eds.), *Life-span developmental psychology: Methodological issues* (pp. 65-86). New York: Academic Press.

Pashler, H. E. (1998). *The psychology of attention.* Cambridge: MIT Press.

Pashler, H. E., & Carrier, M. (1996). Structures, processes, and the flow of information. In E. L. Bjork & R. A. Bjork (Eds.), *Memory* (pp. 3-29). San Diego, CA: Academic Press.

Pepper, S. C. (1942). *World hypotheses.* Berkeley: University of California Press.

Pfeffer, J. (1993). Barriers to the advance of organizational science: Paradigm development as a dependent variable. *Academy of Management Review, 18,* 599-620.

Phillips, D. C. (1990). Postpositivistic science: Myths and realities. In E. G. Guba (Ed.), *The paradigm dialog* (pp. 31-45). Newbury Park, CA: Sage.

Polkinghorne, D. (1990). Psychology after philosophy. In J. E. Faulconer & R. N. Williams (Eds.), *Reconsidering psychology: Perspectives from continental philosophy* (pp. 92-115). Pittsburgh, PA: Duquesne University Press.

Polkinghorne, D. (1992). Postmodern epistemology of practice. In S. Kvale (Ed.), *Psychology and postmodernism* (pp. 146-165). Newbury Park, CA: Sage.

Popper, K. R. (1959). *The logic of scientific discovery.* New York: Basic Books.

Popper, K. R. (1970). Normal science and its dangers. In I. Lakatos & A. Musgrave (Eds.), *Criticism and the growth of knowledge* (pp. 51-58). New York: Cambridge University Press.

Posner, M. I. (1982). Cumulative development of attentional theory. *American Psychologist, 37,* 168-179.

Postman, L. (1972). A pragmatic view of organization theory. In E. Tulving & W. Donaldson (Eds.), *Organization of memory* (pp. 3-48). New York: Academic Press.

Prawat, R. S., & Floden, R. E. (1994). Philosophic perspectives on constructivist views of learning. *Educational Psychology, 29,* 37-48.

Proctor, R. W., & Reeve, T. G. (Eds.). (1990). *Stimulus-response compatibility: An integrated perspective.* Amsterdam: North-Holland.

Quine, W. V. (1953). Two dogmas of empiricism. In W. V. Quine (Ed.), *From a logical point of view* (pp. 20-46). New York: Harper.

Quine, W. V. (1970). On the reasons for indeterminacy of translation. *Journal of Philosophy, 67,* 179-183.

Quine, W. V. (1975). On empirically equivalent systems of the world. *Erkenntnis, 9,* 313-328.

Reber, A. S. (1993). *Implicit learning and tacit knowledge: An essay on the cognitive unconscious.* New York: Oxford University Press.

Reese, H. W. (1991). Contextualism in developmental psychology. In H. W. Reese (Ed.), *Advances in child development and behavior* (Vol. 23, pp. 187-230). Orlando, FL: Academic Press.

Reese, H. W. (1993). Contextualism and dialectical materialism. In S. C. Hayes, L. J. Hayes, H. W. Reese, & T. R. Sarbin (Eds.), *Varieties of scientific contextualism* (pp. 71-105). Reno, NV: Context Press.

Reese, H. W., & Overton, W. F. (1970). Models of development and theories of development. In L. R. Goulet & P. B. Baltes (Eds.), *Life-span developmental psychology: Research and theory* (pp. 115-145). New York: Academic Press.

Rescorla, R. A., Durlach, P. J., & Grau, J. W. (1985). Contextual learning in Pavlovian conditioning. In P. D. Balsam & A. Tomie (Eds.), *Context and learning* (pp. 23-56). Hillsdale, NJ: Lawrence Erlbaum.

Roediger, H. L., III (1980). Memory metaphors in cognitive psychology. *Memory & Cognition, 8,* 231-246.

Rorty, R. (1989). *Contingency, irony, and solidarity.* Cambridge, UK: Cambridge University Press.

Rosenberg, A. (1995). *Philosophy of social science* (2nd ed.). Boulder, CO: Westview.

Rosnow, R. L., & Georgoudi, M. (1986). The spirit of contextualism. In R. L. Rosnow & M. Georgoudi (Eds.), *Contextualism and understanding in behavioral science: Implications for research and theory* (pp. 3-22). New York: Praeger.

Rychlak, J. F. (1981). *Introduction to personality and psychotherapy.* Boston: Houghton Mifflin.

Sagan, C. (1995). *The demon-haunted world.* New York: Random House.

Santillana, G. de, & Zilsel, E. (1941). The development of rationalism and empiricism. In O. Neurath, R. Camap, & C. Morris (Eds.), *International encyclopedia of unified science* (Vol. 2, No. 8). Chicago: University of Chicago Press.

Sarbin, T. R. (1977). Contextualism: A world view for modern psychology. In A. Landfield (Ed.), *Nebraska symposium on motivation, 1976: Personal construct psychology* (pp. 1-41). Lincoln: University of Nebraska Press.

Sarbin, T. R. (1990). Toward the obsolescence of the schizophrenia hypothesis. *Journal of Mind and Behavior, 11,* 259-284.

Sarbin, T. R. (1993). The narrative as the root metaphor for contextualism. In S. C. Hayes, L. J. Hayes, H. W. Reese, & T. R. Sarbin (Eds.), *Varieties of scientific contextualism* (pp. 51-65). Reno, NV: Context Press.

Sarbin, T. R., & McKechnie, G. E. (1986). Prospects for a contextualist theory of personality. In R. L. Rosnow & M. Georgoudi (Eds.), *Contextualism and understanding in behavioral science: Implications for research and theory* (pp. 187-207). New York: Praeger.

Scheffler, I. (1967). *Science and subjectivity.* Indianapolis, IN: Bobbs-Merrill.

Scheibe, K. E. (1993). Dramapsych: Getting serious about context. In S. C. Hayes, L. J. Hayes, H. W. Reese, & T. R. Sarbin (Eds.), *Varieties of scientific contextualism* (pp. 191-205). Reno, NV: Context Press.

Schmidt, F. (1997). Book review of *The Mismeasure of Man. Personnel Psychology, 50,* 485-489.

Schneider, K. J. (1998). Toward a science of the heart: Romanticism and the revival of psychology. *American Psychologist, 53,* 277-289.

Schneider, S. M., & Morris, E. K. (1992). Sequences of spaced responses: Behavioral units and the role of contiguity. *Journal of the Experimental Analysis of Behavior, 58,* 537-555.

Scriven, M. (1964). Views of human nature. In T. W. Wann (Ed.), *Behaviorism and phenomenology* (pp. 163-183). Chicago: University of Chicago Press.

Seligman, D. (1994). *A question of intelligence.* New York: Citadel.

Shanon, B. (1990). What is context? *Journal for the Theory of Social Behavior, 20,* 157-166.

Shanon, B. (1993). *The representational and the presentational: An essay on cognition and the study of mind.* New York: Harvester Wheatsheaf.

Shapere, D. (1984). *Reason and the search for knowledge.* Dordrecht, the Netherlands: D. Reidel.

Shotter, J. (1997). Artificial intelligence and the dialogical. *American Behavioral Scientist, 40,* 813-828.

Shull, R. L., & Lawrence, P. S. (1993). Is contextualism productive? *The Behavior Analyst, 16,* 241-243.

Shweder, R. A., & Sullivan, M. A. (1993). Cultural psychology: Who needs it? In *Annual review of psychology* (Vol. 44, pp. 497-523). Palo Alto, CA: Annual Reviews, Inc.

Skinner, B. F. (1948). *Walden Two.* New York: Macmillan.

Skinner, B. F. (1950). Are theories of learning necessary? *Psychological Review, 57,* 193-216.

Skinner, B. F. (1957). *Verbal behavior.* New York: Appleton-Century-Crofts.

Skinner, B. F. (1971). *Beyond freedom and dignity.* New York: Knopf.

Skinner, B. F. (1973). Answers for my critics. In H. Wheeler (Ed.), *Beyond the punitive society* (pp. 256-266). San Francisco: W. H. Freeman.

Skinner, B. F. (1988). Response to Stich's commentary, *Is behaviorism vacuous?* In A. C. Catania & S. Harnad (Eds.), *The selection of behavior: The operant psychology of B. F. Skinner: Comments and consequences* (pp. 364-365). New York: Cambridge University Press.

Slife, B. D., & Williams, R. N. (1995). *What's behind the research? Discovering hidden assumptions in the behavioral sciences.* Thousand Oaks, CA: Sage.

Slife, B. D., & Williams, R. N. (1997). Toward a theoretical psychology: Should a subdiscipline be formally recognized? *American Psychologist, 52,* 117-129.

Slobin, D. I. (1971). *Psycholinguistics.* Glenview, IL: Scott, Foresman.

Smith, J. A., Harré, R., & Van Langenhove, L. (Eds.). (1995a). *Rethinking methods in psychology.* Thousand Oaks, CA: Sage.

Smith, J. A., Harré, R., & Van Langenhove, L. (Eds.). (1995b). *Rethinking psychology.* Thousand Oaks, CA: Sage.

Smith, J., Staudinger, U. M., & Baltes, P. B. (1994). Occupational settings for facilitating wisdom-related knowledge: The sample case of clinical psychologists. *Journal of Consulting and Clinical Psychology, 62,* 989-999.

Smith, T. L. (1994). *Behavior and its causes.* Dordrecht, the Netherlands: Kluwer.

Snyderman, M., & Rothman, S. (1988). *The IQ controversy: The media and public policy.* New Brunswick, NJ: Transaction Books.

Spear, N. E., & Riccio, D. C. (1994). *Memory: Phenomena and principles.* Boston: Allyn & Bacon.

Spence, K. W. (1956). *Behavior theory and conditioning.* New Haven, CT: Yale University Press.

Spence, K. W. (1960). Operationism and theory in psychology. In *Behavior theory and learning: Selected papers of K. W. Spence* (pp. 3-16). Englewood Cliffs, NJ: Prentice Hall.

Staddon, J. E. R. (1993). Pepper with a pinch of psalt. *The Behavior Analyst, 16,* 245-250.

Steele, D. L., Hayes, S. C., & Brownstein, A. J. (1990). Reinforcement, stereotypy, and rule discovery. *Analysis of Verbal Behavior, 8,* 57-66.

Steier, F. (1991). Introduction: Research as self-reflexivity, self-reflexivity as a social process. In F. Steier (Ed.), *Research and reflexivity* (pp. 1-11). Newbury Park, CA: Sage.

Stuart-Hamilton, I. (1988). Review of *Cognitive Psychology in Question. Quarterly Journal of Experimental Psychology, 40A,* 411-412.

Szapocznik, J., & Kurtines, W. M. (1993). Family psychology and cultural diversity: Opportunities for theory, research, and application. *American Psychologist, 48,* 400-407.

Tarpy, R. M. (1997). *Contemporary learning theory and research.* New York: McGraw-Hill.

Taylor, E. (1996). *William James on consciousness beyond the margin.* Princeton, NJ: Princeton University Press.

Tolman, E. C. (1932). *Purposive behavior in animals and men.* New York: Appleton-Century-Crofts.

Tolman, E. C. (1959). Principles of purposive behavior. In S. Koch (Ed.), *Psychology: A study of a science* (pp. 92-157). New York: McGraw-Hill.

Turner, M. B. (1965). *Philosophy and the science of behavior.* New York: Appleton-Century-Crofts.

Van Langenhove, L. (1995). The theoretical foundations of experimental psychology and its alternatives. In J. A. Smith, R. Harré, & L. Van Langenhove (Eds.), *Rethinking psychology* (pp. 10-23). Thousand Oaks, CA: Sage.

von Glasersfeld, E. (1996). Introduction: Aspects of constructivism. In C. T. Fosnot (Ed.), *Constructivism: Theory, perspectives, and practice* (pp. 3-7). New York: Teachers College Press.

Vygotsky, L. S. (1960). *Razvitie vysshikh psikhicheskikh funktsii* (The development of higher mental functions). Moscow: APN.

Wallach, L., & Wallach, M. A. (1994). Gergen versus the mainstream: Are hypotheses in social psychology subject to empirical test? *Journal of Personality and Social Psychology, 67,* 233-242.

Warren, R. M. (1970). Perceptual restorations of missing speech sounds. *Science, 167,* 392-393.

Wickens, D. D. (1987). The dual meanings of context: Implications for research, theory, and applications. In D. S. Gorfein & R. R. Hoffman (Eds.), *Memory and learning: The Ebbinghaus centennial conference* (pp. 135-152). Hillsdale, NJ: Lawrence Erlbaum.

Wilson, E. O. (1998). *Consilience: The unity of knowledge.* New York: Knopf.

Woolfolk, R. L., Sass, L. A., & Messer, S. B. (1988). Introduction to hermeneutics. In S. B. Messer, L. A. Sass, & R. L. Woolfolk (Eds.), *Hermeneutics and psychological theory* (pp. 2-26). New Brunswick, NJ: Rutgers University Press.

Zahar, E. (1976). Why did Einstein's research programme supersede Lorentz's? In C. Howson (Ed.), *Method and appraisal in the physical sciences* (pp. 211-275). Cambridge, UK: Cambridge University Press.

Author Index

Abelson, R. P., 133, 175
Adams, J. A., 110, 175
Alford, B. A., 125, 175
Allison, J, 124, 175
Altman, I., 4, 11, 175

Baddeley, A. D., 113, 175
Balsam, P. D., 111, 175, 181
Baltes, P. B., 59, 62, 67, 94, 101, 175, 182-183
Barker, P., 5, 29, 132-133, 147-148, 177
Barnes, B., 30, 168-169, 175
Bechtel, W., 4, 27, 97, 159, 175
Bernstein, R. J., 30, 175
Biglan, A., 62, 65, 108, 135, 175
Blackman, D. E., 7, 117-118, 176
Blank, T. O., 56, 176
Bloor, D., 139, 168, 175
Bransford, J. D., 79, 176
Brownstein, A. J., 62, 184
Bruner, J. S., 1, 3-4, 7-8, 11-12, 14, 27, 54, 74, 76, 80, 83, 106, 112, 116, 129, 164, 176
Buss, A. R., 77, 176
Butterfield, E. C., 22, 180

Callebaut, W., 31, 152, 158, 163, 176
Capaldi, E. J., 42, 66, 127, 176
Carrier, M., 162, 181
Catania, A. C., 123, 176, 183
Chaiklin, S., 2, 15, 176

Chandler, M. J., 99, 176
Chase, W. G., 125, 176
Chomsky, N., 50, 125, 176
Cicirelli, V. G., 4, 51, 59-61, 63, 65, 95, 176
Comunidad Los Horcones, 115, 176
Cooper, C. R., 40, 176
Costall, A., 157, 176, 181
Cover, J. A., 30, 176, 180
Crabb, P. B., 57, 176
Curd, M., 30, 176, 180

Dampier, W. C., 23, 176
Davies, G. M., 112, 176
Deese, J., 4, 16, 54, 57-58, 64, 74-76, 165, 176
Dougher, M. J., 77, 177
du Preez, P., 49-50, 177

Earman, J., 32, 177
Efran, J. S., 57, 177
Einstein, A., 26, 41, 132-133, 135, 146, 177, 179, 184
Ericsson, K. A., 125, 176

Feyerabend, P., 5, 36, 139, 145, 148-150, 152, 163, 177
Fish, S., 79-80, 177
Fletcher, G., 80, 177
Floden, R. E., 87, 182
Fodor, J. A, 97, 177

Ford, D. H., 4, 7, 16, 59, 63, 92-94, 96, 98, 102-103, 105, 177
Fosnot, C. T., 10, 166, 177, 184
Fox, N. J., 9, 177
Franklin, B., 81, 177

Geertz, C., 6, 84-86, 177
Georgoudi, M., 56, 77, 176-177, 182
Gergen, K. J., 3, 14-15, 27, 55-56, 62, 69-70, 72, 74, 78-79, 85-86, 106, 128-129, 164-165, 177, 184
Gergen, M. M., 14-15, 72, 78, 177
Germer, C. K., 57, 177
Gholson, B., 5, 29, 132-133, 147-148, 177
Gibson, R. F., Jr., 151, 178
Giere, R. N., 31-32, 178
Gillespie, D., 3-4, 6-7, 12, 40-41, 51, 54, 65, 131, 178
Gillet, G., 86, 178
Giorgi, A., 77, 178
Goodman, R. B., 9, 11, 178
Gross, P. R., 46, 178
Guba, E. G., 11, 82, 115, 145, 166, 178, 181
Gulerce, A., 165, 177

Hall, G., 112, 178
Halliday, D., 96, 178
Harlow, H. F., 133, 178
Harré, R., 21, 27, 73-74, 84-86, 128-129, 166, 178, 181, 183-184
Hayes, L. J., 3-5, 7, 17, 39, 62-64, 105, 107-111, 113-114, 123-125, 129-131, 133, 135, 158, 175-178, 180-183
Hayes, S. C., 1, 3-5, 7, 12, 16-17, 39, 46, 59, 62-64, 67, 105-111, 113-114, 117, 123, 125, 129-131, 133, 135, 158, 175-178, 180-184
Heilbrunn, J., 45-46, 178
Henry, J., 168, 175
Hilgard, E. R., 26, 178
Hoffman, R. R., 56, 178, 184
Holt, N. R., 132, 178
Holton, G., 26, 179
Hommel, B., 168, 179
Hoyningen-Huene, P., 144, 179
Hull, C. L., 100, 131, 158, 179

Irey, E., 110, 181

Jaeger, M. E., 73, 179
James, W., 4, 9-11, 17, 26-27, 39, 53-54, 71, 179, 184
Jenkins, J. J., 112, 179
John-Steiner, V., 21, 179
Johnston, J. M., 106, 179
Jurden, F. H., 62, 179

Kantor, J. R., 39, 179
Kappers, A. M. L., 125, 179
Kauffman, M. B., 59, 63, 93, 99, 179-180
Kawato, M., 125, 179
Kazdin, A. E., 115, 179
Kendler, T. S., 48, 99, 179
Kim, J., 31, 179
Kitcher, P., 30, 36, 141, 179
Klatzky, R. L., 96, 179
Koenderink, J. J., 125, 179
Koerner, L., 110, 181
Kuhn, T. S., 5, 22, 25, 29-34, 36, 131-134, 136, 138, 144-150, 152, 154, 159-160, 163, 170, 175, 177, 179
Kurtines, W. M., 4, 184
Kvale, S., 15, 69, 75, 83, 161, 176-177, 179, 181

Lachman, J. L., 22, 180
Lachman, R., 22, 180
Lakatos, I., 29, 36, 132, 139, 163, 177, 179-181
Lashley, K. S., 95, 180
Laudan, L., 5, 24-25, 29-37, 132-135, 139-143, 146-149, 152-153, 156, 162-164, 170, 172, 177, 180
Lawrence, P. S., 105, 181, 183
Leahey, T. H., 5, 10, 21-22, 180
Lee, V. L., 59, 61-62, 64, 128, 156, 172, 180
Lerner, R. M., 4, 7, 12, 16, 46, 59, 63-65, 67, 92-94, 96-99, 102-103, 105, 177, 179-180
Levitt, N., 46, 178
Liddle, H. A., 4, 180
Lock, A., 165, 177
Longino, H., 135, 152, 160, 180
Lukens, M. D., 57, 177

Mach, E., 10, 17, 25-27, 132, 180
Mackintosh, N. J., 110, 180
Mancuso, J. C., 4, 65, 180
Manicas, P. T., 50, 180
Marr, M. J., 97, 105, 180
McCurry, S. M., 48, 180
McGuire, W. J., 47, 180
McKechnie, G. E., 57, 182
Medin, D. L., 112, 181
Messer, S. B., 77, 177, 184
Minturn, A. L., 112, 176
Misra, G., 165, 177
Morris, E. K., 3, 7, 39, 41, 46, 59-60, 62,
    64, 67, 108-111, 113-114, 123, 129,
    135, 158, 181, 183
Muenzinger, K. F., 109-110, 181

Nead, J. M., 56, 178
Newman, B., 116, 181
Nicolson, P., 10, 181

Overton, W. F., 48, 92, 105, 131, 181-182

Pashler, H. E., 72, 162, 181
Pennypacker, H. S., 106, 179
Pepper, S. C., 6, 39-44, 47-49, 52-53, 56,
    67, 70, 87, 93, 111, 114, 118-119,
    129-131, 133, 136, 151, 178, 181, 184
Pfeffer, J., 5, 181
Phillips, D. C., 140, 181
Polkinghorne, D., 69, 75-76, 181
Pollick, F. E., 125, 179
Popper, K. R., 25, 28-29, 33, 36, 130, 134,
    144, 146-147, 163, 181
Posner, M. I., 72, 181
Postman, L, 95, 182
Prawat, R. S., 87, 182
Prinz, W., 168, 179
Proctor, R. W., 42, 66, 127, 168, 176, 182

Quine, W. V., 32-33, 36, 139, 142-143,
    149, 151-154, 163, 178, 182

Reber, A. S., 79, 182
Reese, H. W., 1, 3, 7, 17, 59, 62-64, 77,
    92, 105, 114, 131, 175-183
Reeve, T. G., 168, 182

Resnick, R., 96, 178
Reynolds, T. J., 112, 181
Riccio, D., 96, 183
Roediger, H. L., III, 50, 182
Rogoff, B., 4, 11, 175
Rorty, R., 9-12, 27, 86, 163, 182
Rosenberg, A., 169, 182
Rosnow, R. L., 54, 56, 73, 176-177, 179, 182
Rothman, S., 168, 183
Rychlak, J. F., 139-140, 182

Sagan, C., 33, 169, 171, 182
Santillana, G. D., 153, 182
Sarbin, T. R., 1, 3, 7, 12, 14, 16, 54, 57-58,
    64, 67, 72, 76, 88, 129, 158, 164,
    166, 175-178, 180-183
Sass, L. A., 77, 177, 184
Scheffler, I., 5, 183
Scheibe, K. E., 58, 183
Schmidt, F., 168, 183
Schneider, K. J., 3, 183
Schneider, S. M., 62, 183
Scriven, M., 20, 183
Secord, P. F., 50, 180
Seligman, D., 168, 183
Shanon, B., 3, 6, 183
Shapere, D., 5, 30, 36, 150, 153, 183
Shotter, J., 83, 129, 183
Shull, R. L., 105, 183
Shweder, R. A., 11, 183
Skinner, B. F., 1, 12, 21, 27, 105-106,
    115-117, 119, 125-126, 176, 183
Slife, B. D., 3, 22-23, 140, 158, 183
Slobin, D. I., 125, 183
Smith, J., 62, 1983
Smith, J. A., 27, 73, 129, 161, 167, 178,
    181, 183-184
Smith, T. L., 106, 183
Snyderman, M., 168, 183
Spear, N. E., 96, 183
Spence, K. W., 20-21, 110, 183, 184
Staddon, J. E. R., 4, 48, 184
Staudinger, U. M., 62, 183
Stearns, P., 73, 129, 178
Steele, D. L., 62, 184
Steier, F., 73, 177, 184
Still, A., 36, 46, 86, 157, 176, 181
Stuart-Hamilton, I., 157, 184
Sullivan, M. A., 11, 183
Szapocznik, J., 4, 184

Tarpy, R. M., 168, 184
Taylor, E., 26, 184
Thomson, D. M., 112, 176
Tolman, E. C., 19-21, 109-111, 184
Tomie, A., 111, 175, 181
Turner, M. B., 27, 184

Van Langenhove, L., 21, 27, 73, 77, 158,
    167, 178, 181, 183-184
von Glasersfeld, E., 10, 184
Vygotsky, L. S., 86, 184

Wallach, L., 3, 184
Wallach, M. A., 3, 184
Warren, R. M., 112, 184
Wickens, D. D., 113, 184
Williams, R. N., 3, 22-23, 45, 140, 158,
    180-181, 183
Wilson, E. O., 46, 167, 184
Woolfolk, R. L., 77, 177, 184

Zahar, E., 132, 184
Zilsel, E., 153, 182

Subject Index

Act:
  historical, 52, 67
  in context, 52, 107
  See also Event, historical

Behavior analysis, 16, 39, 64, 105-114, 118, 123-127, 133
Behaviorism, 5, 21-22, 106-107, 111, 130, 133, 161
  analytic, 62, 64, 67, 105, 107-108, 124
Bruner, J. S., 1-4, 7-8, 11-12, 14, 27, 54, 74, 76, 80, 83, 106, 112, 116, 129, 164

Change, 12, 42-43, 55-56, 63, 69, 73, 93
  See also Novelty
Cognitive attitudes, 36
Constructionism, 5, 7, 17, 23, 114, 118, 138, 155, 165-166
Constructivism, 5, 7, 10-11, 13, 65, 87, 152-153, 166
Context, 2, 6, 16, 28, 34, 42, 45-46, 51-52, 60, 64, 67, 73, 76-77, 84, 94, 107-108, 111-113, 134, 149, 166, 168
  of discovery, 28, 51
  of justification, 28, 51
Contextualism:
  developmental, 59, 91, 99, 104, 109, 119, 122, 129

functional, 91, 105-119, 123, 125-128, 136
modified, 11, 48, 53, 59-60, 65, 68, 91, 104
philosophic, 11, 53-54, 59-65, 68, 70-71, 73, 84-86, 89, 93, 102, 107, 114, 116, 118-119, 127-128, 136, 138, 160
pure, 60
Control, 2, 47-48, 58, 67, 71, 86, 99, 101-102, 107-108, 114-116, 119, 124, 126, 130, 135-136, 156, 160.
  See also Prediction
Cultural psychology, 7, 11, 76

Deese, J., 4, 16, 54, 57-58, 64, 74-76, 165
Demarcation criterion, 25, 28, 34
Description, 6, 26-27, 70-71, 74, 117
Developmental contextualists, 13, 66-67, 91, 93-102, 104-106, 122-123, 129
  See also Contextualism, developmental

Einstein, A., 26, 41, 132-133, 135, 146
Epistemology, 8, 11, 32, 88, 100, 127, 136, 159, 161, 163
Event:
  historic 42, 45-46, 118-119
  See also Act, historical
Experimentation, 1-3, 7-8, 14-15, 54, 58, 61, 63, 68-69, 71-74, 78, 80, 88,

107-108, 115-116, 122, 124, 140,
161, 164-167, 172-173
Explanation, 22-23, 27, 32, 67, 71, 97,
116-117, 135, 145, 153
causal, 55, 71, 73, 77-78, 84, 86, 97

Feyerabend, P., 5, 36, 139, 145, 148-150,
152, 163
Formism, 39-40, 42, 47-49, 52, 70
Functional contextualists, 60, 66-68, 101,
107, 111, 113-114, 116-117, 119,
123-124, 126-130, 132, 135, 160
See also Contextualism, functional
Functional relations, 12, 27, 101, 107,
117-118, 124, 126

Geertz, C., 6, 84-86
Generalization, 24, 71, 108, 121, 161,
167-170, 173-174
Gergen, K. J., 3, 14-15, 27, 55-56, 62,
69-70, 72, 74, 78-79, 85-86, 106,
128-129, 164-165
Gillespie, D., 3-4, 6-7, 12, 40-41, 51, 54,
65, 131
Guba, E. G., 11, 82, 115, 145, 166

Harré, R., 21, 27, 73-74, 84-86, 128-129,
166
Hayes, L. J., 3-5, 7, 17, 39, 62-64, 105,
107-111, 113-114, 123-125, 129-131,
133, 135, 158
Hayes, S. C., 1, 3-5, 7, 12, 16-17, 39, 46,
59, 62-64, 67, 105-111, 113-114,
117, 123, 125, 129-131, 133, 135, 158
Hermeneutics, 1, 9, 14, 23, 77-79, 88
Hypothetical data rotation, 14, 73, 78, 81,
88, 164
Hypothetical imperatives, 33, 163

Incommensurability, 137-138, 149-151,
153-154
Induction, 24, 28, 145
Interpretation, 51, 79-80, 106-107, 116, 165
Interpretive schemes, 116-117, 119

James, W., 4, 9-11, 17, 26-27, 39, 53-54, 71

Kuhn, T. S., 5, 22, 25, 29-34, 36, 131-134,
136, 138, 144-150, 152, 154,
159-160, 163, 170

Laudan, L., 5, 24-25, 29-37, 132-135,
139-143, 146-149, 152-153, 156,
162-164, 170, 172
Lawfulness, 55-56, 58, 62, 66, 68, 88, 122
Lerner, R. M., 4, 7, 12, 16, 46, 59, 63-65,
67, 92-94, 96-99, 102-103, 105
Linear causality, 96, 158
Logical positivism, 3, 21, 23, 27, 158

Mach, E., 10, 17, 25-27, 132
Mechanism, 1, 3, 5, 7, 17, 39, 41-42, 47-
49, 52, 54, 58, 64, 70, 87, 96-98, 101,
105, 107, 113-115, 117-118, 123, 158
Metamethodology, 162-163
Metamodel, 59, 65, 92-93
Metaphor, 7, 16, 39-42, 45-46, 49-50, 52,
67, 107
Metatheory, 1, 4, 8, 17, 52, 99, 121
Methodological rules, 33, 163
Multilevel determination, 13, 43, 47, 54,
67, 93, 98-99, 104
Mutual causality, 96, 104, 109

Narrative, 1, 12, 76, 78-81, 88, 164
Naturalism, 25, 32, 36-37, 77, 163-165, 173
normative, 37, 163-165
Novelty, 16, 42-43, 54-58, 63, 66, 68, 87,
114

Ontology, 11, 70, 100, 106, 127-128, 136,
159-160, 171, 173
Operant, 1, 4, 12, 27, 105-106, 109, 111,
117, 119
Operational, truth theory, 43-44
Operationism, 21
Organicism, 39-41, 47-49, 52, 59-60, 70,
98-99
Overton, W. F., 48, 92, 105, 131

Paradigm, 4-5, 22, 29-31, 36, 70, 84, 105,
132-133, 138, 145-146, 149, 151

Parsimony, 8
Pepper, S. C., 6, 39-44, 47-49, 52-53, 56,
    67, 70, 87, 93, 111, 114, 118-119,
    129-131, 133, 136, 151
Phenomenology, 23, 25, 27, 78
Philosophic contextualists, 43, 54-63, 66-69,
    72-73, 75, 78-79, 82, 84-86, 88, 91,
    105, 111, 116, 119, 127-129, 136, 160
    See also Contextualism, philosophic
Philosophy of science, 4-5, 9, 19-20, 22,
    23, 25, 28, 30-32, 37, 77, 137-138,
    152-154, 158-159, 162-163
Popper, K. R., 25, 28-29, 33, 36, 130, 134,
    144, 146-147, 163
Positivism, 3, 21, 23, 27, 3-32, 115, 158
Postmodern, 9-10, 13, 15, 22-23, 37, 69,
    72, 74-75, 78-81, 83, 87-88, 155-158,
    160-162, 172-174
Postpositivism, 36-37, 148
Pragmatism, 9-11, 27, 39, 44, 133
Prediction, 2, 11, 42, 48, 58, 65, 86, 99,
    107-108, 114-116, 119, 124, 126,
    130, 135-136, 142, 160
    See also Control
Problems:
    anomalous, 35, 148
    conceptual, 35, 147
    empirical, 8, 35, 148
    potential, 35, 148
    solved, 35, 148

Quine, W. V., 32-33, 36, 139, 142-143,
    149, 151-154, 163

Radical empiricism, 9-13, 16-17, 25-27,
    37, 66-68, 88, 106, 117-118, 122, 127
Reductionism, 93, 97-98
Reese, H. W., 1, 3, 7, 17, 59, 62-64, 77,
    92, 105, 114, 131
Reflexive technique, 73, 78, 177
Relativism, 4-5, 7, 9, 25, 30-32, 36-37, 44,
    47, 56, 82, 130, 132, 137, 140,
    144-146, 150-154
    epistemic, 31, 144, 152
    linguistic, 31, 130
    metamethodological, 31
    methodological, 130, 132
Research programs, 29, 48, 132-133

Research traditions, 132
Root metaphor, 7, 39-42, 45-46, 67, 107
Rorty, R., 9-12, 27, 86, 163, 182
Rules of the game, 155, 173

Sarbin, T. R., 1, 3, 7, 12, 14, 16, 54, 57-58,
    64, 67, 72, 76, 88, 129, 158, 164, 166
Science:
    acceptance of, 64-65
    approaches to, 14, 16, 130, 162
    attitudes toward, 15
    causal, 23-24
    conceptions of, 7-8, 23-25, 62, 159
    contextualism and, 46-52, 119
    descriptive, 88
    explanatory, 88
    goals of, 92-93, 113, 115, 123, 146-147
    mainstream, 65-68, 91
    metaphor of, 41-42, 49-50
    philosophies of, 25-37
    psychology as a, 2-5, 77, 81, 83
    rejection of, 3, 54-56, 58-59
    world view of, 40, 47
Separatism, 129-131, 134
Skinner, B. F., 1, 12, 21, 27, 105-106,
    115-117, 119, 125-126
Successful working, 43-44, 114
Synthetic, 12, 47-48, 93
System:
    closed, 50-52
    open, 50-52

Theoretical psychology, 23
Theories:
    analytic, 47-48, 50-51
    cumlativity of, 147
    dispersive, 45, 47-48, 59, 93
    integrative, 12, 47-48, 52, 99
    progressivity of, 35, 147-148, 151, 154,
        171
    synthetic, 12, 47-48, 93
Thesis:
    algorithm, 35
    translation, 35, 148-149
Transactional psychology, 11
Truth criterion, 40-41, 43-44, 114

Underdetermination, 13, 137-146,
    149-151, 153-154

Variables, restriction of, 55, 66, 68
Verification, 28, 44

Worldviews, 11, 39-40, 43-44, 47-49, 52, 54, 63, 92-93, 98, 105, 122, 129-131, 151

About the Authors

$\mathcal{E}. \mathcal{J}.$ Capaldi is Professor of Psychology at Purdue University, W. Lafayette, Indiana. He has published a number of articles on animal learning and memory. He is identified with sequential theory, which suggests that overt instrumental behavior is regulated at least in part by memories associated with goal events such as reward and nonreward.

$\mathcal{R}$obert W. Proctor is Professor of Psychology at Purdue University, W. Lafayette, Indiana. He has published a number of articles on human performance. His major interests currently are in response-selection processes and the codes on which they are based. He is coauthor, with Addie Dutta, of the book *Skill Acquisition and Human Performance.*